MACRO-ECONOMIC MARKET REGULATION

Macro-economic Market Regulation

A. R. G. HEESTERMAN

Senior Lecturer in Econometrics
University of Birmingham

W H

HEINEMANN : LONDON

William Heinemann Ltd
15 Queen St, Mayfair, London W1X 8BE

LONDON MELBOURNE TORONTO
JOHANNESBURG AUCKLAND

First published 1974
434 90720 0 (hardback)
434 90721 9 (limp)

Printed in England by
Willmer Brothers Limited, Birkenhead

Contents

Outline and Introduction

This book discusses problems of economic regulation. Regulation of an economy means intervention by the government in the working of the economy in order to try to make it behave in a certain preconceived way. Regulation of a market economy implies that the regulation does not go to the length of completely displacing the market mechanism. It is more a question of partial adjustment of the market mechanism.

When we discuss market regulation, we face two fundamental questions. *Why* is it necessary, or desirable, to regulate an economic system, and *how* do various instruments of regulation influence the goals of economic policy?

We shall meet the second point, the working of various instruments of regulation, at numerous places in the main text of this book. It is, however, useful to say something at this early stage about the first point, the very reasons why economic regulation is there and should be there. We have, in the first place, to confront the elegant and internally logical and consistent system of neo-classical economics.

I hold that the way an economic system is assumed to work, if incomes and prices have the significance which the neo-classical system attributes to them, is not even a tolerable approximation of the actual working of a modern economy.

It is, however, obviously not enough to maintain that the neo-classical model is *not* a realistic model of the workings of a real economy. One must also indicate how a real economy *does* work, if it does not work as the neo-classical model says it does.

I have, in this book, tried to give a coherent description of the processes and forces which determine the level of activity and the rate of growth of a national economy under various conditions, and the methods by which a public planning authority can influence the development of the economy.

The points where I find that a real economy functions in a way different from the neo-classical model can be classified under three main headings:

Firstly, there are economies of scale. These economies of scale concern the availability of material resources, organization and infrastructure, the size of capital goods, and the scale on which knowledge is applied.

Perfect competition cannot, of course, exist under conditions of increasing returns to scale. There is no perfect competition, and this constitutes the second main point where I beg to differ from the neo-classical model.

A major inadequacy of exchange prices, as indicators of costs, arises in connection with the introduction of newly conceived methods of production. The return on new investment in new methods of production once they are undertaken—despite informal resistance and lack of complete information about technical possibilities and despite uncertainty about the sales prospects of the additional amounts of product coming from the new production facilities—is systematically greater than the financial costs of new investment.

Under these conditions the level of demand for products is not merely an equilibrium which arises out of the interaction of market forces but an object of regulation. It determines not only the degree of utilization of existing resources, but also the sales prospects for future increments in production, and hence the expected return on new investment and, via induced technical progress, the rate of growth of the economy.

There are also resources, in particular natural resources, gifts of nature, which are limited and should be treated as cost factors, but are not always so treated. Or if they are treated as cost factors, their price is lower than would be justified in order to ensure that the demand does not exceed the available supply.

The reasons for this undervaluation of the costs of natural resources are twofold. Firstly, natural resources are free gifts of nature and have no need to live from their earnings, whereas human beings who supply labour require earnings. Secondly, we may recognize certain resources as a cost factor but still object against imputation of their value to a private individual. Under those circumstances it is the duty of the state to intervene in order to preserve scarce resources.

For example, I would, as a citizen, most strongly object to a proposal that we should pay as private individuals for the privilege of enjoying a clean beach with a clean sea to swim in. Nevertheless, the clean sea is a scarce resource, and it is proper for the state to charge any firm or local authority which pollutes it a cost for being allowed to do so, if it is allowed at all.

I do not, however, fully share the Rome Club's somewhat pessimistic conclusion [29] that it is under all conditions imperative to reduce the rate of economic expansion to virtually zero, in order to preserve natural resources. Even so, the existing rate of growth of mondial production is not enough to provide full employment of labour on a world-wide scale.

For the first time in history we can, if we wish, apply conscious regulation to the economy of the whole world. There are, however, two criteria for the establishment of a suitable level of mondial production. They correspond to the desirability to provide employment for people who want a job, and to contain the consumption of natural resources at a level which will keep the earth a decent place to live in. Unfortunately, at the prevailing price structure, these two criteria contradict each other.

The qualification 'at the prevailing price structure' is, however, worth mentioning. Even so, it remains to be seen if the criteria would coincide at any conceivable and politically enforceable price structure.

If not, the conclusion would be that we have to organize our society in such a way that a job is not necessarily a prerequisite for a full human life and a place in society. Regulation of our material economy would then be geared to the requirement of preservation of natural resources and an equitable distribution of the products obtained from them.

The material is presented in the following order:

The beginning of the book, the first chapter and to a lesser extent the second, *introduce* a number of concepts to the reader. In this respect the book is a textbook. I have tried to present my material in such a way that the book does not require much previous knowledge of economics.

Some concepts like income, prices, costs, inflation, etc., are generally known and accepted economic terms. Other concepts, like the oligopolistic market equilibrium and the distinction between the private and the social return to new investment, are not so standard.

The middle part of the book contains a somewhat larger number of discussions, *capita selecta*, on economic regulation itself. There is, of course, no separate theory of economic regulation, only a theory about the way an economy functions, and it is possible to draw policy conclusions from this theory.

Important aspects of the theory of economic equilibrium and economic growth are, however, discussed in more detail in this middle part of the book than could be done with the introduction of the basic concepts.

Most of this theory is equally applicable to a 'Western' type of market economy with elements of regulation by the government as well as to an 'Eastern' type of publicly planned, but decentralized economy. Indeed, there is a possible type of economic management which could theoretically be arrived at from either side.

The permanent full-employment strategy requires associated administrative controls in order to prevent inflation. In the more extreme cases of pursuance of this strategy the result becomes virtually indistinguishable from what one would obtain if one introduced decentralization and cost calculation in a publicly planned economy.

The final, ninth chapter confronts my theory of economic equilibrium with existing economic theory. I have tried to indicate the links with, as well as the differences from, some other economic theories.

Note added in proof

My observations about the undervaluation of earth rentals have suddenly (end of 1973) gained a degree of actuality which I had hardly expected so soon. I considered amending the text but have refrained from doing so. A textbook cannot hope to keep up with actuality. Moreover, I submit that the situation is still substantially the same for many products, even when oil now commands a realistic price.

1

Survey of the fundamental concepts

1.1 TOTAL INCOME

Suppose we ran an economic system without money. Various consumption items, such as bread, butter, sugar, cheese, etc., as well as services like local bus rides, haircutting, etc., would be produced, and people would come and have what they needed. The bread and cheese would be made, brought to certain distribution points, and people would come and collect what they wanted. The haircutter would be in his shop, and cut anyone's hair, because he was a haircutter and that was the job assigned to him.

For these everyday things this would even be a practicable way of running things. It would, however, not be so simple with, let us say, the building of a house. Everyone would want a nice, roomy, centrally heated house, and could so many fine and large houses be built? And what about refrigerators or travelling to Hawaii? In short, we cannot give everyone all the things he likes.

Production is limited by the available amounts of various natural resources, such as land and minerals, and not least by the fact that most production requires labour. This last refers not only to the basic production of the various articles themselves; there is also, and to a quite considerable extent, the fact that the articles have to be brought to, and made available for, the people who need them.

The human labour needed for the bread on our table is not only that of the baker, but also the labour of the van-driver who brought the bread from the bakery to the shop, and that of the electrician who fitted the baker's oven, the miller who ground the wheat, and quite a number of other people, some of them in distant parts of the world.

The function of money income is to limit the demand for the services of production factors—both the human factor, labour, and the material factors, natural resources—to their actually available amounts.

The budget limit, imposed by society's organization, on the expenditure on various desirable articles, should correspond to the real limits on their availability, as imposed by the technical factors, such as the amounts of the various production factors that are available.

1.2 PRICES

The concept of income has significance only in conjunction with prices. The price of a house with a private swimming pool is more than can be financed out of the income of ordinary people, except at the cost of sacrificing other, more necessary items of expenditure. Therefore, few people order a house with a private swimming pool, despite the fact that some would like a house with one.

This is precisely the purpose of the whole system, because building swimming pools costs a lot of labour as well as land and only certain amounts of both are available.

The point seems obvious, and is generally taken for granted. It is, however, not quite so obvious as it is generally assumed to be.

The cost involved in *selling* chocolate bars, securing them against just being picked up, adding their purchase on a cash register, and actually cashing the money, is a quite noticeable fraction of the purchase price. It could well be that the production of as much chocolate as anybody would like would cost less than producing and selling a somewhat smaller amount.

Therefore, if the sole purpose of the pricing system were to avoid wasteful use of resources, we should, from that point of view, consider supplying chocolate and other mass-produced articles free of charge. This argument has also been raised with some success in defence of free public transport.

The monetary economy has, however, its own logic. If cameras, watches, and houses cost money, how is the baker to get his fair share of these money-costing things, if bread is to be produced free of charge?

1.3 MARKET EQUILIBRIUM AND MARKET REGULATION

One other assumption implied in the classic economic model is the equality between supply and demand. The user's demand for, and the producer's or owner's supply of, an article are functions of the price of that article; supply and demand are equal to each other at the market clearing price but not at any other price.

For example, let the following five users or potential users be willing each to purchase one unit at the following prices:

user 1: at any price below	100
user 2: ,, ,, ,, ,,	60
user 3: ,, ,, ,, ,,	45
user 4: ,, ,, ,, ,,	20
user 5: ,, ,, ,, ,,	5

Let there also be six producers, with costs of 56·1, 56·2, 56·8, 57·0, 57·1, and 57·2, who are willing to produce one unit each at any price above their costs, but who will leave the industry if their costs are not recovered. The price will then be in the interval between 56·2 and 56·8. Users 1 and 2 will buy, whereas users 3, 4, and 5 will stay potential users. The two units purchased by these two users will be supplied by the producers with the lowest costs, 56·1 and 56·2. The other producers, with cost prices from 56·8 upwards, will stay potential suppliers.

The market-equilibrium assumption is much more realistic than the stronger assumption of perfect competition (to be discussed in section 1.6), but some qualifications must be made.

Many prices are set at a standardized level, because the seller is a large organization, and his price setting does not allow for local and short-term temporary variations. As a result the customer may find at some time that the supplier is sold out. The supplier may also close certain distribution outlets (shops, warehouses) because they are unprofitable at the set uniform price, even where it would be possible to make them profitable by charging a special local* price. Furthermore, supply may, in any meaningful sense, be in excess of demand, because the supplier is left with unsold stock.

This point may be brought within the scope of the market-equilibrium model, by assuming that the supplier prefers to stockpile, in anticipation of selling later at the set price. He then becomes temporarily a purchaser himself.

This is, however, a somewhat artificial construction as the producer has no preference for his own stock, but simply has not, so far, done anything to bridge the discrepancy between supply and demand. Nevertheless, there is an element of realism in the idea of market adjustment by the price. Increases in the price do indeed reduce

* Compare the system of 'delivery charges' as used by some English motor car manufacturers.

demand and stimulate supply, whereas a price reduction does the opposite. There is thus a possibility for price adjustment to result in equilibrium between supply and demand.

The notion of the price as a regulator, which equates the supply offered at the prevailing price to the amount asked for purchase at the prevailing price, limits but not altogether excludes the possibility of price regulation by the government. At present we will not investigate the desirability of public control over prices, but merely discuss its technical aspects, in particular the conditions under which it is likely to be effective. We must, however, distinguish between different types of public price regulation, namely, simple price setting by law, price-adjusting market interference, and compulsory market regulation. Simple price setting is possible, only within a limited interval, and it can be altogether impractical if economic conditions change faster than price regulations can be adapted.

In our example, changes in the price between 56·2 and 56·8 affect neither the supply nor the demand. Supply is equal to demand for a certain range of prices. Therefore, in the interval between 56·2 and 56·8, the price can be regulated by the government, without disturbing the equilibrium between supply and demand. In a large market for a uniform product, covering a wide geographical area, this 'no response' interval is likely to be very small indeed. The possibility of controlling prices, simply by making transactions at higher or lower prices illegal, is, however, slightly greater than one would expect from the notion of a complete absence of response to changes in the price. Some discrepancies between supply and demand can and are accommodated by the supply which is offered for sale but not actually sold, and the demand which is asked to be supplied but not actually supplied. A large and systematic difference between supply and demand persisting over a period of time is, however, bound to make any price control ineffective. Producers who could make a profit at the prevailing official price and even at a price well below it, but who cannot sell their product at the official price, are likely to sell below the official price, offering special price concessions to attract customers despite their legal obligation not to do so. On the other hand, if there is a queue of customers and a supplier knows that he can serve only half of them, there is a temptation to overcharge, to refuse to sell at the official price unless an unofficial extra payment is made on top of the official price. In short, simple price regulation can be effective only if the control is operated at a level not too far from where a 'free' equilibrium price would have found itself.

One solution to this problem is for the government to restrict either the supply or the demand. If the demand for milk at the set price is less than the supply, then the government must either buy the surplus or persuade a sufficient number of dairy farmers to become ex-dairy farmers by buying off their farms. The cost of such a policy to the government depends greatly on how *elastic* the demand and the supply are. We will say that the price elasticity of the demand for milk is 0·1 if a 10 per cent increase in its price causes a 1 per cent drop in its demand. And the price elasticity of its supply is said to be 0·2 if an increase of 10 per cent in its price causes a 2 per cent increase in its supply. The fraction of the production to be taken out of the market, in order to cause a certain shift in the price, is then the sum of the two elasticities multiplied by the desired price adjustment. Hence if the demand and supply elasticities are 0·1 and 0·2, then to cause an increase of 20 per cent in the price, it is necessary to take $0{\cdot}3 \times 20$ per cent $=$ 6 per cent of the production out of the market. Price-adjusting market regulation is therefore likely to be costly, except where both price elasticities are low.

For society as a whole, however, a compensation is sometimes possible by supplying the surplus to certain underprivileged categories of consumers who could not otherwise have bought the product. American surplus grain has been sold to India and paid for in non-convertible* rupees.

Price regulation can also be underpinned, not by purchasing surpluses, but by directly restricting the supply (or the demand) by means of a permit system. Import quota are the most widely known example of this type of compulsory market regulation. Certain importers are licensed to import specific amounts of a particular product; or registered producers are allowed to produce certain permitted quantities, and import or production outside this quotum is illegal. In the opposite case of excess demand, compulsory market regulation is commonly known as distribution.

1.4 COSTS

The total of all the financial outlay necessary to produce and sell a

* The United States government was getting Indian rupees which could, however, only be spent in India, because India was unable to exchange them for U.S. dollars.

certain article is the *cost of production* of that article. This cost of production does not only include outlay on the various materials, etc., which are necessary for the technical production process, i.e. for actually producing the article. Economically, the article as finally purchased by its end-user is a different article from the one that comes from the machines in a factory.

The final product must be made available to its end-user and this incurs such costs as transport or, for example, advertising; without advertising the end-user would be only a potential user, as he would be ignorant about where the article could be obtained.

1.5 OPPORTUNITY COST AND RESOURCE VALUE

The fact that one manufacturer uses loan capital, while another had issued shares (i.e. the factory is collectively owned by the shareholders) does not make a difference to the cost of production.

If the factory makes so little profit that the dividend is less than the interest on government bonds, then the shareholders would have been well advised to buy the bonds instead of the shares.

It is therefore assumed that interest on the required capital is a part of the production cost, irrespective of whether or not it is actually paid. This idea can be generalized. If a company owns an office, the rent of the office which the company could obtain by not using the office but letting it to another company instead, is the opportunity cost of using the office, even if no rent is paid.

The concept of opportunity cost gives rise to a somewhat special interpretation of *total cost* as well.

Total cost, when interpreted as including the opportunity cost of the alternative use of a firm's own resources, does in fact include a minimal 'normal' return on the invested capital, and 'profit' will mean 'extra profit', i.e. in excess of any alternative use of the same capital.

In a market economy the costs of a particular firm are transmitted to the users of the product as the price they have to pay for it.

The regulating functions which this price is meant to fulfil are two:

(*a*) To restrict the demand for any product to the amount which is available or can be produced, or which society can afford to produce.

(*b*) To ensure that the opportunity cost incurred by society at large, because the purchase of an article by one user prevents its use for other purposes, is paid by the purchaser.

For produced items, the cost of the product is obtained as the cumulation of the costs of the producing and supplying firms.

There are, however, resources which are not produced. They are primary inputs, *production factors** like human labour, uncultivated, non-irrigated land, or mineral deposits. These production factors are not themselves produced and do not therefore incur a cost of production.

The function of costs is, however, precisely to limit the demand for production factors to their availability. Production factors should have a price which is transmitted as costs to the users of products, even if the production factors themselves have no cost of production. The price of a production factor is therefore indicated with a different name, the *rental value* or *imputed cost* of the production factor.

In a market economy, the operation of an imputed cost as paid price generates an income to the owner of the production factor. This income of the owner of a production factor is, of course, equal to the cost to be paid by its users.

1.6 COMPETITION

Two assumptions are conventionally made under the general catch phrase: 'assume perfect competition'. They are:

(*a*) *Competitive behaviour*: Every entrepreneur or would-be entrepreneur makes the quantity dispositions which maximize his profit at the existing prices.

(*b*) *Competitive market conditions*: The cost of new acquisition, and the value to be realized by disposing of (e.g. selling or letting) such firms' assets as machines, buildings, etc., are one and the same and every firm can at any moment, if it so chooses, cease to produce and realize the value of its assets instead.

The result of these two assumptions is, first of all, that no firm will continue to operate if the proceeds of its product are less than the total of its (opportunity) costs. It will, if faced with such an unfavour-

* The term 'production factors' will sometimes be used in a wider sense, describing anything which is not *currently* produced, e.g. including produced capital goods, machines, vehicles, etc.

able ratio between proceeds and costs, choose not to produce, but realize the value of its assets instead.

Furthermore, whenever the proceeds of some article are greater than its cost, potential entrepreneurs will become actual entrepreneurs, obtain the means to produce that article, and start producing it. The result will be that the price of the article is soon back at its cost.

These are strong assumptions and some sweeping results may be obtained from them. Some of these results sound plausible and a certain amount of confusion has arisen from them, because people have assumed the conclusions to be relevant in the real world.

The real world is, however, by and large more adequately described by the alternative assumption of traditionalism. Established organizations are expected to meet certain requirements; if they satisfy these requirements they function satisfactorily and they will go on to behave as they have been used to do.

The point may be illustrated by an example. In India there is a low level of wages and an abundant supply of labour. According to the postulate of perfect competition I should now borrow a lot of money, buy or rent a number of machines, set up a factory in India to produce motor cars, or tables, or any suitable article, export the product to North America and Europe, and sell it for good money. I will, however, do no such thing and I cannot do it, even if I wished, because no one will lend me the required capital and because I do not have a European or North American sales organization. But what about the established American or European manufacturers? They could close their factories, or some of them, sack the high-paid labour, and produce the same article in India at much lower cost. They do not and as a result India is, so far, still a poor country.

We will replace the assumptions of perfect competition by a combination of weaker assumptions, which are:

(*a*) An established firm will change its sales and marketing policy if, and only if, it can increase its profit by a marginal adjustment of its dispositions.

(*b*) New firms will enter an industry if at some level of activity, which is comparable with that of an established firm, an outsider can expect proceeds from production which leave a positive profit over costs, where the costs include the opportunity cost of investing the same capital elsewhere.

(*c*) Firms which do not make proceeds at least equal to average cost will not replace worn-out capital equipment and will eventually leave the industry.

1.7 RETURNS TO SCALE

Under this heading we discuss first of all the *assumption of divisibility*. According to this assumption it is always possible to apply a production process at an arbitrary scale. For example, if a factory can produce a million tonnes per year of a certain product and its machines contain 500 tonnes of steel and the building 7,000 tonnes of concrete, then one assumes that one can also build a factory one-hundredth of the scale, which can produce 10,000 tonnes of the same product, with machines containing 5 tonnes of steel in a building containing 70 tonnes of concrete.

Like the assumption of perfect competition, this is convenient for economic textbooks, but not generally true in the real world. It is not true for the steel and the concrete, as many machines are of a standard size and type. It is even less true for an advanced-technology production process, where fundamental research into the process and the design of the installations gives rise to a substantial fraction of the total cost.

Half the research and half the design produces not half the output, but none at all, at least by this particular method of production. As a result the producers who operate on the largest scale have the widest choice in the type of process they can use to produce their product. A large firm can, of course, use the same method of production as a smaller one, if necessary by building several factories. The smaller producers cannot, however, use all the production methods that are available to the large producers, as some of them assume a large scale of operation.

The indivisibility of certain technical means of production, as discussed above, causes increasing returns to the scale of operation of individual firms.

When we look at the demand for the product of a whole *industry*, there is yet one further dimension. The level of demand for the product of an industry influences not only the demand for the product of each firm in the industry, it also influences the distribution of production between the efficient and the less efficient firms.

In any industry there are bound to be some firms of less than average efficiency, who will continue to operate as long as they can recover cost. The expansion of the industry's production capacity by new investment will, however, come mainly from firms which employ the newest and most efficient methods of production, at good profit. An expanding demand for the end-product is therefore associated with the cost structure of the more efficient and expanding firms, not with the average cost of the industry as a whole.

The result of this indirect 'industry-demand' effect is, just like economics of scale in the narrower technical sense, that an *additional* unit of product costs less than the firm will in fact charge for it in order to stay financially viable. The point will be discussed in more detail in sections 1.9 and 1.12.

1.8 AVERAGE AND MARGINAL COST

The meaning of the term average cost will be obvious. It is the ratio between the total proceeds of a productive activity in the production of a certain article and the total of all outlay (the total cost) necessary for producing this particular amount of this particular article.

The meaning of the term 'marginal cost' is not altogether so self-evident and we can distinguish two different meanings of the term.

There is firstly marginal operating cost.

At present the air transport industry is plagued by a substantial discrepancy between its production capacity and the demand for the product. With a largely empty plane, the marginal cost of transporting an additional passenger from London to New York is the cost of burning a little more fuel, because of higher load, and serving the passenger some refreshments and a meal.

While this is an extreme case it is clear that marginal operating cost can, and will normally be, well below average cost. There are, however, exceptions. The marginal cost of transporting an additional holiday-making family from England to France with their car is probably well above the average, as this is likely to be by aircraft, the maritime ferries being already fully booked.

The other concept of marginal cost is that of (marginal) full production cost, the full cost of an additional unit in initially planned full-capacity production.

If one assumes divisibility then the cost of an additional unit of initially planned full-capacity production is the same as the average cost of production. However, this assumption is not made in this book, and the marginal full production cost is generally less than the average cost. In particular, with an advanced-technology production process, the marginal full production cost does *not* include the cost of the fundamental research to develop the production process at all, nor the cost of designing and testing new types of installation. It does, however, include the cost of building a new factory, once the first factory of such a type is established.

1.9 THE OLIGOPOLISTIC MARKET EQUILIBRIUM

The term *oligopoly* was coined by E. H. Chamberlin [5], [6]. While I acknowledge Chamberlin's legacy, my theory of oligopolistic competition is somewhat different from his. Chamberlin believes in U-shaped cost curves. I believe in L-shaped cost curves. The *ex-ante* cost per unit of output, to be incurred when planning production on a certain scale is, for a number of products, a decreasing function of the scale on which production is planned, and the limit to a further increase in the scale of both firms and plants is the size of the market in which they operate.

The convention* in mainstream economics is to treat monopoly as a special market form, where due to some external circumstances, the free entry to the market has been blocked and oligopoly is treated as a milder form of monopoly. A monopolist is assumed to maximize his profits with respect to his sales price and the volume sold. Maximization of profits, with respect to small changes in the sales price and the volume produced and sold, allows continuity with the traditional† activity of the producer; it is a credible assumption and we shall maintain it.

* The facts about industrial concentration, including its relation with market size, have been noted by those who cared to look at the facts themselves instead of presupposing competition; *see*, for example, Reynolds [37], pp. 41–2, referring to an earlier work by Bain [3*a*]. In a general way most leading economists are aware of the existence of a problem, even if the emphasis in what they believe to be the actual situation in industry may be different from mine. *See*, for example, Samuelson [39], section 23. An integration of the theory of limited competition with the theory of macro-economic equilibrium is, however, almost completely lacking in established economic theory.

† An increase in the amount sold, obtained by sales promotion, i.e. *without* price concession, is always welcome. The question is whether or not a firm is willing to make a price concession in order to obtain increase in sales.

We shall see that this assumption is quite consistent with considering oligopoly as *the normal market form under conditions of increasing returns to scale.*

From the buyer's point of view the amount purchased is a function of the price. There are, however, two different demand functions to be considered. When we consider the purchaser's demand for a particular type of product it is mainly an expression of his preference for the article in question and his ability to pay it. When we consider the demand for the product of a single firm the price elasticity expresses the purchaser's alertness, i.e. in buying the product of another firm instead if that is cheaper.

Let us assume that the demand for the product of firm X (manufacturing a certain type of product) drops by ϵ per cent for each 1 per cent increase in the price charged by firm X. This is commonly expressed by saying that ϵ is the elasticity of demand. If a firm is a monopolist then ϵ is equal to the industry-wide elasticity of demand, arising out of the demand function for the product as such. If there are more firms producing the same article, then ϵ will be greater than the industry-wide elasticity of demand for the product itself. A firm's profit position is maximal only if it is impossible to make more profit. The net additional revenue, which would arise from a 1 per cent increase in its sales, less the price concession needed to obtain it equals the associated increment in its cost, i.e. its marginal cost.

If the price elasticity is ϵ, this means that ϵ per cent additional sales are obtained by a price concession of 1 per cent. Conversely, the price concession associated with 1 per cent additional sales will be $1/\epsilon$ per cent. Hence the additional revenue arising from an additional 1 per cent sales is $1-1/\epsilon$ per cent of the level of the revenue. It follows that if the price elasticity is less than 1, the relation between the volume of sales and the revenue obtained becomes inverse, and a firm can actually *increase* its revenue by charging a higher price and selling less.

For the aggregate demand for a product a price elasticity of less than 1 is, however, quite common. It follows that a monopolist would, under those conditions, always benefit from increasing his price. But then, under those conditions, i.e. with a price elasticity of less than 1, there will *not* be a private monopoly. The only monopoly which would be stable under those conditions would be that of a public corporation, which does not maximize profit.

If a private firm were a monopolist, it would increase its price—

thereby raising total proceeds—to be more than total cost, and then even higher, as long as the firm remained a monopolist. This would mean that the price is raised above the average cost of a potential competitor; the latter would now become an active competitor and the firm would cease to be a monopolist. From that moment onwards the price cannot be raised further, because otherwise the outsider would quickly increase its market share. The price elasticity for the product of a single firm has been increased to above 1.

A firm would also have to consider its cost. It would be satisfied* with its present sales policy if the additional revenue from a 1 per cent increase in the volume of sales (i.e. $1-1/\epsilon$ per cent of the level of sales) would equal its additional cost, which should then also be $1-1/\epsilon$ per cent of the level of sales.

By our weaker assumptions of competitive behaviour (*see* section 1.6), we may assume that total revenue is approximately equal to total cost and that the figure $1-1/\epsilon$ is the ratio between marginal and average cost. This ratio is largely a technical datum, however, and does not depend on market conditions. Market conditions, therefore, *adapt themselves to the technical conditions.* The number of firms in the industry will increase until a price elasticity for the demand of a particular firm's product is realized, which will equate $1-1/\epsilon$ to the ratio between the marginal and the average cost.

Far from being an abnormal market condition, oligopoly is the inherent result of increasing returns to scale. The price elasticity of demand is, however, not only a function of the number of firms in the market, but also of its size (e.g. the total turnover in the industry and the geographical density of the market).

Sheer physical distance between one firm and another may give rise to some degree of separation in an economic sense and shield the two firms from each other's competition. It is nowadays possible to transport products from one end of the earth to the other, but there are transport costs as well as state frontiers, with the associated barrier of customs formalities, etc. Because the distance barrier is there at all, we find in a large country more firms than in a small country with otherwise similar conditions. However, because the distance barrier is imperfect, there are in a country which is twice the size of another country with comparable economic conditions, less than twice the number of firms.

* *See* the end of this section for a mathematical exposition.

If an economic frontier between two countries is removed this will reduce the total number of firms, but not to the same number as there were formerly in one of the two countries. As a result we find the largest production organization in the country with the largest national product, i.e. the United States, and also the greatest degree of remaining competition—in the sense that there are still several firms in any industry compared with only one national firm in many European countries.

The effect of the size of the market on the 'normal' firm-size is reinforced by the economics of scale themselves. Due to the preponderance of large, well-equipped firms in a large market, a firm needs a low average cost to be economically viable in such a large market.

An important modification of the oligopolistic market equilibrium arises if firms are unequally endowed with technical knowledge and managerial skill. Economics of scale caused by technical indivisibilities play a role in sustaining almost any form of oligopolistic market equilibrium, unless the oligopoly is a publicly supported cartel. The degree of concentration is, however, greater than would be indicated by technical indivisibilities alone if there is inequality in efficiency between firms. The resulting oligopolistic market structure then allows the efficiently producing firms to make a surplus profit, a monopoly rent, over and above the normal return to their investment.

Suppose the staff of firm *X* in industry *A* has made a number of technical discoveries and inventions which, in combination with efficient organization, allow firm *X* to produce at lower cost per unit of product than any other firm in industry *A*. A combination of ignorance, inertia, technical secrets and patents of firm *X*, together with plain conservatism, prevents the lead of firm *X* to be followed to the full in the rest of industry *A*. In other words firm *X* has a special resource at its disposal, called superior efficiency. This superior efficiency is not an exhaustible resource and neither does it cost much money. Firm *X* may or may not pay its staff a higher reward than is paid elsewhere in industry *A* for otherwise comparable work, but this salary differential is unlikely to involve an amount of money comparable with *X*'s exceptionally high productivity. Firm *X*'s specially high productivity results in a monopoly rent in the form of an extra profit for the owners of the firm. If firm *X* behaved competitively in the sense that it maximized its profit with respect to the volume of its production, without considering the relationship between the volume and the price, it would increase its sales, thereby driving its competitors out of the market. As long as firm *X* is one among many fairly small firms, it will, of course, do just that. The ability to understand and apply efficiently the most productive methods of making the *A*-product is, however, a scarce resource, possessed to an unequal degree by different firms. This fact by itself reduces the number of firms in an industry, and increases the average market share of an individual firm in the industry beyond the point which would be indicated by economies of scale on its own. This is obvious for the leading firm *X*, but it is also true for those firms in the industry which respond to *X*'s challenge, either by entrenching their position by means of a brand-name, advertising, etc., or by making an effort to increase their own productive efficiency and survive despite *X*'s competition. As some of the less efficient firms are forced out of the market, their clients are taken over, partly by *X*, the initial challenger, but also by other surviving firms.

Once competitors are relatively few and far afield, each protected by its own distribution network, brand-name, advertising campaign, etc., firm *X* can only hope to increase its market share further by making a more substantial price concession, at the cost of its own profit margin, and an oligopolistic equilibrium has established itself.

Now consider the possibility of an outsider entering the market, in order to copy firm *X*'s success story. In the first place, the outsider must have confidence in its own ability to recruit a similarly competent staff, who will be able to match or at least approximate the leading firm's efficiency. Just to make reasonable profit like the other firms in industry *A*, in a market where the leading firm has a lower cost of production and can start a price war, is not an attractive prospect. Secondly, if there are economies of scale an outsider cannot enter stealthily as operations must be started on a fairly large scale, although perhaps on a smaller scale than the leading firm. The outsider must therefore reckon with the possibility that firm *X* will react to its entry into the market by starting a price war, e.g. by offering the product at its true cost price, temporarily sacrificing its (firm *X*'s) monopoly rent, in order to prevent the outsider from gaining an established market position. Such an event would probably change the structure of the market for a longish period to come. One or more of the less efficient among the established firms might be forced out of the market, but on the other hand some other established firms might make a determined effort to become more efficient in order to survive. The potential competition of an outsider would to some extent limit the possibility of reaping a monopoly rent on a technical lead, but not eliminate it. As a result the co-existence of several largish but not fully dominant firms of unequal efficiency is a more or less stable situation.

A final point concerns the reasons why customers are willing to buy from one manufacturer, despite the fact that the same product is offered for sale at a lower price by several other manufacturers. One reason may be simply transport costs and at least one author, Greenhut [12], has developed a theory on those lines. An inference from the theory is that the monopoly rent inherent in a site close to a large concentrated body of customers and/or favourable supply positions (in the vicinity of a port, ore deposit, etc.) is appropriated by the owner of the site, rather than by the firm operating there. I beg to differ, however, and submit that a purely locational theory based on transport costs does not explain the concentration in industry actually observed. If transport costs were the only problem, then nothing would stop another firm hiring a site immediately adjoining that of an established firm and attempting to underbid him. The result would be, of course, that the owner of the first firm's site would have to reduce his rent, or risk his tenant going into bankruptcy. An equilibrium would be reached only if all available sites in the relevant area had been occupied.

Economics of scale, unequal efficiency and lack of knowledge, and 'irrational' customers' behaviour, play their part as well.

The distinction between an oligopolistic situation, where the relatively less efficient producer is protected by the cost of transporting the product of a more efficient rival into his vicinity, and the situation where the less efficient producer is protected by customers' lack of competitive behaviour is of some practical relevance. If the protection is entirely due to 'irrational' behaviour, the government can realize the objectively efficient situation, where only the most efficient firms can stay in business, by imposing a maximum price equal to the average cost per unit of the most efficient producer. This, in effect, compels the leading firm to offer at the competitive price and forbids the customer paying more than he needs. If, however, the protection of the less efficient firm is the result of transport costs, then a maximum price has the same outward effect, but the customer is paying more than he needs, because of the maximum price, which drove the technically less efficient but locationally better situated local supplier out of business and requires the customer to pay higher transport costs.

Mathematical Note

Those familiar with optimality conditions will recognize that the sales policy of pp. 12–13 could be formulated as a programming problem:

$$\text{Maximize} \quad (p-c)q$$
$$\text{subject to} \quad p = p(q,d)$$

with respect to p and q, c and d being exogenous.

Here p is the price, q the quantity, c the (marginal) cost, and d the index of demand, representing the purchasing power in the market.

The price is a function of the quantity offered, q, and the level of demand. The assumption of a price elasticity of ϵ implies that we can represent the side condition by

$$\frac{\partial p}{\partial q} = \frac{1}{\epsilon}\frac{p}{q}$$

We obtain the Lagrangean

$$L = (p-c)q+\lambda[p(q,d)-p]$$

and the optimality conditions

$$\frac{\partial L}{\partial p} = q-\lambda = 0; \text{ hence } \lambda = q$$

$$\frac{\partial L}{\partial q} = p-c+\lambda\frac{\partial p}{\partial q} = p-c+\frac{p}{\epsilon} = 0$$

Hence $\epsilon = \dfrac{p}{p-c}$

1.10 SOCIAL VERSUS PRIVATE COST UNDER PERFECT COMPETITION

The social cost of one unit of a particular article (either a product or a production factor) is (the money equivalent of) the amount of other goods, which society has to forego, as a result of disposing of that one unit of a specific article.

One of the results which one obtains from the assumptions of perfect competition (*see* section 1.6) and divisibility (*see* section 1.7) is the identity between the private cost of an article, i.e. its price, and the social cost of the same article. The argument runs as follows:

With perfect competition a producer will increase the level of his production, as long as he makes a profit, and new producers will enter the market; this they can do because the production processes are divisible, hence they can start on a small scale and, by assumption, all the materials, etc., are obtainable for them at the same cost as to the established producers.

Conversely, production will drop whenever any productive activity incurs a loss. As a result, all prices will be equal to the cost of production, where the cost of production is reckoned to include the opportunity cost of disposing otherwise of firms' assets, i.e. a normal return on the invested capital.

As a result we have the following identity:

Return on production factors (labour, land, mineral resources, and capital stock)

plus

cost of semi-finished products, reprocessed as inputs into other productive activities

(*plus* profits, which are zero)

equals

total turnover

equals

value of semi-finished products

plus

value of finally disposed end-products, i.e. sales to end-users.

We may cancel the value of the semi-finished products on both sides of the equation and find that the value of the finally disposed output equals the revenue on production factors plus any profits (which are, however, zero under conditions of perfect competition).

The prices associated with this competitive equilibrium allow us to distinguish two types of productive activities: those used, for which proceeds are equal to costs, and those not used, for which proceeds are less than costs. Under perfect competition only efficient methods of production can earn their costs.

There are no productive activities for which the proceeds are actually greater than the costs (including opportunity costs) which must be incurred to operate such a process. They would long ago have attracted so many firms that the price of the product would have been forced down, back to the level of costs. No collection of productive activities can result in a return on production factors in excess of the full-employment value of the total available supply of production factors. Furthermore, at the competitive prices, profits are impossible. The full-employment value of the production factors evaluated at the competitive prices is, therefore, an objective limit on final production delivered to the various end-users, also evaluated at the competitive prices. The evaluation of the production factors, by the competitive prices, and the corresponding costs of the various products reveal a restriction—a 'social budget limit'—which must be satisfied by every combination or every 'bundle' of outputs obtained from the available supplies of production factors. This may be expressed

$$\Sigma p_j f_j \leq \Sigma r_i y_i$$

where quantities f_j indicate the final outputs of particular types of products, as delivered to the end-users, and the p_j indicate the corresponding prices; y_i are the available supplies of the various production factors, with r_i the corresponding prices of production factors.

This conclusion is valid, irrespective of actual prices, and even independent of the way society is organized. The 'social budget limit' does not arise from any financial arrangement, but rather from the objective circumstance that only limited amounts of production factors are available. Even if production is directed centrally by the state, and distributed on an army-type rationing basis, it is still true that the final production, if evaluated at the prices which would exist under perfect competition, cannot be more than the corresponding evaluation of production factors. For this reason, the competitive prices are also known as *efficiency prices*. There may be several sets of efficiency prices. For example, in a thinly populated country, undrained land covered with wood and marshy shrubs might be available at no cost. However, when population increases this second-quality land would become scarce, and the price of land in general would rise, causing a change in the whole price structure.

Associated with each set of efficiency prices is a corresponding inequality, limiting the final production value to be obtained from any possible combination of productive activities. They are collectively known as the *efficiency frontier*.* Furthermore, under conditions of perfect competition (which presupposes divisibility), the market mechanism is a method of implementing efficiency prices as actual prices, thereby creating a situation whereby any productive activity which is not part of the efficient collection of processes results in a loss.

1.11 SOCIAL VERSUS PRIVATE COST AND CAPACITY UTILIZATION IN AN OLIGOPOLISTIC MARKET

Consider by way of example† two ways of obtaining fertilizer:

(*a*) *By import*:

Marginal cost per unit (loss of the alternative possibility of importing something else): 200.
Fixed cost: nil.

(*b*) *By domestic production*:

Marginal cost per unit (labour and materials): 100.
Fixed cost (design and construction of fertilizer factory): 1,000.

The first point to be noted is that, as long as one considers a demand of less than 10 units, it is cheaper to import, both in terms of the true social cost, and in terms of the cost to a manufacturer or importer. If total demand is *more* than 10 units, say $10+a$ units, the true cost is $2{,}000+100a$ by domestic production, and not $2{,}000+200a$ by import. The cost which society must forego in order to obtain an additional unit of fertilizer is precisely the same as it was before we dropped the assumption of divisibility.

Once it is decided to produce fertilizer at all (instead of importing it) the fixed costs are incurred, and from that point onward the results of the previous section 1.10 are valid for any additional use of fertilizer. However, if the efficiency prices (and the full marginal production cost of an additional unit of output) are to be established by the market, we must assume that firms behave competitively, in the sense that they

* A more detailed discussion of this problem can be found in my book *Allocation Models and their Use in Economic Planning* [17].

† No particular reference to fertilizer as such is meant, but rather an illustration of the general principle.

will increase their output whenever the additional revenue from one unit of output, *disregarding the impact of the level of output on the price*, is more than the marginal cost.

The market mechanism cannot, however, establish the true social cost, when there are increasing returns to scale. To illustrate this proposition let us return to the fertilizer example and assume that demand is 15 units. Any firm which considers building a fertilizer plant has to assume a market penetration of at least two-thirds. Quite likely no firm will risk the venture and the effective cost of fertilizer will remain at 200 per unit, by import. Now suppose demand is 50 units. In that case no major risk is involved in the venture of building a fertilizer plant. However, as long as there is only one firm it will be tempted to charge a price only just below the cost of import and a second firm will enter the market.

In the oligopolistic situation which will now establish itself *two* firms will produce each an output between 15* and 35 units and sell at a price which must be less than 200, otherwise import will regain a more than marginal share, but not less than 167, otherwise the smaller firm will be driven out of the business†.

The true cost to society of an *additional* unit of fertilizer is, of course, 100.

Furthermore, the financially stronger firm will have to consider that it can only maintain its higher market share by *keeping* the price permanently below a level at which a smaller competitor can operate profitably.

Now suppose the government were to prohibit imports, and at the same time imposed a maximum price of 135. The smaller, less equipped firm would be driven out of business‡: one monopolist would produce all the 50 units, presumably at the set maximum price of 135, and the fertilizer would be produced at its true minimum cost of 6,000 for 50

* The lower limit of 15 is somewhat arbitrary, but more realistic than either the 10, at which point it is just possible to compete with imports, or 25, a 50 per cent market share.

† Under conditions of surplus capacity either of the two firms may be tempted to start a price war in the hope of increasing its market share. However, when production is at full capacity, the increased sales have to be matched by additional investment, even if other overheads, like research organization, central administration, service and distribution network, remain substantially unchanged.

‡ At 140 the price would equal the average cost of a firm which supplies just half the market, i.e. 25 units.

units, giving rise to an average cost of 120 per unit. So far, so good. The cost of an *additional* unit of fertilizer would, as before, be 100. Now suppose the demand for fertilizer is graded according to the quality of the land. For example, we might have:

COSTS AND PROCEEDS PER 300 UNITS OF AGRICULTURAL EXPORT VALUE

	Land quality 1	*Land quality 2*	*Land quality 3*	*Land quality 4*
Gross production value	300	300	300	300
Labour, etc.	100	100	100	100
Remaining	200	200	200	200
Required fertilizer	0·40	1·01	1·40	1·90

If fertilizer is supplied at the true social cost of 100 per additional unit all four grades of land will be worked. However, this assumes that the fertilizer factory is not only subject to price control, but also that it is subsidized, to the extent of its fixed cost. If the fertilizer factory is required to cover its total cost from its sales revenue, the price must be at least 120, and only land qualities 1, 2, and 3 will be worked, unless the price is more than 142, in which case land quality 3 will not be worked either.

With an oligopolistic market (price in the range 167–200), only land qualities 1 and 2 will be worked, except in the borderline case when the price is 200. Finally, if there is no domestic production of fertilizer, only land quality 1 is worked.

The position is somewhat, but not widely, different if an oligopolistic market structure is due not to economics of scale alone, but is reinforced by technology and information limits, e.g. the scarcity and unequal quality of technical specialists and efficient managers. There are in this case two concepts of marginal cost, but the true relevance of one of them is somewhat limited. There is a discontinuity at the point of full employment of the industry's existing capacity without any expansion. The gain to society, to be obtained from abstaining from a unit of the product of an industry which is at this point of discontinuity, is the price as well as the average cost of the least efficient firm, provided its resources can be re-employed elsewhere. If the least efficient firm leaves the industry and releases its resources, we may assume their value on re-employment to be the same elsewhere. This is how a competitive economy is supposed to work. This marginal product is valid only in the case of genuine structural change, that is, if the resources are indeed at once employed elsewhere. The alternative value of the resources which are released by a firm temporarily, because of a recession-type setback in demand and recalled once demand picks up again, is likely to be none at all, because this happens when there is unemployment in the rest of the economy as well. On the other hand in a growing economy the marginal full production cost is a weighted average of the marginal full production costs of the separate firms in the industry. The weights are, however, not proportional to the various firms' size in the existing flow of demand, but the shares in any expansion of production. The largest positive difference between sales price and marginal full production cost is enjoyed by the most efficient firms and they will be the first to expand. The result is that the marginal cost is well below the average cost, in a technological oligopoly, just as in a scale-of-operations oligopoly. The two causes of oligopoly lead to virtually the same market structure.

Both forms of oligopoly are characterized by a tendency to generate surplus capacity, at any rate in a growing economy. This surplus capacity *within* an industry and an individual firm should not be confused with the visible, macro-economic surplus capacity, which is represented by unemployment of labour. Both types of surplus capacity can be present at the same time, but it is also quite conceivable that surplus capacity within an industry prevails even with full employment of labour. Surplus capacity inside an industry means that the people who are employed and paid by the industry, and the machines which are available and in good working condition, can in fact produce more than can be sold at the prevailing price. Firms will naturally not expand their production capacity if there is no prospect of selling the increased output. They can, however, overestimate the future increase of demand, either of the industry as a whole or their own ability to increase their market share. Or they can lose market share to other more aggressively selling firms in the same industry.

This is not specific to an oligopolistic market structure but is rather the result of the uncertainty inherent in any economic system except a theoretical (and not actually existent) perfectly planned command economy. What is, however, specific for the oligopolistic market structure is its limited ability to redress the balance.

A firm which has surplus production capacity will first of all hope that this surplus capacity will be eliminated by a further increase in demand and sales, and it will increase its sales promotion. If there is no prospect of this resulting in an elimination of the surplus capacity within reasonable time, the least efficient of the firm's own production units will be closed down. The one effective means towards driving the less efficient firms out of the market is a reduction of the leading firm's quoted price to a figure well below the average cost per unit of a weaker rival. The leading firm will not do this, because of its impact on the receipts from the already established market share.

This 'ultimate remedy' will be considered only if the magnitude of the surplus capacity is of such a size, that the increased sales for a surviving leading firm, as a result of the elimination of a rival, can be produced without additional investment from the existing production facilities. For a smaller surplus capacity, co-existence with the rival at a price which enables both firms to survive even with surplus capacity, or else a take-over and an amalgamation of the rival's most efficient parts with the leading firm and release of the rest of his resources, is more profitable.

A combination of rising costs and under-utilization of available capacity may have already brought the weakest firms to the verge of bankruptcy without any specific action by a stronger firm. This does not necessarily mean that the less efficient firm will indeed be driven out of the market. A market leader is likely to choose precisely such a moment to raise his own price, because the weaker firms will be only too glad to follow.

We conclude that in a market economy, working under conditions of increasing returns to scale (indivisibility), there is a systematic difference between private and social cost, the private cost being higher than the true social cost, resulting in failure to produce efficiently.

This conclusion applies to *any* form of market economy where a firm or production organization is required to meet its cost from its sales, not only the 'capitalistic' one where the firm is working for profit. Before one draws the further conclusion that the market mechanism should therefore be abolished, at least for certain sectors of advanced-technology production processes, one has to answer one crucial question: can the theoretically possible, efficient production, actually be achieved by any other method of organization?

1.12 INVESTMENT AND INTEREST

Within the model of competitive equilibrium, interest is a price, just like any other price, and indicates the ratio between the social cost of present and future production.

Suppose we compare the costings of two methods of producing the same product. Producing a million pounds' worth of a particular article by the present, rather obsolete production methods will cost a million pounds' worth of labour and materials. Producing the same amount by the most efficient production methods will require only half a million pounds' worth of labour and materials, plus a once-for-all initial investment outlay of two million pounds. The new installations must, however, be produced by the capital-goods producing sectors of the economy. If the product were offered for sale from now onwards for the lower price of half a million, it would immediately drive out all the production by the obsolete existing methods of production, and an enormous instantaneous demand for capital equipment would arise. Therefore, we charge the new production method with a capital charge, of just under 25 per cent, and the cost price of the new production method is nearly the same as for the old one. The demand for capital-goods machines, etc., is now kept within the limits of what can be produced by the capital-goods producing industry, because the new process is introduced only gradually.

This follows the general idea of a limited incentive for a productive activity as such, the return to be appropriated by a factor in limited supply, rather than by the productive activity itself. As long as the price of a red stone is in excess of the cost of a white stone plus a few minutes' work and a bit of red paint, there is no rational limit to the activity of painting white stones red, and the attempts of the red-stone painters to outbid each other will bring the price of a red stone down to the cost of production. This may be a sound idea in the case of an essentially repetitive activity; but it does not work in the case of investment, which is limited by new ideas about investment projects to initiate as well as by the limitation of the market, e.g. the possibility of selling the products from the newly built factories, machines, etc.

There is a noticeable discrepancy between the market rate of interest and the return on new investment, as far as this figure can be assessed independently. Rates of return on new investment in the order of 20–40 per cent are not uncommon, whereas the market rate of interest barely covers the reduction in real value of the capital sum by inflation.

At this point, it seems useful to discuss in some detail the relation between the return on investment and the role of new inventions. The calculation of the rate of return to which I refer* is based on the idea of *embodied* technical progress. This means that the whole of the increase in productivity arising from the installation of a new machine, which 'embodies' a new invention, is attributed to the investment rather than to the invention as such. Personally, I hold that technical progress is by and large *induced*,† i.e. the decision to invest and modernize now, if taken under conditions of continuous full employment, itself creates the conditions for new inventions.

The cost side of an economy-wide rate of growth is reflected in an individual firm's costs, in the form of higher labour costs revealing the obsolescence of traditional methods of production. The benefits of induced technical progress are, however, for the greater part external to any investing firm. The result is that:

(i) A firm which does not invest, while the economy at large grows, becomes obsolete and is eventually driven out of business.

(ii) No firm can pay, to a capitalist-shareholder or money-lender, the full social return which arises out of the investment financed with the shareholder's or lender's money. If it did, it would not be able to pay increased wages. This is not to say that the market rate of interest is a valid indicator of the return on new investment to an average firm, let alone to society. It is the minimum requirement to be satisfied by all financially viable investment projects. 'Only just' financially viable investment projects may be initiated by firms who are less efficient than the average. This inferior efficiency may be because of their small scale of operations—they cannot freely choose the most efficient methods of production because they require capital goods of a certain minimum capacity, which a small firm cannot

* *See* sections 5.4 and 5.5 of my book *Forecasting Models for National Economic Planning* [16]; also J. Sandee's *Possible Economic Growth in the Netherlands* [40]. Sandee does not explain the calculation of the capital–output ratio in detail, but I learned it from him as I was working under his direction at the time. *See* Sandee, loc. cit., p. 173.

† This notion of induced technical progress is by no means the accepted *communus opinio*. There is still, by and large, the assumption that technical progress is exogenous and only its rate of implementation at a particular point in time by investment can be influenced by economic policy. *See*, for example, R. Solow [43].

utilize to the full. The inferior efficiency can also result from being ill informed.

In both cases the orderly expansion of demand requires that even these relatively less efficient firms get their chance. Furthermore, 'only just efficient' investment projects include miscalculated projects. Uncertainty is one reason for operating a market rate of interest which is well below the average return on new investment. Suppose a new method of producing a certain product is expected to result in a return of product value less operating cost equal to 50 per cent of the initial investment. If, however, by miscalculation the actual return of product value less operating cost is only 10 per cent of the initial investment, it is still economical to continue operation, since the initial investment has been spent anyway.

The relation between investment and sold production is indirect, the intermediary being effective demand for end-products, which regulates the demand for production capacity and should correspond (with a certain margin) to it.

If under the influence of an increasing demand for the end-product a number of firms expand their production capacity, this establishes a return to the corresponding investment. This is because without the possibility of importing or producing the capital goods concerned, the government could not have allowed demand to expand in the first place; if it had done so, this would have resulted in excess demand and rising prices. The realized return on investment includes the return made by the most efficient as well as by the least efficient firms, and is therefore higher than the minimum.

On the other hand the rate of interest is to a large extent government controlled and this control is exercised at a level which allows firms to cover costs. If firms actually invested whenever this promised a return in excess of the rate of interest, this would result in over-investment. The economic life span of capital goods would be shorter than would be called for by efficiency: investment in new equipment for expansion of production would have to be restricted by a reduction in aggregate purchasing power to keep total demand, including the demand for capital goods, within the limits of what could be produced. New investment for expansion will not be undertaken if there is no prospect of selling the increased production, irrespective of the profitability of the investment. New investment for increased productivity, for producing the same amount of products with less costs, is not necessarily prevented by stagnating demand. Many industrial concerns, however, base their investment decisions, expansion and modernization alike, on an internally required rate of return, which is well above the market rate of interest. As a result their actual decisions may well be more efficient than would be the case if they maximized profit, i.e. behaved according to the competitive model and initiated any project which promised a return greater than the market rate of interest.

The notion of a 'full' social rate of return which is higher than the finance-capital rate of return needs qualification. I shall argue in other parts of this book:

(*a*) That the prevailing price structure systematically underestimates the true costs of exhaustible natural resources; and
(*b*) That a resource-sparing price structure implies a lower return on new investment.

The true social return on additional investment is therefore not as high as calculations of the macro-economic return on new investment would indicate. My guess is that the balance of these two contradictory arguments is that the true return on new investment is nevertheless well above the market rate of interest.

1.13 TECHNOLOGY AND PRICES OF NATURAL RESOURCES

Suppose the following to be the breakdown of the requirements for producing an industrial product by mechanized and by non-mechanized methods:

	Non-mechanized	*Mechanized*
Labour	0·5	0·1
Machines	—	1·2
Raw materials	0·5	0·5

Let us for the sake of simplicity assume that the units are in value at the currently prevailing prices and that, so far, the non-mechanized production is the predominant method used by the traditional firms. This is in line with the figures and with market equilibrium. The amount of product is measured in value as well and the price is 1·0 per unit of value of the product, which is equal to the cost of production by the least efficient method of production.

The return on additional investment, if the increased production can be sold, is the difference in the variable costs of the two methods of production, i.e. $1{\cdot}0 - 0{\cdot}6 = 0{\cdot}4$ per 1·2 units of new investment, which works out as a rate of return of exactly one-third.

We have seen in the previous section that this is quite compatible with a much lower financial return and with market equilibrium, of a kind, as well. The difference between the full social rate of return and the financial rate of return to a firm is eventually absorbed by increasing labour costs, and in the meantime the stability of the market is maintained by its oligopolistic structure.

How do costs of raw materials fit into this picture? A large part of the costs of a material, as paid by a firm, consists of the costs of its extraction from the earth and any further processing which may be needed, like the refining of an ore and the generation of (hydro-electric) electricity from flowing water. There is, however, a residual cost which represents the scarcity value of the natural resource itself. Recall section 1.5. The imputed cost of a production factor is that price of the production factor which limits its demand to the available (or affordable) supply.

Mechanization economizes on labour while the demand for raw materials, implied by a given level of demand for end-products, is not directly affected.

The demand for energy is, of course, increased. To maintain full employment of labour in the presence of increased labour productivity one needs, however, an increased demand for end-products, resulting in a further increase in the demand for natural resources. This leads to what we might call the *principle of compensating factor-substitution.*

If the demand for raw materials rises, then a part of the existing demand for raw materials should be redirected towards other production factors. Either raw-material intensive products should become more expensive, prompting final users to buy other products instead, or else raw-material intensive processes should become unprofitable and the use of substitutes encouraged. The same is true for other resources like fresh water, etc.

Mechanization affects the relative prices of labour and raw materials because the increase in production requires additional raw materials. If we take the figures of our example, the productivity of labour in producing this particular product increases by a factor 5 between the first introduction of the mechanical method and its complete dominance. Full employment of the same number of people will be maintained only if production increases by a factor 5 in that same period as well. In that case the expected result would be either a corresponding rise in the required supply of raw materials, or else a rise in the price of raw materials so as to redirect demand in the direction of labour-intensive products and away from raw-material intensive products.

The most extreme case would arise if total raw material supply were already at a maximum limit and could not be increased. In that case total consumption of final products could rise only if the consumption of raw-material intensive products were to be reduced in absolute terms.

One would suspect that to be possible only if the price of raw materials rose more than that of labour. In actual fact, the prices of raw materials have been relatively stable* during most of the post-World War II period. Only quite recently (1972, 1973), newspaper reports indicate a rising tendency for the prices of crude oil, foodstuffs, and some metals. Because of the still incomplete statistical record it is difficult to assess the importance of this change in trend.

In any case, we would wish to understand how the situation of stable prices of raw materials and rising wages could prevail for such a long period of time. In the first place technical change has not only been labour-saving but also material-saving. The development of various man-made materials is a case in point. Nevertheless, the amounts of raw materials extracted from the earth have *not* been kept stationary but have increased dramatically.

The means towards achieving this result have been more systematic prospecting and improved mining technology, allowing extraction at greater depth, under the sea, etc. An economic system which is based on the continuation of such a development assumes that there *are* no limits to natural resources, in an economically relevant sense, and that if perchance a particular material runs out we can always find a substitute. If, however, the true position is that there is a limited total of exploitable materials, we indulge in the wasteful consumption of scarce resources at the cost of their availability to future generations.

One would infer that at some stage the mere fact that the earth's

* I copied the 1968 (base 1963) raw material indices from Table 176 of the 1970 U.N. *Statistical Yearbook* and computed 1968 (base 1963) indices of average earnings in industry from Table 175 of the same publication. I did this for Australia, Canada, France, West Germany, Italy, Japan, Sweden, the United Kingdom, and the United States.

The range was: raw materials 98 (West Germany) to 115 (United Kingdom) and for labour 126 (Australia as well as the United States) to 174 (Japan).

resources are limited will enforce a different tendency, where natural resource limits will become a restriction on further increase of industrial production.

A related point is pollution. From a purely technical point of view pollution is the converse of resource depletion. The one relates to the fact that there is only a limited amount of certain minerals inside the earth, and even less within the reach of men. The other problem, pollution, relates to the fact that the earth's surface, the air, and the seas can contain only a limited amount of the waste products of these same minerals. The one crucial economic difference is that ore deposits are owned or controlled by governments or private individuals and companies, who cash the implied rental on a specific geographically located source of supply. The air and the seas on the other hand are freely available to everyone until such time as appropriate restrictions on dumping waste in them are introduced.

In both cases we have the twin problem of creating a material-efficient and 'clean' technology reprocessing by-products to useful or at least harmless substances, rather than throwing them away, and of maintaining a price structure which penalizes failure to make use of the available technical possibilities in this respect, simultaneously encouraging the development of the required processes.

The position of food and other agricultural materials is slightly different. The amount of immediate extra production which can be obtained by over-intensive use of arable land and pasture, or by hunting whales and other species of animals to extermination, is much more limited than the amount of additional minerals which can be extracted from the earth by more intensive mining.

Agricultural prices have nevertheless been remarkably stable during most of the post-World War II period, but have risen sharply in quite recent times (1973). As pointed out by Elizabeth Stamp in Oxfam's *New Internationalist* [43*a*], this is no mere freak: the resource limit is beginning to make itself felt.

1.14 MONEY

Income consists of payments in money arising from other people's expenditure. For this reason there is a certain technical relation between the stock of money in a country and its level of income per time period.

Suppose, for the sake of simplification, that all income consists of monthly salaries payable on the last day of each month, all expenditure consists of consumption, while all companies are integrated production and distribution companies selling directly to the public. Suppose, furthermore, that people spend all their money each month. Then on payments day all the money is with the trading companies. On the first day of the next month it is all in the hands of private people who will during the month bring it back to the various shops, etc., to exchange for consumer goods. Clearly, under these conditions, income per year will be twelve times the stock of money. In reality the stock of money has to be more than one-twelfth of the annual income, mainly for two reasons:

(*a*) Private people will want to keep at least some cash left at the end of the month, and firms will want some cash left at the beginning of the month.
(*b*) Not all firms sell directly to final consumers, and intermediate payments for semi-finished products and various services must be made in money as well.

On the other hand, not all money is cash. A bank account and the associated right to write a cheque is as good as cash.

Money comes into the economic system by the following channels:

(*a*) *The State Budget*

The state's expenditure may be greater than its revenue from taxation and such incidental revenue as public ownership of shares, etc. If the difference is financed by a long-term loan this has no monetary effect, at least not directly. But the difference may also be financed by printing banknotes and then the money supply is increased.

(*b*) *The Banking System*

If the manager of branch *X* of bank *Y* tells Mr Z that he will allow him an overdraft of £200 to finance the purchase of a new car, this effectively increases the money supply by £200. It will, of course, only be recorded statistically at the moment that the car dealer presents Mr Z's cheque, to be exchanged either for cash, or for a positive balance in his own, the car dealer's, account. Furthermore, if the cheque is paid into an account, instead of being paid out in cash, the banking system does not as yet make any payment over the counter at all. But for all practical purposes (e.g. the car dealer's further use of his bank balance), the transaction has increased the amount of money in circulation until such time as Mr Z has paid back his overdraft, either by paying in cash or by a transfer from someone else's positive account. The effective amount of money in circulation is then the cash, plus the *gross* total of all positive bank balances, without subtraction of overdrafts.

(*c*) *From Abroad*

If a firm sells abroad it receives payment in a foreign currency. This foreign currency will be exchanged via the banking system, and eventually by the central bank of the country we are discussing, against national currency. While this increases the central bank's holdings of foreign currency, it also means an increase in the country's internal circulation of its own national currency. Conversely, imports have to be paid for and this means that the amount of money in circulation is affected by a country's external balance of payments—exports less imports.

(*d*) *Lending Transactions by the State, the Central Bank, and Foreign Countries*

If Mr A borrows from Mr B, then A's stock of money is increased and B's stock of money is reduced. Hence there is no change in the money supply unless A uses it to clear a bank overdraft or B finances it by a bank overdraft; we would classify this change in the stock of money as a change in bank overdraft, i.e. cause (*b*) above. However, money in the vaults of the state or the central bank or in a foreign country is not money in domestic circulation: for this reason public loans and foreign loans affect the money supply.

These channels—the public budget, overdraft on bank accounts, the balance of payments, and foreign and public loans—are the basic channels by which money comes into or leaves circulation. They may, however, occur in combination and one and the same transaction may involve two or more of them. For this reason it may sometimes be necessary to think carefully before one is sure of the monetary effect of some transactions.

A loan between one private firm and another inside the country is monetarily neutral, a loan from abroad is not neutral, but a foreign loan by the government is neutral.

1.15 THE MULTIPLIER

The effect known as 'the multiplier' arises from the interaction of two relations. The one is the definition of total (national) income as the sum of all expenditure—less the amount spent abroad (imports) plus the amount spent by foreigners—on paying for goods and services produced in the country in question.

Income is always someone else's expenditure, but not all expenditure gives rise to income inside the country and some income may arise from foreigners' expenditure. Now one of the items of expenditure is consumption. If, for the moment, we leave out the complication of foreign trade then production (or rather the statistical record of production, which is its proceeds) is identical to the producers' income as well as to the purchasers' expenditure.

In an aggretated economic system, a 'national economy', the items of expenditure are:

(*a*) The *consumption* of private households and families, e.g. the expenditure on (and hence the production of) bread, butter, cameras, ladies garments, film shows, etc.

(*b*) The *investment* by production organizations (enterprises, firms), e.g. the expenditure on (and the production of) machines, factory buildings, shop and office buildings, typewriters, measuring equipment, computers, and the like, and also any increment in traders' stock, as well as work in progress of construction.

(*c*) The *public expenditure* on goods, services, and salaries. This comes in two categories: *public consumption*, e.g. purchase of salt and grit for the roads in winter and the salaries of the civil servants, and *public investment*, e.g. the construction of roads, bridges, public buildings, etc.

To be consistent with the convention that expenditure is production (except when purchased abroad) the salaries of the civil servants must be classified as part of production. They are, of course, part of income as well. The identity between production and its outlets is then expressed as:

$$pro = co + iv + pe$$

(production = consumption + investment + public expenditure)

At the same time consumption is a function of income and hence of production. While (sold) production is identical to *earned* income it is not the same as *disposable* income. Taxes and such financial commitments as social security benefits come between them, as do financial benefits like social security payments, which are not income from production but are disposable personal income. It is possible to express all these factors by suitable relations (equations), but at present we will express consumption *ceterus paribus* (i.e. no change in taxes, etc.) as a function of production:

$$co = \alpha\, pro + \beta$$

One other discrepancy between consumption and production is personal saving.

The value of the coefficient α will be in the interval $0 < \alpha < 1$ (the 'marginal propensity to consume') and also it will normally be less than the average ratio between production and consumption. People will want to eat, to have at least some roof over their heads, and some minimum of clothing, more or less at any cost. From an increment in their income they will, however, spend or rather not spend a substantial fraction on personal savings (and on paying the marginal rate of tax). As a result the constant β would be positive.

We may now substitute the expression ($\alpha\, pro + \beta$) for the consumption to obtain:

$$pro = \alpha\, pro + \beta + iv + pe$$

or

$$pro = \frac{1}{1-\alpha}(\beta + iv + pe)$$

Now at a marginal propensity to consume of, let us say, two-thirds of any addition to gross productive income, this would mean that any increase in either investment or public expenditure would eventually result in an increase in production of about three times the original expenditure impulse. All this would not materialize at once. For example, if the government decided to build an additional road at £10 million, then this is in the first instance £10 million more production, until such time as the contractors of the road have paid their workmen and these (additionally hired) workmen have found time to spend their wages. In the second instance, then, the consumption expenditure which arises from the £10 million increase in income will be £6⅔ million. The manufacturers of the various refrigerators, ice-creams, etc., bought by the contractors' labourers as well as by the workmen and shareholders of the suppliers of the concrete and other materials, now all experience increased sales. Therefore, in the third instance, the manufacturers of consumer goods also hire more labourers and pay more dividends, and a further instalment of additional consumption will arise. The eventual result would be £10 million for the road and £20 million additional consumption.

This concept of 'the multiplier' or 'multiplier effects' will come up in a number of places when we discuss the results of, for example, increasing public expenditure.

The following comments on this concept are useful at this stage. Firstly, the multiplier effect operates in value terms. What happens to physical production is another matter. For example, in a situation where production is already as high as is technically possible, when there is full employment of labour and all machines are in constant use, the results of an increase in public expenditure will be, more than anything else, higher prices. In fact, if production in physical terms is really unchanged consumption will be less when public expenditure is more, and consumers will find they can buy less for more money. Secondly, the multiplier effect is reduced because the income which people can spend is not the same as what they earn, and the difference has a systematic tendency to *stabilize* earned income and consumption with it. The main items of difference between earned and spendable income which are relevant as stabilizers are unemployment benefit and progressive taxation. If a man loses his job his earned 'primary' income drops virtually to zero, but the reduction in his spendable income is much less (*a*) because he gets unemployment benefit and (*b*) because he now pays virtually no tax at all. There are other differences between primary, earned income and spendable income, such as, for example, pensions but they have no particular stabilizing effect.

One other question is what happens to the amount of money in circulation. Clearly, the increase in the level of production and income, whether real or only nominal, requires an increased stock of money in order that the higher income may circulate. An increase in public expenditure does bring more money into circulation, but not necessarily to the required amount. Hence, the two phenomena, the expenditure impulse and its multiplier effect on the one hand and the increase in the stock of money originating from that expenditure on the other hand, must be treated as separate entities.

1.16 CAPITAL–OUTPUT RATIO AND ACCELERATOR

The installation of factories, machines, and other appliances makes it possible to produce more products with the help of the new capital equipment. If on the average the production of a steady flow of output, measured in value as £1 million per year, requires a stock of capital equipment which costs £2 million to produce, we say that the (average) capital–output ratio is 2. Production is not produced solely by machines. Nevertheless, we have seen that by *replacing* older, rather obsolete production methods by new ones, we can obtain additional production and the sole *additional* requirement for the attainment of this additional production is new machines.

Hence, if it requires £3 million's worth of new capital equipment to increase production by £1 million, without also increasing the use of labour and raw materials, we will say that the *incremental* capital–output ratio is 3. Furthermore, the concept of the incremental capital–output ratio has been extended to value added and profit. If we can produce more products, worth £3 million, using additional labour and raw materials worth £1 million, by installing £4 million's worth of new machines, we will also say that the incremental capital–output ratio is $4:(3-1) = 2$.

Incremental capital–output ratios in the order of 2 or 3 are astoundingly low if we interpret them the other way round: an investment of £3 million produces a product flow of £1 million each year. Even so, the capital–output ratio is a potential source of violent instability if the relationship works the other way round.

If, for whatever reason, the demand for end-products increases by £1 million, and this is likely to be a permanent situation, firms will want to adapt their production capacity to the new higher level of the demand for their end-products and order £3 million's worth of new capital equipment. To make matters worse, investment itself is also a final destination, and the demand for investment goods will generate new demand for investment in the capital goods producing sectors of the economy.

This is the *accelerator* mechanism. The accelerator does not, however, have the same general validity as the multiplier. The accelerator response to changes in demand is limited by the following factors:

(*a*) Investment in a particular industry or a particular type of equipment cannot become negative. Hence, if under conditions of recession the overall level of demand drops, there is still a certain positive demand for new investment in replacement of worn-out or obsolete equipment, even if most firms have idle production capacity which they might want to sell off, if they could.

(*b*) The production of capital goods is limited by the technical production capacity of the capital goods producing sectors of the economy.

(*c*) Investment in any given period of time is limited not only by technical limits on production but also by investing firms' ability to pay for new investment. In this connection we must distinguish between a planned investment programme and realized investment. Hence, a £1 million rise in the demand for end-products may well result in additional investment programmes which would cost £3 million, but the percentage of any programme which will be implemented in any separate period of time will drop, because of the financial constraints on firms' ability to pay for new investment.

The accelerator mechanism will be discussed in more detail later, in particular in sections 6.4 and 9.7.

1.17 THE CIRCULAR FLOW AND ITS OPEN ENDS

The concepts of production, income, and expenditure are linked by the fact that expenditure is on products and that income arises out of production.

For example, if I go to the barber to have my hair cut, this is my expenditure because I have to pay the barber. My payment to the barber is also the barber's income. His actual work is part of the national product.

The link between production and expenditure is further emphasized because the actual record of production, its statistical measurement in national income statistics, is based on the criterion that money is paid for it.

For example, an artist may have worked very hard on a painting and both he and his colleagues consider it a beautiful piece of work. National income statistics do not, however, measure the artist's product by his personal effort, nor by the artist's own or his colleagues' opinion about the result, but by the fact that he obtains money for it.

Let us make the simplifying assumption that there is no outside world to be traded with, i.e. that all production, income, and expenditure are within a single 'closed' economy. Then, in such a closed economy, production, income, and expenditure are one and the same, they are all *identical.*

Note that production is not identical with the technical capacity to produce. It may be a sign of effective economic regulation if the actually realized production is not much below the technical limit to production, as imposed by objective circumstances like labour supply, capital equipment, availability of raw materials, etc. Production *is*, however, the amount actually produced which is identical to expenditure and to income.

Although the totals of expenditure, production, and income are identical in a closed economy, this identity is lost when we refer to the production, the income, and the expenditure of a particular sector within the economy, enterprises, families, government, etc. The expenditure is split into 'expenditure categories', according to the sector and the assumed purpose of the purchase. One 'follows' the products to their users. The main *expenditure categories* are:

Private Consumption

This would include purchases of food, clothing, housing (rent), television sets, etc., by ordinary people.

Investment by Firms

This concept of 'real' investment should be distinguished from such financial investment as purchase of a share, bond, etc. The productive investment by firms is the actual purchase of tangible capital goods—machines, buildings, etc. Although the main purpose of financial investment is to finance real investment, the two can in fact be different,* as a result of a variety of financial manipulations.

* Depending on the precise definition of what a financial investment is. I assume in any case that the mere accumulation of money is not an investment.

Public Investment

Construction of roads, public buildings, etc., is public investment but it does not include investment by state-owned firms. State-owned firms should be treated as part of the enterprises sector. Some countries count material expenditure on armaments as public investment, which is, however, contrary to the main criterion concerning the nature of investment, its envisaged contribution to production.

Public Consumption

Salaries of the army and civil service are the main items here. These are income to the public servants, and expenditure of the public authorities, on behalf of the community at large. To maintain the identity between the three aspects of economic activity here, one postulates that government is a service produced by public authorities for the community at large.

Inventory Building or Stockpiling

This is mainly temporary accumulation of products in the trade channels. The *income* is split into two main categories, namely:

Earnings from Employment

Wages and salaries, employers' contributions to pension funds, etc.

All Other Incomes

This is the full difference in value between the gross proceeds from production and the payment to labour, not just profit. For example, payment of interest on a bank loan* by a firm is not profit, but it is non-labour income to someone. Rents are another example of non-labour income.

In an open economy with foreign trade, income and expenditure are not identical. There is first of all a sometimes quite noticeable discrepancy between expenditure and production. A substantial part of the national expenditure is not on domestic production but on imported products. Similarly, an approximately equally sizeable part

* Interest on the public debt is treated as a transfer payment, because it does not originate in production.

of domestic production is destined not for sale in the domestic market but for export. The financial counterpart of the difference between imports and exports is the country's external *balance of payments.*

Unless a country's national currency is an international reserve currency* (a position which has its own complications), exports as well as imports are and must be paid for in gold or in the money of other countries. A national government or a central bank† possesses, however, only a limited amount of foreign currency and cannot, or does not want to, borrow unnecessarily. Therefore it is desirable that imports should be approximately equal to exports. This means also that national expenditure should be approximately equal to production. Approximate equality between national income and expenditure is, however, a *result* of successful economic regulation rather than a necessary event. There are also discrepancies between domestic production and national income. In an industrially developed‡ country they are of lesser quantitative importance than the differences between production and expenditure, both in absolute terms and in their fluctuation.

The other main 'open end' in the circulation system is the government and its economic policy.

Public expenditure is part of production. More important is, however, the *difference* between the payments by the government for its expenditure and the payments of taxes to the government.

Income after tax is of practical relevance to the private sector in order to determine its expenditure. The private sector's expenditure should be less than its full productive income, otherwise there would be no room for public expenditure. It is, however, wrong to assume

* A reserve currency is a national currency in which other, smaller countries with less well-established international trading positions keep part of their own reserve of foreign currency. For example, Western European countries' central banks keep balances in US dollars and sterling area countries keep balances in English pounds.

† Authorized issuing institute of the national currency and official holder of the country's foreign currency reserve. This is in substance a public function and today most central banks are run by or owned or controlled by the government. Historically many of them originated as private banks and most of them have still a certain degree of autonomy.

‡ In some of the oil-producing underdeveloped countries this is not at all the case. Income, accruing to expatriate capital, e.g. oil companies, is often a figure in the same order of magnitude as the income which accrues to the producing country!

that taxes should always match public expenditure in the same period of time. There are other sources of disequilibrium in the economic system, and fiscal policy is one of the instruments which can be used to compensate their effects. Nor are taxes the only difference between productive and spendable income.

These differences all come under the general heading of *transfer payments*, that is, payments which cross the boundaries between different sectors of the economy (and therefore occur in the national income statistics) but are not considered as originating in production. Examples of such 'non-productive' payments are state-financed social benefits, grants to students,* and interest on the public debt. Interest on industrial bonds is part of the productive income of capital and not a transfer payment.

Finally, expenditure can be different from spendable income because of borrowing and/or the use of cash or bank balances accumulated in earlier periods; or, in the opposite case, it can be different because of net lending to the banks, the public sector or the rest of the world, or the accumulation of cash or bank balances with money character. The availability of cash or bank balances to particular persons or institutions enables them to finance expenditure in excess of their currently disposable income. The availability of a relatively large amount of money in the economy, over and above what is strictly needed for circulation, can therefore cause a temporary rise in expenditure relative to current spendable income. If this happens, productive income will subsequently rise as well and the whole level of both income and expenditure will be pushed upwards.

Equilibrium, or a kind of equilibrium, can nevertheless be restored at a higher level in three ways or in a combination of them:

(*a*) Production, and hence income and expenditure, fails to respond, because production is at a physical limit. If this is the case the expansion in the volume of production can change into an inflationary rise in prices, more money being paid for the same amount of products.

(*b*) The money 'leaks' out of the private sector of the economy, into taxes or abroad. Under a system of progressive taxation,

* The 'productivity' of a particular payment may indeed be an object of discussion and it may be doubted if the work of a student is less productive than that of, for example, an army officer in peacetime, who receives a salary.

the state's revenue from taxes rises faster than its proportional fraction of national income, and a rising level of income generates a surplus on the public budget. A money-leak abroad arises because the national currency is exchanged by the central bank for foreign currency, in order to pay for imports, and the money leaves the country.

(*c*) Although the total amount of money may remain substantially the same, the 'surplus' character disappears because the 'normal' ratio between income and the amount of money in circulation is restored at a higher level since the income has risen.

Conversely, the government can also consciously *manipulate* the stock of money and the price at which it can be borrowed, the rate of interest.

Since the public budget is one of the channels by which money comes into circulation, a budget surplus or deficit has a monetary effect, as well as a direct effect on spendable income.

The government can also decisively influence other channels by which money comes into circulation. The total of all measures which influence the stock of money as an object of policy is the government's *monetary policy*.

The main money and income streams which go through the economy can be summarized as in Figure 1.

The arrows in the diagram indicate the direction of the money flows. Some of the flows of money have material counterparts, like products sold, labour performed, etc. These material flows should then be visualized as going in the direction *against* the arrows, as the arrows indicate their payment. The 'taps' on values indicate points where the flows are regulated by various public policies.

The object of regulation is to ensure that the rate of flow through the system is approximately equal to its technical capacity. Unlike what would be the case in a simple fluid system, the rate of flow depends on the relation between public spending on the one side and the other two controls, taxes and monetary policy. We should envisage the throughput capacity of the system as dependent on the level in the production tank.

The true measure of economic performance is, however, not just money and income, but the amount of products which can be bought

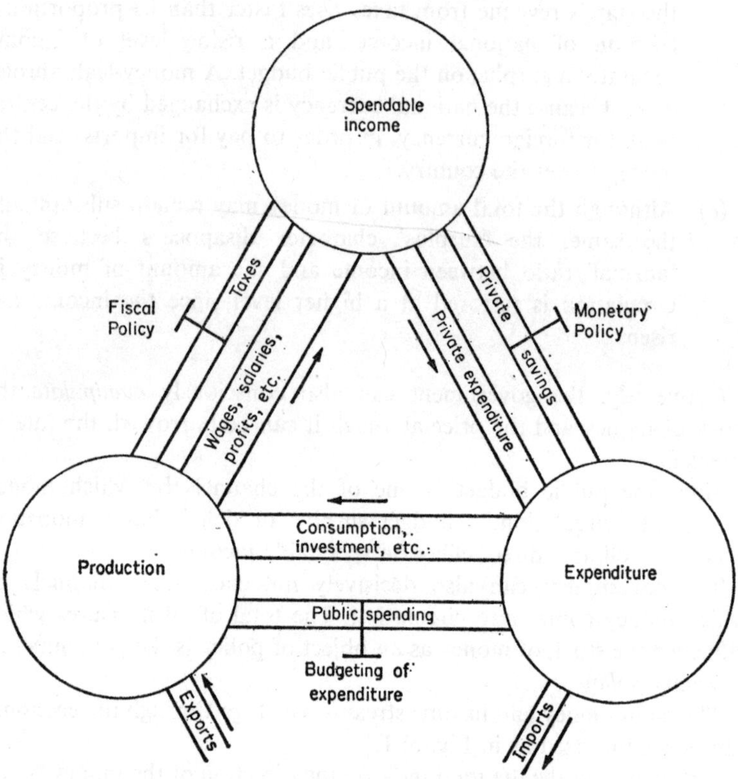

FIGURE 1 Visual presentation of the circular flow

by them. This means that the system is at full capacity if the income stream is equal to the cost of full-employment production.

It will therefore be argued in this book that public control over price level is an instrument of economic regulation on the same footing as the more traditional fiscal and monetary policy.

1.18 INFLATION, DEMAND PULL, COST PUSH, AND MONEY

Incomes are accounted per unit of time and credit transactions involve the comparison of payments at different points in time. Therefore, it is desirable that a sum of money, written in a contract as salary, a pension or a loan, shall command about the same amount of products at a later point in time. Otherwise people will not know the real value of future payments of salary, pension, etc., nor of the repayment of a loan. Alas, this stability condition has been violated, sometimes on a tremendous scale. This has occurred mostly, but not completely exclusively, by way of rising nominal values of incomes and prices. The condition of rising prices, and hence of a falling real value of money, is known as *inflation.*

According to our analysis of the cause of inflation, we distinguish two types: 'demand pull' and 'cost push' inflation.

Suppose there is, for example, a deficit on the public budget and a consequential increase in the amount of money in circulation, then people's expenditure out of their disposable income and any credit they obtain can become greater than the value of the available supplies of various products, if measured at the previously prevailing prices. This causes 'demand pull'. There is, popularly expressed, 'too much money chasing too few products'. The equilibrium will reassert itself by an increase in the financial valuation of the same amount of products, that is, by increase in the price level until the value of the available products is equal to expenditure. If, however, earnings from employment rise first, while there is no shortage of products, prices will rise as a result. This is so, partly because of the rising labour cost and partly because people can, anyhow, afford to pay higher prices.

Incomes do not, however, rise uniformly at the same percentage for everybody. Rising prices, and the fact that other people are receiving increased earnings, prompt claims for increases by groups who have not received an increment in earnings so far. This will result in a further rise in the price level and the groups who received the initial increment demand more in order to restore their purchasing power. Furthermore, once inflation is under way people will try to *over-compensate** the erosion of the purchasing power of their earnings, and 'cost push' is in full swing. The increased nominal income cannot, however, be kept circulating without an increase in the amount of money in circulation.

With rising incomes and prices firms (and people) have to pay ever-increasing sums of money. If the amount of money does not keep pace with the income it must circulate, there will come a moment when a firm just does not have the cash available to pay either its

* Otherwise the spiralling process would eventually dampen, because prices of imported products do not increase (at least for a fixed exchange rate).

staff or some bill for materials. If this occurs on a large scale a *liquidity crisis* develops and firms will have to do something about it.

One solution to the problem is to go to the bank and borrow. That would mean that additional money is brought into circulation by the banking system. If cost push is financed by increasing the money supply afterwards, the two types of inflation can be distinguished only by the presence of unused production capacity. If for whatever reason (for example, because the government has ordered the banks *not* to increase their supply of credit), firms are unable to obtain credit they must contain their expenditure. If firms' deteriorated liquidity position prompted them to resist further increases in earnings per worker, this would contain inflation. It is, however, equally possible that firms will reduce the number of their staff and the amount of their purchases. This will create unemployment.

It will be argued in this book that modern industrial economy has an inherent tendency towards cost-push inflation. If this is so, full employment of labour and stable prices are compatible only under a regime of incomes policy, which will contain inflation by means of administrative controls.

A special kind of cost-push inflation (almost a separate type of inflation) arises in connection with resistance to price and income reductions.

Technical change and the equilibrium between supply and demand may call for a change in the price *structure.*

For example, in section 1.13 we saw that mechanization, combined with an unchanged supply of natural resources, calls for a rise in the earth rentals imputed to ore deposits, etc., relative to labour, which becomes the factor in abundant supply.

If relative prices can only be changed by price increases, the price structure can only be changed if the average price level increases.

2

Regions

2.1 THE CONCENTRATION OF INDUSTRY

Why does a firm choose a particular country, city or region in which to build a factory instead of another?

Apart from specific locational factors*, such as the presence of ore deposits, etc., there are certain *general* factors which influence the economic viability of a high-productive, science-based production organization. Among the *economic*† factors which are relevant we may mention:

(*a*) Availability of educated, skilled, and trained manpower, preferably of all grades from semi-skilled to academically trained and with experience of similar work in other production organizations.

(*b*) Access to a sufficiently large and preferably expanding market. Under this heading two points are noticeable:
(b_1) Availability of an efficient transport and communications network, and
(b_2) Position within a prosperous region.

These conditions presuppose a certain *infrastructure* of public services, e.g. educational institutions and transport facilities, but they are also to a considerable extent self-perpetuating.

One of the sources of skill and training is possessing experience in similar work in another firm. Prosperity is also where the established firms in other sectors of economic activities are. They are further reinforced by market forces. Because of economics of scale, the leading production centres set the price, thereby preventing economically

* *See* H. O. Nourse [36].

† The political stability of a country, e.g. the likelihood that the next government will nationalize without compensation or that production will be interrupted by civil war, is, of course, a quite relevant *political* factor.

viable production of certain types of products outside the established regions altogether.

As a result of these considerations the industrially developed countries have become the specialized suppliers of advanced-technology products.

2.2 INFRASTRUCTURE

The infrastructure of a country or region is the collection of facilities, traditionally the result of public investment, which could not be made profitable to private enterprise except at the cost of an undesirable high price, if at all. The provision of adequate infrastructure facilities is a main characteristic of an economically developed region. The reasons for financing a particular project from public funds are mainly the following:

(*a*) The operation of the project, its service, is itself characterized by important economies of scale.

Nuclear electric-power generators should not charge the electricity consumer with the full cost of their development. If they do, the further expansion of the electricity industry, not involving a comparable cost of development, is hampered.

(*b*) Major users of the service operate production processes characterized by increasing returns to scale, and can only operate while charging a price in the neighbourhood of the true (marginal) cost if they themselves obtain other products or services *below* the true cost.

The training of students is not by itself characterized by important indivisibilities. But the provision of education at zero or low cost to those qualified to follow it makes it possible for science-based industries to obtain scientifically trained manpower at a price well below its training cost.

(*c*) The service provided is complementary to the use of under-employed labour.

The provision of more than adequate infrastructure facilities below their cost in an otherwise backward region may help industry to pay wages where it would not otherwise be able to do so. We will come back to this point at a later stage.

Many traditional infrastructure facilities are examples of lack of divisibility. A railway must consist of at least one track of a standardized width and, if it is to link two cities at all, it must cover the full length between them.

The concept of infrastructure is, however, limited to such things as railways and ports, with telecommunications and electric power generation as borderline cases, not only by the intrinsic merits and demerits of public ownership but also by tradition. We should, however, realize that the intrinsic arguments are sometimes valid for other facilities as well, and that they are dependent on the economic conditions in a particular country.

The United States internal market is sufficiently large to accommodate a number of steelmaking firms of a sufficiently large size to be able to use any known production method, and several units of them as well. The production of steel in Algeria, if economically viable at all, would have to be by a single firm, a monopolist, and its marginal cost would be well below its average cost.

2.3 ECONOMIC FRONTIERS

An economic frontier is an obstacle to the movement of goods and services and/or production factors whether it is a natural obstacle, like a mountain range or sea or whether it is a social and political barrier. Among the latter the frontiers of nation states are by far the most obvious and conspicuous. The existence of an economic frontier compels economic regions to certain adjustments which would not otherwise arise. They arise because of the asymmetry between the mobility of products and the lack of mobility of production factors. There is some—often considerable—possibility of transporting and trading goods and services across economic frontiers, but rather less mobility of production factors and in particular of the production factor *par excellence*, labour.

I mentioned the concept of an *underdeveloped* region in its general context of unequal development of industry, rather than as a special problem on its own. Rural Wales is in many respects just as underdeveloped as, for example, Egypt or Ceylon. The Welsh have, however, the alternative of moving themselves to a suitable job in the nearby Midlands. Between England and Wales there is no economic frontier of any importance and between Ceylon and England there is. It is wrong to identify economic frontiers wholly with national frontiers.

There are, for instance, now virtually no economic frontiers between the member states of the European Economic Community. Nevertheless, the nation state which is also an economic region is a useful frame of reference. In what follows, with the exception of section 2.6 where we are specifically dealing with regions inside a national economy, we will assume that a national economy is also a region.

A region can, of course, be part of a national economy, a problem to be discussed in that section. In the rest of this book we assume nation regions, i.e.

(i) There is a central policy-making body which decides economic policy.

(ii) There are no economic frontiers inside the region, except by the will of that central policy-making body.

(iii) There are economic frontiers with the outside world.

2.4 THE DISPERSION EFFECT

In section 1.15 we discussed the multiplier mechanism. Broadly speaking the multiplier effect means that the total effect of some initial change in the level of economic activity (an expenditure impulse) is a multiple factor of the initial effect.

Observed within a particular geographical area, the multiplier may drop to a figure which is only just above 1. To make this quite clear let us consider the economy of a single street. One of the people who lives in that street loses his job. This does not affect his neighbours in any significant degree because the people all do their shopping outside the street. If, however, one of the local factories in a small town is closed this will affect the local shopkeepers, small craftsmen, etc. Yet the number of people employed by the factory may be a similar percentage of the town's population as the one man is of the number of people living in the street.

The equivalent of this on the national level is the *import leak*. If there is an increase of one unit in public expenditure the effect of this in an open economy is not the same as in a closed economy. The reason is firstly that imports will change. In section 1.15 we assumed for a closed economy:

$$pro = co + iv + pe$$

In an open economy, this would now be:

$$pro = co + iv + pe + exp - imp$$

(production = consumption + investment + public expenditure + export less import)

Now assume that import is a fixed fraction of production (import fraction):

$$imp = \gamma\, pro$$

We maintain the same relation for consumption as given in section 1.15 and substitute ($\alpha\, pro + \beta$) for consumption and $\gamma\, pro$ for import. We will, in this example, assume that the marginal propensity to consume is equal to the average ($\beta = 0$), and obtain:

$$pro = \alpha\, pro + iv + pe + exp - \gamma\, pro$$

or

$$pro = \frac{1}{1-\alpha+\gamma}(iv + pe + exp)$$

which reduces the multiplier from

$$\frac{1}{1-\alpha} \text{ to } \frac{1}{1-\alpha+\gamma}$$

The import leak is not so much a characteristic of a national economy as of any open economic system with outside trade connection where part of the multiplier effects will materialize elsewhere instead of within the geographical unit which is the object of study.

2.5 THE BALANCE OF PAYMENTS

The requirement to maintain some sort of balance between incoming and outgoing payments, if necessary by means which are harmful in other respects, is one of the realities to which national governments and national economy planners in both developed and underdeveloped regions have to adjust themselves. This is not the case when just a geographical part within a country is considered. It is true that the effect of various factors will be to establish some sort of balance. This is, however, an automatic self-adjusting mechanism and does not require special actions by the public authorities which may be harmful in other respects. For example, if a factory goes bankrupt this will cause loss of production and loss of jobs. The multiplier effects of such an event are cushioned by unemployment benefit. This stabilizing effect cannot always be allowed to operate in an open economy. If a major exporting factory goes bankrupt the loss to the national economy cannot always be cushioned. The unemployment benefit would tend to stabilize imports and this is not possible in the face of a loss in export earnings. On the other hand, if the country had a surplus on its balance of payments in the initial situation, the authorities may be able to cushion the effects of any setback, just as in the case of an unemployment problem in a single city.

The term 'balance of payments' is not fully defined and we may distinguish several balances according to which payments are included. The surplus of all payments coming into the country over all payments going out of the country is the total balance of payments (cash basis). For any incoming payment, either the receiver of that payment, or the central bank after changing the money into national currency, becomes the holder of a sum of foreign exchange; the reverse will apply for an outgoing payment. Hence, the total balance of payments is also the change in the country's holdings of foreign exchange, provided the criterion of registration is the same.

The total balance of payments can, however, be quite misleading as an indicator of a country's true financial position. For example, suppose that speculators expect a devaluation of the currency of country *A*. They will sell any holdings of *A*'s currency, exchanging them into the currencies of other countries. This results in an influx of foreign exchange into these other countries but this is no proof of their financial strength.

Another measure of the balance of payments is the *balance of payments on goods and services* (transaction basis). It is obtained from customs statistics of exports less imports; the proceeds of such services as shipping, insurance, and airline transport are added to it and the cost of the use of similar foreign services is subtracted. Even the definition of what services are can make a noticeable difference. The United Nations [46] recommend that income on bonds, shares, interest, etc., from or due to countries abroad, as well as the payment of wages and salaries to frontier labour (people living in one country and working in another), should be classified as a separate category 'factor-income from (or due to, as the case may be), abroad'.

If we want to indicate that payments concerning rent, dividend interest, and salaries (i.e. income of production factors, capital, and labour) is included, we should therefore speak of the balance of payments on *goods and services and incomes* (*transaction basis*). The words 'transaction basis' refer to the fact that the goods have passed the frontier, the services have been rendered, but payment may not coincide with the actual transaction. If we mean the balance of the actual payments arising from these causes, we will speak of '*cash basis*' instead of 'transaction basis'.

Yet another group of payments may be included in the balance of payments. These are the *transfer payments*. Transfer payments originating in the private sector of the economy are: money sent by immigrants to relatives in their former homelands, grants in support sent by parents to children who are students abroad, donations to charitable funds abroad, etc. Transfer payments originating in the public sector are: contributions to international organizations, foreign aid, etc. Also, because it is not countervalue to production the interest on a public loan is not a factor-income, and hence must be booked as a transfer payment. (All productive income must correspond to production.)

The balance of payments on export and import of goods and services, factor-incomes, and transfer payments is also termed the balance of payments on *current account*. The rest of the balance of payments is then the *capital account*.

The capital account can be split into the *long-term capital account* (bonds and shares, and transfers so to establish or increase the capital of subsidiaries abroad) and the *short-term capital account*.

The United States government reckons it is normal to have a net increase of ownership of foreign assets by US citizens and companies. This gives rise to the concept of the *basic balance*, i.e. the current account plus (less) a correction which is the average norm for the long-term capital export. The remainder capital account is then the short-term capital account plus any casual variation in the long-term export of capital, e.g. purchase of shares, bonds, etc.

2.6 THE COST-BENEFIT BALANCE OF METROPOLITAN CONCENTRATION

The case for spatial concentration of industry and trade has been most instructively argued by J. G. M. Hilhorst [19]. Hilhorst's argument is, in a way, broadly analogous to the arguments about *regional* concentration, as summarized by me in section 2.1. His main specific argument for *urban* concentration is, in fact, Adam Smith's argument of specialization, division of labour. Concentration of economic activity on a relatively small space makes specialization both of people and organizations possible, without incurring undue transport and communication costs. (This refers both to transport of and communication of persons, and to the transport of products.)

In this connection, Hilhorst argues the desirability of a policy of deliberate concentration of resources on certain centres. This may be good development economics, but in an established industrial country urbanization and regional inequality are established facts, usually through historical accident rather than from design and planning.

As a result of industry's general tendency towards concentration there is, within most established industrial countries, a noticeable disequilibrium. Italy's division into an industrialized northern part and a semi-underdeveloped south is probably the most prominent case. One part of the country is industrially developed and prosperous: outside this 'metropolitan' area there are certain 'problem regions' with a lower degree of prosperity. The difference in prosperity is reflected both in the level of earnings and in the presence of unemployment. The less prosperous regions suffer from a certain amount of unemployment, even when there is full employment in the metropolitan area. At the same time industry often prefers to expand within the established metropolitan area, despite the fact that it can obtain labour at lower cost by moving out of the metropolitan area. The international analogy to this phenomenon is the division in the world between the economically developed and the less developed countries.

There are, however, two essential differences between the problem of unequal development inside a national economy and in the world at large.

One aspect of difference is the balance-of-payments requirement. A national government can channel its own funds into one region of the country or into another; it can also by its policies influence the geographical distribution of expenditure by the private sector of the economy. In short, there is no balance-of-payments requirement between different regions of a single country.

The other salient aspect of economic difference inside a national frontier is the existence of a national level of income aspiration.

Differences in earnings, in the order of magnitude which exist between developed and underdeveloped countries, are completely unacceptable inside a national economy. Some measure of equality in regional income distribution is a political requirement, accepted by all citizens within a single national unity. We will, in this section, discuss the problem of regional economic inequality as it presents itself to the national government.

Full employment throughout the country represents more employment in total than full employment in the metropolitan area only. Therefore, unless one aims at a reduction in the productivity of labour, one can only convert partial full employment in the metropolitan area into genuine full employment throughout the country by policies which also produce an increase in the total national production. This leaves as an open question where the increase in production is to come from.

As will be seen from Chapter 6, the government can, by suitable macro-economic policies, increase the demand for production—and for employment as a consequence—up to the level of national full employment. If the government does just that, and leaves the rest to market forces, the likelihood is that a substantial part of the additional demand for labour will be in the metropolitan area.

The result will be that in the metropolitan area the number of jobs and vacancies will be greater than the number of people from that area itself who are looking for a job. There will be some increase in the demand for labour outside the metropolitan area, but full employment for all will only be achieved by large-scale migration. Those who cannot find a job in the less prosperous regions will have to move to the metropolitan area.

Such a development may not be agreeable to the inhabitants of non-metropolitan regions on the grounds that, even if it relieves poverty, the economic dominance of the metropolitan area is increased even more and the non-metropolitan areas may lose their cultural identity.

The migration of the unemployed to more prosperous regions as a solution to the problem of unemployment can also be criticized on strict economic grounds.

The alternative is a conscious policy of regional development, stimulating the dispersion of employment from the metropolitan area to the rest of the country.

The central government can disperse its own offices, it can offer special fiscal facilities to new investment in the less prosperous regions, and it can give preferential treatment to the less prosperous regions in terms of infrastructure provisions. It can build roads, ports, etc., in the less prosperous regions, despite the fact that the expected demand for such facilities is less than for similar facilities in the metropolitan area itself.

Such a policy of regional development by special facilities can be defended on the grounds that it avoids additional investment in the metropolitan area in housing and related infrastructure investments like streets, and so on. Although it is not possible to quantify the arguments for and against metropolitan concentration with a reasonable degree of accuracy, they can at least be surveyed and this will be done in the rest of this section.

First of all, the fact that people move to areas with increasing population means that houses and flats have to be built for them and their old houses will stay empty and be demolished. Up to a point the cost of additional urban housing is represented in the price structure. Urban metropolitan-area wages are generally higher than those paid for the same type of work in the less prosperous areas, and the difference in housing costs is the main justification for this difference.

All the same, industry by and large prefers to stay and expand in the metropolitan area despite the fact that labour costs are higher than in the less prosperous regions.

We must also consider the difference between the market rate of interest and the alternative use of the investment in industry, the full social rate of return. Rents, including the relatively high urban rents, are calculated on the basis of the market rate of interest. That is what the property-developer and landlord or, for that matter, the owner-occupier who finances the purchase of his own house by a mortgage, actually pay.

The true cost of this additional housing requirement to society at large is not just the interest on this investment on urban housing, but the alternative return on a similar amount of investment elsewhere in the economy, according to the full social rate of return.

To build a house costs, let us say, £5,000 and a labourer who moves to an urban area will pay interest on this building cost, either as owner-occupier on his mortgage or as rent to his landlord. That puts the cost of moving to the metropolitan area to the labourer, assuming

7 per cent interest, at £350 per year. That is also roughly the wage difference to an employer hiring labour in the metropolitan area instead of moving himself to a less prosperous area.

Now suppose the government uses a fiscal incentive, persuading an industrial firm to build a new plant in a less prosperous region instead of in the metropolitan area originally intended, and which thereby creates local employment for 1,000 people. These 1,000 people may or may not regret that they will continue to live in their old houses instead of in the new modern flats which they would have obtained if they had not found a local job.

The additional product value produced by the firm hiring the 1,000 labourers in their own non-metropolitan region may be less than the firm would have produced if it had built the new factory in the metropolitan area instead and the people had moved. The most likely reason for such a differential productivity would be the higher costs of transport and communication. This assumes that the firm's main suppliers and clients, as well as its own central administration, are situated inside the metropolitan area.

We may assume that the cost of this productivity difference is equal to, or perhaps slightly more than, the difference in labour cost which arises out of the higher metropolitan housing cost. Instead of supposing such a productivity difference we could also assume that the firm, which was only prepared to invest outside the metropolitan area after being offered a special incentive, behaved irrationally in not choosing the region with the lowest labour cost in the first place. We cannot exclude the possibility that firms do behave irrationally in this way, but the case for a positive regional policy does not depend on such an assumption. Let us therefore put the cost of the productivity difference at £350,000 per year.

Now consider the alternative use of the metropolitan construction industry's production capacity, or of the resources used by the construction industry. When it is not needed for building additional houses this freed production capacity is 1,000 × 5,000, i.e. £5 million.

The government can adjust its macro-economic control over the demand for end-products, thereby creating additional demand for equipment as well. Another firm in the metropolitan area, persuaded by the increased sales of its end-product, can build a new factory *as well*, provided this replaces an existing one which produced less output with the help of the same amount of labour. Total employment in the metropolitan area cannot, of course, be increased without building more houses.

The return on this industrial investment may be much higher than the £350,000 per year which is made on the investment in housing. There are two reasons for such a differential. One is in part social–political. Housing is often provided at the cost of building, giving a price below the equivalent of the free-market financial rate of return on the initial investment. This can be achieved by subsidies or by special government-backed loans to non-profit organizations or to local authorities who provide low-cost housing on a non-profit basis. The reason can be social justice and equity, because it helps large families, or it can be a facet of a controlled incomes policy.

Low-cost urban housing reduces the need for a difference in wages between rural and urban labour. This makes it possible for a national incomes policy to be based largely on national, uniform rates of pay for a particular type of work, and this has obvious administrative advantages. However, even if tenants pay a full 'economic' rent, this 'full' rent is not genuinely the full cost to the nation of allocating resources to housing instead of industrial investment.

The other, more technical-economic, aspect of the problem is the difference between the financial and the full social return on new investment in industry.

As we saw in section 1.12, the return on investment in industrial modernization, including the part of this return which accrues to labour in the form of higher wages, is systematically higher than the private financial rate of return.

At a full social rate of return of, for example, 24 per cent, the increase in production as a result of the substitution of a £5 million new and modern factory for an old one, would be £1·2 million per year.

The factors considered so far would put the net gain to the nation, as a result of avoiding the metropolitan concentration, at £1·2 million less £350,000 for loss of centralization efficiency, i.e. £850,000 per year. This calculation may be inaccurate, because both types of expansion of production would require additional infrastructure investments.

Industrialization of a so far largely rural region will require public investment in roads, electricity supply, and so on. The costs of these new infrastructure investments may well be higher than the alternative, a further strengthening of the metropolitan infrastructure. In the metropolitan area it becomes a question of extending an already existing structure whereas some of the non-metropolitan facilities may be completely new to the region in question.

On the other hand, the metropolitan area may require infrastructure investments of a quite different type as a result of its increase in population and industrial activity. These are of a kind specifically related to the high density of population and for combating congestion, such as for example an underground railway system. Furthermore the wage differential may not fully represent the costs of 'ordinary' urban investment even at the financial (interest) rate. The increase in metropolitan population results in additional investment in houses, but also in 'social' infrastructure (like schools, hospitals, etc.), as well as in local infrastructure in new residential areas (streets, water supply, telephone lines, etc.).

A further dimension of the problem arises if we assume imperfect mobility of labour.

So far, the case for spreading industry is based solely on avoiding additional investment in urban housing and associated infrastructure. It presupposes that full employment of labour is achieved either way, by industry moving to the people, or the people moving to industry.

Now suppose the people just do not want to move. They stay in the less prosperous regions, even if it means living on unemployment benefit or working a family farm with more people than are needed. In that case, any further demand for labour in the metropolitan area will result in inflationary pressures, because the supply of labour from the less prosperous regions is not forthcoming, and the local population in the metropolitan area itself is already fully employed.

If that is the true situation the case for industry to move to the unemployed labour, if necessary by fiscal incentive or even outright subsidy, is considerably strengthened. The reason is that the local labour used for the construction of the infrastructure in the less prosperous regions, for the construction of the factory and for the operation of the factory as well, is not a true cost to society since the alternative is regional unemployment.

3

Short-term economic policy in an industrially developed market economy

3.1 THE AIMS OF ECONOMIC POLICY

One of the characteristics of an industrially developed country is that a sophisticated infrastructure is already established. It is true that, from a long-term point of view, this infrastructure will need to be modernized and extended. The performance of the economy in any year is, however, not significantly influenced by further extensions and improvements of the infrastructure. Accordingly, the short-term objectives of economic policy are:

(i) To maintain a balance-of-payments equilibrium with the rest of the world.
(ii) To maintain full employment among the available labour force.
(iii) To increase *per capita* consumption.
(iv) To maintain stable prices.

We can now review the impact of various instruments of economic policy on these four aims.

One further aim of economic policy, maintaining a satisfactory long-term rate of growth, is to some extent related to the way the short-term instruments of economic policy are operated. A full discussion of this problem is, however, not within the scope of this chapter.

3.2 INCOMES POLICY

Some form of administrative control over the average (total) personal income is necessary for the proper management of an industrial economy. Its primary and essential function is simply to ensure that total income fulfils its function—to ensure that the claim on real resources, production factors, arising from the way people spend their money, is within the limits of what can be produced. In this respect, incomes policy is an instrument towards the control of consumption. However, firms must also recover their costs from the proceeds of their sales, and for this reason an incomes policy is also an important determinant of the general price level. The most effective way to achieve control over incomes is by making collective agreements, negotiated by trade unions, subject to approval by a public or corporate agency set up for this purpose.

Objections to an incomes policy have been, or could be, made on the following grounds:

(*a*) That an increase in wages and salaries does not increase total spendable income because it reduces profits.

(*b*) That it is unfair to labour as long as there is not at the same time a control on prices and on paid-out profits, i.e. dividends.

(*c*) That the same aim can and should be achieved by means of fiscal and monetary policy, i.e. that direct control over incomes is unnecessary.

(*d*) That administrative control over incomes, like price controls, are likely to be ineffective; if other (e.g. monetary) factors make for rising incomes, then incomes will rise anyway, no matter what laws are made to regulate them.

(*e*) That with each 'pause', each temporary restriction on incomes, pressure for more and bigger rises will occur at the end of the pause.

Let us examine firstly points (*a*) and (*b*).

The first, (*a*), is simply not true. It is true that if wages and salaries rise while production and prices remain constant, then gross profits before tax will fall by an equal amount. However, spendable personal income before tax will rise, because of the following differences between gross profits before tax and personal spendable income from profits:

Corporation Tax

A fall in profits by companies means a fall in the taxes paid by these companies and the corresponding reduction in their after-tax profits is less than the increase in their wages and salaries bill.

Retained Profits

Profits of companies do not become personal income until they are paid out as dividends, and not all profits are paid out.

A Differential in the Savings Ratio

If a rich man earns more money he feels less inclined to spend it at once than a poor man who sees all sorts of nice things in the shops which he could not afford hitherto.

Point (*b*), that it is unfair to labour, is a matter of politics and social justice. It can, however, be answered. The full case against it rests on the—undesirable—*results* of cost-push inflation and the way this inflation has to be counteracted by monetary and fiscal policy. An exposition of this full case must be deferred and we limit ourselves to the narrower aspect of the labour market itself.

First, there is an administrative argument. Price controls, other than on standardized mass-produced products, can be evaded and with relative ease, while income controls are not so easy to evade. The chief loophole for products is the creation of a new brand, a new model, etc., which is technically a *new* article.

Now consider the economic arguments. The argument *for* control over incomes rests on the case that the competitive price mechanism does not work properly and that control over labour income is an effective method to restore it. The typical situation which asks for public control over negotiated wages and salaries is where, in a particular sector of production, a few firms face a single trade union that puts in a claim for increased rates of pay for a particular grade of labour doing the same type of work in all the firms.

How does this situation appear to the management of any one of the firms? The claim for a higher wage rate is not all that objectionable, as long as the firm can pass the higher cost on in the form of a higher price charged to the purchaser of its product. Since the claim affects all firms in the industry this is indeed possible, although some loss of sales will occur for the industry as a whole. But this is the lesser of two evils, compared with a strike.

The wage rate earned by certain groups of workers in certain industries may rise in consequence to well above that of workers who possess similar skills and do roughly the same kind of work in another industry.

In a perfectly competitive situation this would not be possible; one of the firms in the industry would break out of—or refuse to join—the agreement, hire workers at or slightly above the old wage rate instead of at the new increased one, and would then be in a position to underbid the other firms in the market for the end-product. Or, if this did not happen, an outsider would step in and do the same. It is because there are only a few established firms which, in an oligopolistic market, compete with one another only to a limited extent, that makes it possible for the trade unions in a particular industry to increase their rates of pay. Nevertheless, the consequences of such inflationary wage settlements are likely to be, in the end, an increase in unemployment, although this need not be in the industry where wages rose most strongly.

The willingness of management to resist inflationary wage settlements, which do cause a temporary reduction in profits, is further eroded by the fact that the actual decisions are taken by salaried managers, who have a strong motivation to keep the firm in business but not necessarily to maximize profits by resisting wage claims. This relation between high wages and unemployment arises specifically in the 'open' industrial economy. In such an open economy a substantial fraction of the products and raw materials consumed by the domestic economy are produced abroad and imported. Correspondingly, the country is required to export a substantial fraction of the products it produces. If it were not for this 'complication' of international trade, it would be possible, although somewhat meaningless, to double everyone's income and all prices, making no one any better or worse off. The money needed to circulate the double nominal value of production and income would, of course, also be twice its former amount.

This is not so in an open economy, at least not at an unchanged rate of exchange.

With rising domestic costs, the country's export industries will sell less in the international market. They may, or they may not, sell at a higher price. The net result may well be that they sell less product for the same money.

Again, imports of foreign products, which have not risen in price, will claim a higher share in the domestic market. The money value of the sales in the domestic market will follow fairly closely any increase in the nominal income of the bulk of the population. Higher wages will most certainly imply higher turnover in terms of money. However, if foreigners with non-increasing costs increase their share in the domestic market, the domestic sales of the domestic industry will rise by less than its costs.

This is also the overall result for the sales of the domestic industry in internal and external market combined.

If the import fraction is, let us say, 25 per cent, then for every one per cent increase in the rate of pay of domestic labour the costs of the domestic industry rise by three-quarters of one per cent. If prices increase in proportion to costs, this means that the real increase in standard of living, for those who remain employed, rises by only a quarter of one per cent for every one per cent increase in the wage rate. The total value of sales by the domestic industry in money terms will rise by less than three-quarters of one per cent, if at all. If prices are increased in proportion to the rise in costs, then, with a semi-stationary turnover, less product will be sold and the technical demand for labour is reduced. If prices are not put up, firms do not have the means to pay the higher wages and they shake out labour for that reason. The inflationary process will be stopped—after unemployment has manifested itself.

It might be thought that, since foreign trade brings competition back in the domestic market, it should also restore the 'normal' result that prices, including those of the various grades of labour, settle themselves at a level where supply equals demand.

This does not actually happen, however, except for those industries which keep their own labour cost down, even if they rise elsewhere in the economy. The explanation is technical change and the unequal productivity performance of the various sectors of the economy to which it gives rise.

In this connection it is useful to distinguish between 'leading' and other industries. Leading industries are those which realize the highest increases in productivity, while at the same time expanding their sales to such an extent that they need to recruit additional labour, despite the reduction in the labour requirement per unit of output. These will generally be export industries, because the domestic market will not have room for a sharply increasing output of one sector.

The level of aspirations and the rate of increase in the rate of pay considered as 'normal' throughout the economy is pushed upwards by these leading sectors.

Pay increases in these leading sectors are possible because of genuine increases in productivity, possibly augmented by a trend of rising prices in the world's economy at large, as represented by the prices of the foreign competitors of the leading sectors. For the rest of the economy, however, the result is a 'cost push'.

The 'normal' and proper result of such an unbalanced increase in productivity would be that leading industries would use their increased productivity to increase their market share, both in the domestic market and in the international market, at the cost of their foreign competitors who have not similarly increased their productivity.

There would be an increase in the wage rate per worker throughout the economy. Such a 'following' of the pay rate given by the leading sector(s) is only natural. One cannot expect people to be satisfied with a lower income, just because they happen to work in a stagnating industry. This general pay rise may be less than the rise which is realized in the leading industry. Even so, it weakens the competitive position of the other sectors of the economy, relative to their foreign competitors, in so far as these competitors do not experience similar increases in labour costs. The same result would arise if these foreign competing industries also experienced rising labour costs, but kept their cost per unit of product constant by increasing their efficiency. The non-modernizing sectors of the economy would lose their market share and employ less people. That would be no particular problem, as long as the leading sectors of the economy absorbed the labour released by the others. But that will *not* happen, if organized labour in the leading industries is allowed to make full use of its bargaining position.

Raising the wage rate in the leading sectors above the macroeconomic full employment level does not cause unemployment in those leading sectors, because the leading sectors need to recruit more people from the rest of the economy even so. Instead, the unemployment arises somewhere else in the economy.

Now consider the final objection against a controlled incomes policy, the 'pent-up pressure' argument. This is not really a valid argument against incomes policy as a permanent system because of the self-perpetuating element in inflation. Wage claims which are bound to cause unemployment arise, among other things, because of the rising cost of living and the anticipation of future erosion of the real value of wages. Incomes policy should be a permanent system rather than being switched temporarily 'on' and 'off', because if the controls are switched off while prices are still rising, then it is indeed possible for the spiral to gain a new momentum.

Finally, there is an administrative aspect. To control inflation effectively it is probably sufficient to control either incomes or prices. If incomes are controlled, competition, even the limited oligopolistic competition, will restrain prices. If prices are controlled the requirement to recover costs will restrain wages. There are relatively fewer grades and qualities of labour than there are types of product. To cover an important point in the price–cost nexus more or less completely requires fewer individual controls, if that point is the price of labour, than if that point is the overall price level of end-products.

3.3 THE RATE OF INTEREST AND ITS IMPACT ON INVESTMENT

First, recall the general propositions about the function of a monetary system. According to the 'perfect competition' model any activity which gives rise to a profit is pursued, and there is no rational upper limit to it other than the actual possibility to pursue it. Therefore, at the prevailing prices, all productive activities including investment should for the average firm just about cover cost. In this view, the rate of interest will drastically affect the profitability of investment activities as any change in the rate of interest makes the difference between profit and loss.

I now restate my own view on this point. Owing to the presence of increasing returns to scale* the price of the end-product has to cover more than the (full) marginal cost, as accounted at the prevailing prices, in order to cover the overheads of the firm's organization and research system, and to finance rising payments to labour as well. Therefore the normal investment project should yield a positive profit, a surplus profit over and above the costs of labour, materials, and interest. The same proposition may be formulated the other way round. The price of some cost items must be *less than* the price of the end-product, minus the price of any other cost items which contribute directly to the productive activity in question. It is my proposition that the rate of interest is such a price. The price of an end-product, less the cost of the current inputs material and labour, leaves a surplus, which covers not only the cost of an investment activity but also a fair share of the overheads of a typical industrial organization. There-

* *See also* sections 4.3 and 4.4 concerning the increasing returns to expansion and new investment, because of the effect of investment on technical innovation.

fore, as long as a firm is in business at all, it will invest, never mind the rate of interest, whenever it can *sell* an increased production, and has *available* the financial means to invest. This relation of investment to the increment in sales and production, rather than to the rate of interest, applies to advanced-technology production where we can expect increasing returns to scale.

In more traditional production sectors like the letting of flats, houses or offices, the rate of interest is a major cost item, and there may be no surplus profit; as a result the rate of interest may influence investment to a much greater extent than in manufacturing industry.

One other investment activity (of a kind) *is* affected by changes in the rate of interest. I am referring to inventories—stocks of mass-produced articles and materials not yet used as parts of a finished product or sold to the end-users. The purpose of keeping a stock is to be able to supply any customer even if he appears unexpectedly. Stocks are normally financed by some form of credit. Now if, at an increased rate of interest, the cost of keeping a larger stock goes up, a firm will take a greater risk* of having to say at some stage to a customer: 'Sorry, we can't supply, we have run out of stock.'

The direct effects of the rate of interest on the level of investment are therefore largely limited to an investment in dwellings, offices, and inventories, whereas the investment in machinery and equipment is primarily affected by other factors, notably the volume of sales and the availability of credit.

The latter factor comprises two things. Firstly, there is the credit-worthiness of a particular firm, i.e. whether it makes a profit at all and the ratio between its outstanding debts and its own capital. Secondly, quite a few governments have in effect introduced credit rationing by directing the banking system not to increase their total lendings above a particular figure.

3.4 THE RATE OF INTEREST AND THE SUPPLY OF MONEY

Let us, for the sake of argument, assume that the relation between the rate of interest and the supply of money is a purely one-sided one,

* Note the analogy between this theory of stockbuilding and Keynes's theory of interest concerning the keeping of cash or bank balances.

i.e. that the government through the central bank and through open market policy controls the rate of interest and that the banking system will lend to anybody, who is creditworthy, at the set rate. The control over the rate of interest is exercised for short-term credits by means of the central bank's lending policy, i.e. the central bank itself lends to banks at a specific rate. This is not always an effective control because the other banks can create new credit themselves. Conceivably, though, there could be restrictions on such actions by banks (*see also* section 3.6). The medium- and long-term rates of interest are controlled by the Treasury (Ministry of Finance) by means of open market policy; in this government bonds are bought whenever their price falls below the ratio between their nominal rate of interest and the desired effective rate of interest, and they are sold again if their market price rises above that ratio.

These transactions change the amount of money in circulation by the channels 'creation of credit by the banking system' and 'net government lending'. The additional money supply, which will be associated with a reduction in the rate of interest, will be used by the rest of the economy for two purposes.

In the first place the ratio between the transaction balances held and the amount of turnover to be circulated by the available sum of money would change. With a lower rate of interest people would be more inclined to hold cash or a bank balance, just in case they should have to make an unexpected payment, whereas with a higher rate of interest they would want to be rid of their debts or buy an interest-bearing bond instead. We might call this the 'reserve balances' purpose.

Secondly, the lower rate of interest would stimulate expenditure. This could either be investment, e.g. purchase of capital equipment financed by a loan, or it could be the purchase of durable consumer goods financed by hire-purchase. Seen as a single transaction, this might possibly not change the amount of money in circulation, because the seller would use the money received to pay off his debt to a bank or he might buy a long-term bond. He might, however, spend the proceeds of his sale and as a result the level of general economic activity, the total turnover, would increase and a larger amount of money would be needed to keep the higher turnover going. This might be called the 'increased expenditure' purpose.

Now consider the effects of the money supply on the rate of interest. We assume an influx of money by one of the non-interest channels, namely from the government (increased public expenditure, reduced taxation) or from abroad (increased export).

The 'reserve balances' effect might, with a bit of oversimplification, be formulated by saying that the ratio between the total turnover (i.e. national product) and the money stock needed to sustain it is a function of the rate of interest. The (at first sight somewhat remarkable) result of this assumption is the *compensation effect.* Given an expenditure impulse, the effect on production *at an unchanged rate of interest* is completely determined by the multiplier effect of the initial expenditure impulse, and the quantity of money will adjust itself.

Any discrepancy between the amount of money needed for circulation and the amount of money supplied in first instance will be corrected automatically by the banking system. At a given rate of interest there is only one ratio between the amount of money in circulation and the production value (income) it keeps circulating. It assumes that the control variable, the rate of interest, is kept at its existing level. Naturally the government can refuse to do this: it can float no loans, neither sell nor buy any of its own outstanding bonds, and can forbid the banking system to create any additional credit. This line of action is also consistent with the assumption that the 'velocity of circulation'—the ratio between the stock of money and the level of production—is a function of the rate of interest. When the amount of money is kept constant, the rate of interest will adjust itself to the required ratio.

3.5 INCOMES POLICY AND FISCAL REGULATION OF DOMESTIC DEMAND

The main instruments which control domestic expenditure, are: incomes policy, i.e. the control over gross income from employment; and direct taxes on personal income (income tax, wages tax), on profit (corporation tax), and on production or sales (turnover tax, value added tax, purchase tax).

We will now review the effects of these instruments on the relevant short-term targets of economic policy, namely full employment, stable prices, and equilibrium in the balance of payments.

Incomes policy has quite a significant impact on production and employment because the cost price of the national exporters affects their competitive position in foreign trade. Even where labour is not particularly dominant as a direct cost item to some of the exporting industries, it may still be an important cost factor to some of their suppliers and influence their prices. Keeping down the domestic labour cost helps national exporters to compete in foreign markets and hence influences the volume of exports.

This emphasis on competition might seem to contradict the notion of oligopoly as the 'normal' market form in a science-based capital-intensive industry, but this is not really the case. The oligopolist argument does indeed mean that industry's resistance to inflationary wage increases is reduced. It does not mean that the balance-of-payments effect of any inflationary settlements is less than in a more competitive situation.

An industry which experiences cost increases and at the same time increased nominal income in the home market will, while this does not occur in its foreign-competitors' home countries, reduce the fraction of its production going to export, in the face of a buoyant home market and competition abroad.

This 'export effect' is typical for a relatively small or medium-sized country where export is an important part of production. In a *closed* economy, without any foreign trade at all, the short-term effect of an increase in labour-income on the level of employment would in all probability be slightly positive. A number of prices, like rents, electricity tariffs, etc., are fixed for some time. These change-resisting prices occur typically in those sectors of the economy where capital rather than labour is the main direct cost factor and the full effect on prices would take time to become apparent. Meanwhile higher nominal incomes are also, to some extent, higher real incomes and generate an increase in consumption. The impact on investment would, under these conditions, depend on whether or not firms could obtain credit. With falling profits the possibility of financing new investment from their own profit is reduced; but the possibility of making new investment economically viable is probably increased, because of the increased consumption-led demand for the end-product.

The effect of incomes policy on *prices* is all too obvious: higher labour costs mean higher prices, except where they are compensated by increased productivity. Nevertheless, higher nominal incomes mean higher real incomes (at least for those who stay in employment) even after a somewhat longer period of time. The reason is that a substantial part of the goods and services we buy comes from abroad and the price is not affected by domestic labour cost at all.

The combination of lower exports (because of reduced competitiveness) and rising imports (because of rising consumption) means that a rise in domestic labour income has a pronounced effect on the balance of payments.

Now let us consider the effect of direct taxation. The main effect of direct taxes on income and profits is to restrict expenditure, on import and domestic production alike, while leaving prices and costs substantially unaltered. This has an influence on both employment and the balance of payments. The effect on the balance of payments is however, from the imports side only.

Direct taxes produce some of the effects which we discussed for incomes policy, but also give effects in the opposite direction. Higher *gross* labour income means less employment and less foreign exchange. Higher *net* income (labour or otherwise) means more employment, because of the associated increase in domestic expenditure, but less foreign exchange, because imports rise and exports are not affected. The exception to this proposition would arise when, as a result of a firm incomes policy and a resulting situation of export-led growth production is already at its limit of technical-physical capacity. In that situation taxation would not change the already existing situation of full employment, but a reduction in domestic expenditure would allow industry to reduce its delivery times and accept more foreign orders. It presumes a situation where customers were queueing for the products. The effect of direct taxes on prices is not significant, except in the indirect sense that a change in the level of employment may affect labour costs in the first place, and then prices as well because of costs.

The effect of indirect taxes when charged on domestic expenditure is largely similar for employment, production, and the balance of payments to that of direct tax. The effect on prices is obviously different, as indirect taxes increase the prices of the products on which they are charged. Indirect taxes charged on export products would reduce exports, which is, of course, precisely why they are not generally so charged. We should, however, pay some attention here to value added tax. Unlike a turnover or a purchase tax, it is not strictly a cost-price increasing tax at all. Purchase tax is charged on the gross price irrespective of cost, and the sales price has to cover the cost of wages, materials, etc., plus the tax. Value added tax, on the other hand, is charged on the difference between purchase and sales price, and is not paid unless there is any value added. However, in so far as V.A.T. puts up the price, it does so irrespective of destination, and this can include export, unless there is a refund of tax on exported products. Import duties, in contrast, specifically hit imported products, and will therefore reduce imports even more than they would already because taxation generally reduces the volume of domestic expenditure. They may, therefore, actually stimulate the level of domestic production despite the reduction in the total amount bought. They have one great disadvantage from a long-term point of view, though: they strengthen the oligopolistic element in the inland market.

3.6 THE AUXILIARY ROLE OF MONETARY INSTRUMENTS

The monetary instruments by which domestic demand can be influenced are threefold:

(*a*) *Restrictions on Credit Transactions*

Certain types are regulated, hire-purchase being the most obvious example. The law may require that hire-purchase is only permitted for a certain maximum repayment period or that at least a certain deposit is paid; any transaction with a longer repayment period and/or lower deposit becomes illegal. This type of regulation has an obvious social function, to protect people against being spendthrift, but variation in the time limits and percentages can become an instrument of economic policy, a means of regulating the demand for consumer goods.

(*b*) *Credit Rationing*

Legislation (or a non-law arrangement) may compel the banks to restrict the creation of credit to an amount specified by the Treasury, Ministry of Finance, or central bank.

(*c*) *Manipulation of the Rate of Interest*

This is carried out by the Treasury, Ministry of Finance, or central bank on the lines indicated in section 3.4. If that manipulation aims at restricting the money supply and imposing a high rate of interest, it will usually be underpinned by credit restriction.

In the preceding section (3.5) we listed incomes policy and fiscal instruments as 'the main' instruments for the control of domestic expenditure. The reasons for relegating monetary policy to the role of a secondary or auxiliary instrument are as follows.

The direct effect of the availability of credit—either consumer credit (hire-purchase) to finance consumption, or bank credit to finance business expenditure (inventories, investment)—is temporary. Once the consumers, or, in the case of inventories and capital goods, producers have reduced their expenditure, with for the time being their income unchanged, their cash position will improve. Once the cash position of the relevant economic agents is adjusted, expenditure is always primarily a function of income.

The monetary effects (a reduction in the stock of money in circulation) and the temporary cut in expenditure may, of course, result in a reduction of production and income as well. That, however, is precisely what is *not* intended in most cases. If there is a balance-of-payments problem, one would want to restore the balance of payments without hitting domestic production.

At this point it is useful to refresh our knowledge of the accounting identities involved. Domestic production is equal to domestic income (wages plus profits) plus net factor income paid to non-residents. This links production to income by its financial proceeds. However, the product must go somewhere, and domestic production is equal to domestic expenditure (consumption, investment, stockbuilding, and public expenditure on goods, services, and salaries) plus the part—exports less imports—sold abroad. On the financial side, the private sector's spendable income available for expenditure on goods and services (i.e. consumption, investment, and stockbuilding) is the productive income (that is, production less factor income to abroad) less any other type of financial outlay. Temporarily, 'any other type of financial outlay' may be an increase in one's cash position. In the long run the available 'other types of outlay' are taxes, pension premiums, etc., not an increase in cash or bank balances, because one is bound to spend the money again.

The difference between the private sector's productive income and its expenditure (income less expenditure) is its payment of taxes to the government, net of compensating transfer payments like subsidies, pensions, etc., plus any increase in the private sector's net ownership of financial titles. However, even if a lack of equilibrium on the balance of payments corresponds* to a similar disequilibrium in the government's budget, it does not follow that this disequilibrium can only be corrected by changing either public expenditure or the tax rates. In particular, stimulation of export (incomes policy, devaluation) may influence tax revenue at the same *rates* of taxation.

We conclude our review of these two monetary instruments, control of hire-purchase and bank credit, finding that, if there is a fundamental discrepancy between imports and exports, these monetary instruments are not effective in the long run, whereas other instruments, incomes control and fiscal policy, are effective.

The effects of hire-purchase control and credit control are essentially temporary. This conclusion is in effect a corollary of the technical nature of these two instruments.

The position is different for the rate of interest. The rate of interest is a cost item. It could conceivably influence decisions with respect to production at the lowest possible cost, i.e. the choice between capital-intensive processes on the one hand and labour-intensive or material-intensive processes on the other. If we maintained the postulate of divisibility and assumed the existence of a competitive market equilibrium, then an increase in the rate of interest would mean less new investment and more continuation of existing (labour-intensive and/or material-intensive) production processes. In fact, as far as the price–cost nexus has an appreciable allocation effect, it is the consumer's price elasticity with respect to a capital-intensive *product*, namely the use of a house or a dwelling, which is most noticeable.

More than half of the (cost of the) rent of a house is the interest on the building cost and, in any 'squeeze' or stop, the building industry is always hit hardest. If interest rates rise, the letting of houses becomes unprofitable except at a higher rent and the would-be owner-occupier has to face more interest on his mortgage. Therefore, both the would-be tenant and the would-be owner-occupier will look for a smaller house of which the cost remains within their budgets.

It is, of course, possible to shelter both the families in search of a home and the building industry from the effects of a higher rate of interest; it can be done by offering a special, privileged rate of interest to certain categories of house purchasers or builders, such as municipal councils, housing associations, etc., or—with a somewhat different

* The two are not normally identical because there may be, among other things, capital export or capital import, even in the long run.

political bias—to owner-occupiers. Such a measure also reduces the allocative effect of the 'full' rate of interest. Another restriction on the regulating effect of the rate of interest concerns productive investment in industry, and more particularly, capital-intensive advanced-technology projects. In those sectors the marginal cost, even the marginal full production cost (i.e. the average cost of the newest type of an additional plant or production unit) is less than the average cost for the industry as a whole. The industry has fixed costs, for example amortization and interest on the existing less-modern equipment, and the overheads of research organization, central administration, etc. Since the price of the end-product has to cover the average cost, the profitability of the new investment is not at all marginal as long as the additional output can be sold. What actually happens during a squeeze is something quite different from a reduction in investment due to the reduced profitability of new investment projects. Firms are short of cash. With an already slackening demand it becomes more difficult to pass any rise in cost on to the end-user, and the rate of interest is one of the cost items. Even so, many firms would probably try to obtain additional credit, rather than cancel their investment plans. They will then be told by the banks that they cannot have the additional credit; a squeeze is characterized by rising interest rates *and* tight credit in the sense of lack of availability of new credit. Simple lack of cash will therefore force firms to review their expenditure plans, including plans for capital expenditure. Current expenditure is, however, hit at the same time, and one of the results of a squeeze is usually a shake-out of labour.

In both cases we see a reduction in the operated production-capacity or a cancellation of plans to increase production capacity. This 'squeeze' works as it does, because firms are not using their full production capacity. If there were no idle capacity firms would raise their prices.

Having read the above analysis of the effects of monetary policy one might wonder why, in actual fact, the monetary instrument and in particular interest policy are often the first to be used in any balance-of-payments crisis.

The answer is twofold. One aspect is the impact of the rate of interest on the *capital* account of the balance of payments. If, under a system of fixed exchange rates and convertible currencies, the rate of interest in country *A* is higher than in country *B*, people who have money available will put it in a bank account in *A* rather than in *B* in order to gain the higher rate of interest. As a result foreign currencies are offered to the central bank in country *A* for exchange into the *A* currency. A temporary deficit on the current account of country *A*'s balance of payments is compensated for by manipulating the capital account in the opposite direction. The device amounts to the nation borrowing from abroad. By raising the rate of interest the authorities encourage foreigners to lend their money to banks in country *A*.

The other, even more dubious, aspect is that of 'confidence'. Many people in 'the City', in banks, and in other financial institutions *believe* that to increase the rate of interest is to cure a balance-of-payments deficit. In actual fact the influx of money from abroad enables the banks to lend more to domestic clients than they could have done otherwise, and a squeeze will not bite if the immediate 'cover up' by means of foreign borrowing is too successful. True or not, this belief by itself means that the mere announcement of an increase in the rate of interest may sometimes alleviate fears of a possible devaluation. This 'confidence' aspect can, however, quite easily backfire, because people will infer from an announcement of an increase in the rate of interest that there is a balance-of-payments problem.

3.7 FORBIDDEN INSTRUMENTS

The economies of most of the industrially developed countries are roughly parallel to those of their main trading partners, i.e. they mainly trade with other developed countries which are faced with approximately the same problems. This has given rise to certain codes of conduct, certain expectations of behaviour, sometimes informal, sometimes put down in international agreements. The point is that some instruments are, from a purely national point of view, quite effective in furthering certain targets of national policy—but at the cost of the non-attainment of similar targets by other countries. Because other countries are in the same position, they can retaliate and a considerable disruption of international trade would be the end-result. Because of this there is an open or tacit understanding *not* to use such instruments except in very extreme circumstances.

These forbidden instruments all relate to a one-sided regulation of foreign trade by national governments in furtherance of national aims of economic policy.

The underlying problem is the relation between production and imports. If there is underemployment of labour and/or underemployment of real capital (production installations, machines) at home, this may be alleviated by increasing domestic expenditure. Other things being equal, this will cause a rise in imports and hence a deterioration of the external trade balance. The result of this situation is, that once a country is faced with the combination of unemployment at home and a deficit on its external balance, regulation of domestic expenditure cannot cure both problems since the cure of one problem makes the other worse. It is, therefore, tempting to adjust the control of expenditure (taxes, public expenditure) entirely for the domestic requirement of full employment, and to cure the balance of payments by simply prohibiting or hampering imports of certain categories of goods which are also produced at home. As long as domestic production is at its limit of technical capacity there is no point in restricting imports, irrespective of the balance-of-payments situation. The monetary income inside the country will be spent somehow and it is the 'normal' assumption that this income level is in line with the capacity to produce. While this is so, the result of restrictions on imports will be redirection of the money income to other non-restricted products, which in the absence of any increase in domestic production will also be imported.

The proposition *for* import restriction will arise when it is possible to redirect the money income from foreign products to domestic products, of which more will be produced. The instruments which come in this category are:

Import Duties

All articles of a certain specification are charged with a tax at the moment they enter the country. Import duties are still relatively 'respectable', compared with such other instruments as import licences.

Import Licences

Certain traders are licensed to import only certain quantities (quota) of articles; a licence is required for this and import of these restricted articles by anyone else is prohibited.

Foreign-exchange Control

The central bank supplies foreign currency in exchange for domestic currency, but only for certain purposes and not to any amount.

While the above three instruments restrict imports, substantially the same result can be obtained by special facilities to exporters, such as the following:

Export Loans

Export loans are mainly relevant to the capital-goods producing sectors. Foreigners who buy capital goods are helped with special low-interest loans by the government of the exporting country or by a bank owned and controlled by the government.

Export-credit Guarantees

The buyer of the article obtains a loan from a private bank, negotiated by the foreign purchaser or by the exporter/manufacturer, on terms which the bank is willing to agree to only because the government guarantees the loan.

These last two instruments are also used as instruments for international aid or they may be presented as such. In the latter case the transaction is presented as help to the foreign purchaser who is in a developing country, not as help to the exporter/producer to get the better of exporters from other industrial countries.

This is not so with one other, rather less respectable, method:

Subsidies to Exporting Firms

Subsidies to exporting firms are seen by foreign competitors as unfair competition.

Devaluation

The last instrument, devaluation, is where the central bank revises downwards the price of the domestic currency relative to gold and other foreign currencies. The result is that exporters are able to compete more effectively with foreign competitors because their costs, in terms of other currencies, are reduced. At the same time imports become dearer and importers find it more difficult to compete with domestic producers of the same product.

4
Economic Growth

4.1 IS ECONOMIC GROWTH DESIRABLE?

Throughout the rest of this book we have worked on the assumption that economic growth is desirable for its own sake, that we want the fruits of more production and increased efficiency in the form of more motor cars, television sets, holiday trips, etc.

The desirability of these things is, however, questioned by some people. The critique concentrates on two propositions:

(*a*) More consumer goods mean more industrial fumes, more noise, less unspoilt nature and these are side-effects we do not want.
(*b*) Anyhow, people do not become happier because they get richer. Once a certain standard of living is reached which guarantees a basic existence, there is no virtue in a further increase.

Proposition (*a*) is valid but as an argument against economic growth in general it nevertheless rests on a misconception.

Consumer welfare consists in the ability to enjoy the good things in life to our choice. If it becomes impossible to enjoy the breathing of clean air, the drinking of clean water, the contemplation of unspoilt scenery, and silence, then that is a deterioration in consumer welfare for those who value clean air, clean water, the beauty of unspoilt scenery, and silence. But, alas, all these have become scarce commodities which we may exhaust, just as we can exhaust, say, the supply of crude oil.

We therefore want machines and consumer goods which are more economical in their use of these scarce commodities: we want machines and cars which do not cause pollution, do not make so much noise, and preserve such natural scenery as we have. The controversial element about the hitherto 'free' amenities and their abuse by industry arises because we live in an exchange economy and these amenities are nobody's property. As a result a manufacturer is not compelled to recognize the use of these amenities as a cost, until legislation forces industry to economize on their use. This can be done by a non-price system, but an even more sophisticated way is by selling licences to emit smoke, make noise, etc., making the abuse of public amenities a cost like any other. Factories which emit smoke, mines which spoil the countryside view, motor cars which pollute the urban streets, washing powder which causes the rivers to become foul—all should be taxed. The tax should be based not only on their share in the cost of construction and maintenance of the community facilities which they require (roads, ports, sewage works, etc.), but also on the other scarce public resources which they use, e.g. the mineral reserves in the case of the mine. The tax should also take account of the destruction of amenities and so penalize dirt, noise, and stink. Once all this is done, the likelihood is that industry will find cleaner and less obnoxious production methods and produce also 'cleaner' consumer goods.

The second proposition, that we do not want additional material prosperity at all, contains a consistent and respectable philosophy but it is one where the implications need consideration. It would call for a radical re-valuation of such things as regular work, money, and property. For the great majority of the human race it is in any case an esoteric speculation, because people do *not* enjoy a standard of living which guarantees basic existence. We shall not pursue the point any more.

4.2 THE SOURCES OF ECONOMIC GROWTH

Production grows because

(i) More machines, labour, and materials are used.
(ii) New production processes are introduced.
(iii) Existing methods of production are used in different combinations, enabling a more economical use of existing resources.

The same change in activities may be considered under all three of the above headings, depending on the point of view. For example, a farmer may buy or rent a harvesting machine: the labourer who used to do the harvesting with a scythe takes up a job in a factory in the nearby city and an additional machine is installed there.

The extra machine produces more output. The additional product of the factory, say a textile factory, is used to replace imports and additional industrial consumer goods are imported instead.

We find:

(i) Additional capital and labour (in the textile factory).
(ii) A new process (on the farm).
(iii) A different use of imports.

We further note that additional investment is associated both with expansion on existing lines (in the textile factory) and with the introduction of a new process (the harvesting machine). Together they make it possible to increase output from an unchanged amount of labour.

Since increases in production always involve several and usually all the basic elements of economic growth at the same time, our classification is bound to be based on outward symptoms. We classify different types of economic growth according to the aspects which are most in the foreground, because they give rise to social side-effects, such as migration, change in people's mode of living, etc. The most noticeable socially observable aspects of economic growth are:

(*a*) An increase in the total number of employed people. This is, of course, a fairly obvious case of economic expansion without too much change in the economic structure.
(*b*) Absorption of additional labour in expanding sectors of the economy by reduction of largely concealed unemployment elsewhere. Agriculture is an obvious source of labour. It may or may not be associated with changes in the method of working on the farm. The crucial point is that hitherto productivity on the farm could not easily be increased, because of lack of alternative employment.
(*c*) Absorption of additional labour in expanding sectors of the economy while other, less productive, sectors of the economy shed labour by actually contracting. For example, a country may become specialized in machine building and export many machines. A traditional handicraft weaving and spinning industry may now gradually vanish because people work in the machine-building industry instead and, for the wages earned in the industry, can buy themselves imported textiles as well as other factory-made consumer goods. The country as a whole will then export machines and import textiles.

The rationale of such a specialization is that people get more textiles or other consumer goods by making machines, an activity in which they are specialized, than directly by making textiles.

Increase in productivity within an industry is based on the same principles: innovation and re-allocation of resources. A new method of producing is introduced. Right away, one can only introduce a new productive activity by absorbing additional resources. If there is no increase in the total supply of labour and raw materials then this can only be done by discontinuing existing activities. The new method of production is, however, more economical in its use of at least one resource, otherwise the new method was not a more efficient one. The same amount of final product can now be produced from the input of less labour and/or raw materials. The surplus of inputs can therefore be allocated to additional production, either of this particular product or of another product. Note that *investment* is not by itself a separate source of economic growth.

New machines contribute to production only in combination with labour and material inputs, which have to be re-allocated. For example, someone may invent a motor which will produce the same amount of power as a motor currently in use but uses only 75 per cent of the amount of fuel and only 25 per cent of the labour for maintenance and servicing. We would then account as the evaluated return on the investment the difference in the exploitation cost of the two types of motor, of which the older type is assumed to be still available and in good technical condition.

At the same time, without the invention of the improved type of motor, there might not be any purpose in investing in new equipment at all. If one is limited to a precisely known collection of production processes, there will come a moment when all productive resources, labour, raw materials, etc., are already being used in running the most efficient among the known processes.

4.3 INDUCED TECHNICAL PROGRESS

In the previous section we discussed technical innovation as a cause of economic growth. However, the invention of new types of machines and production methods is just as much the result of economic factors as a cause of economic growth.

There are three aspects to consider in this two-sided relationship between economic growth and technical change.

Firstly, men learn by experience and are stimulated by the example of others, if these other people are successful. Consequently an environment where new machines and production methods are being tried out and come to useful production stimulates more invention.

Secondly, inventors as well as industrial executives are subject to various non-price influences*. One important influence is the attitude of organized labour towards technical innovation. If the demand for the end-product of a factory stagnates it could, in theory, still increase its profits by introducing more efficient production methods and firing a part of its staff. Under conditions of stagnating overall demand this will imply the personal hardship of unemployment.

Under such conditions, therefore, organized labour is conditioned to opposing new and more efficient methods of production, because it means less employment, whereas under other conditions it would have meant higher wages out of increased production.

The cost of a macro-economic policy which maintains unemployment of a few per cent instead of full employment is therefore more than just those few per cent of lost production. It is also the lost benefits of more efficient production, because rationalization plans were shelved or not even formulated in view of the opposition of organized labour.

The third consideration is that technical progress can be organized and institutionalized, and this is the success story of the large-scale industrial concern working under general economic conditions which favour innovation, i.e. in an expanding market.

The professional inventor working on behalf of a large-scale industrial organization is not only progress-orientated: he is also in a position to benefit from the firm's own investment programme in the sense that he can learn from the problems which arise in the actual application of the results of his and his colleagues' earlier inventions.

* I take the following from G. E. Sandström in a work on the history of construction and the construction industry [41]: 'Building and construction have been the most backward of the major industries in the application of mechanized facilities and methods. Indeed, it seems from available, albeit spotty evidence, as though in building at least there actually was a reversion from a modest use of machines on medieval sites to the exclusive use of human labor . . . The mechanization of the construction industry did not begin in earnest until after 1945. . . . As long as there was a rural proletariat available as recruiting ground for construction labor, there was no need to consider investments in labor-saving machines . . . '

4.4 THE PRICING IMPLICATIONS OF INDUCED TECHNICAL PROGRESS

There is a case for implementing an advanced-technology project, despite the fact that till now the new production method is actually more expensive than the old one. One assumes that, once established, the new production method will be perfected and improved in various details and that the cost of production of new types of machine will come down, once they are established. One hopes the new method of production will be cheaper than the old one in future, once it is properly tried out. Apparently there is a certain level of loss on an investment project which can be justified because of the external economies arising from it, namely that particular project's contribution to induced technical progress.

The same argument applies just as well when a newer, advanced-technology method of production is already established and results in costs equal to or lower than the ones which arise from the older method of production.

The reader will remember the theory of interest discussed in section 1.12. The 'efficiency' rate of interest is that at which the total cost of production (including interest and amortization*), calculated for the most modern and efficient methods of production, is equal to the operating cost incurred by continuing production by the existing methods. It will allow obsolete and modern equipment to co-exist and operate side-by-side for a transitional period, while at the same time preventing further investment in obsolete equipment, for which no adequate return on new investment can be obtained. If the market rate of interest were to be set according to this criterion in the presence of induced technical progress, it would presumably mean that a firm of average technical capability would be able to finance the newest and most efficient types of capital equipment known to its management and research staff. However, there would be a definite positive relationship between the rate of expansion of output and the rate of technical innovation. New investment would always be in the most modern types of equipment; the faster the expansion of output, the more

* The accounting term *amortization* means reservation for eventual replacement. If, for example, the equipment is expected to last twenty-five years, the operating profit should cover not only interest but also finance replacement after twenty-five years.

need for new investment—and the more new investment, the more induced technical progress. It is a typical situation of increasing returns to scale, although in a dynamic context. The increasing returns to scale (or, more strictly, to the rate of growth) would apply to the expansion of an industry as a whole, but also to the individual firms within each industry. The thriving and expanding firms would be able to establish a technological lead* over their competitors, because their research and development staff would work with, and see applied within their firm and its subsidiaries and clients, a greater variety of types of sophisticated equipment than in the competing firms.

Following the general notion of the oligopolistic equilibrium† we should not expect complete monopoly. A dominating firm could perhaps, if it so chose, outbid its rivals and become a monopolist, but only at the cost of its own profit. In the resulting oligopolistic situation the leading firm will make a positive profit (or 'surplus profit') on its newer equipment while breaking even on the somewhat older parts of its capital stock. This 'surplus profit', which is made over and above the normal return on productive investment, is the firm's monopoly rent on its technological lead.

On the other hand, a firm which more or less followed the lead given by the dominating firm would be able to make a normal return on its new investment, without any surplus profit. A leading firm will, of course, base its decisions about the level of its investment in any year primarily on the prospect of selling the end-product of the increased productive capacity; it will take the fact that new investment is profitable for granted.

4.5 MARKET CONDITIONS WHICH FAVOUR ECONOMIC GROWTH

In order to restrict the purchasing public's demand for goods and services, money income is limited to the amount which can be produced, and to just that amount. The technical limit on what can be produced and the financial limit on what people can buy (and hence

* Other authors, like Arrow in his article on learning and doing [2], assume that the market does not pay a firm for the induced technical progress arising out of its own productive activities; instead it is assumed that the benefits of induced technical progress arise solely in the form of external economies. I beg to differ.

† *See* section 1.9.

on what producers can sell) are meant to be at the same level. The 'production capacity' is, however, somewhat elastic. The demand for goods and services is not for a theoretical concept called 'total production' but is for specific articles asked for by individual people, or for capital goods, machines, and buildings required by individual firms and public authorities.

If one trader runs out of a particular article but has more customers wanting to buy that same article, the customers will be disappointed. Some of them will buy elsewhere, some will buy something else, and some will spend less money than they would have done otherwise. With a further increase in purchasing power, more traders as well as manufacturers will run out of stocks. Manufacturers will step up production until they cannot increase it any more, because of the technical limits on production facilities. It is clear, however, that the amount of the various articles obtained by the purchasing public can increase considerably before all production facilities are at their limits of technical capacity. Indeed, such a situation is unlikely to arise at all.

Normally there is 'reserve' production capacity, which enables industry to supply the goods and services asked for by the purchasing public without having to disappoint too many customers. A national economy's capacity to produce goods and services in the next year may be elastic, but this is even more the case with the technical limits on producing more goods and services in, for example, ten years from now. There is, of course, the strictly technical-economic aspect of having to build or buy machines, factories, etc., in order to increase production in the future.

At least as important is the limit of imagination and foresight and the lack of encouragement towards the introduction of more efficient methods of production. One important reason for ignoring the technical possibilities of increasing production is an expectation that it cannot be sold anyhow. The expectation of future increases in the income available to the purchasing public is the dynamic counterpart of present income, because firms will plan to increase their production only if they expect to be able to sell more in the future. A firm which behaved genuinely competitively would take the initiative to find and introduce more efficient methods of production; it would try to expand its sales by offering the product for sale below the cost price of its rivals who use less efficient methods of production. In reality, many firms will *not* behave like that; they may already supply a substantial share of the total market for their product, and cannot expect to increase this share without a price concession which costs more than the firm stands to gain, or they simply may not be all that active and are inclined to follow the market. For the less-than-fully-competitive firm the increase in its own sales is closely related to the increase in the total sales of its product in the entire industry.

Suppose in a certain industry it is technically possible to increase production by 50 per cent on the basis of the existing production organizations, and without increase in labour force. Suppose, also, it is expected that demand for the product is to rise in the next five years by 20 per cent. It would be possible to raise productivity by 50 per cent and sack 30 per cent of the labour force. But, more likely, the decision will be to increase productivity by 20 per cent and shelve any further modernization plans until, it is hoped, the demand for the end-product rises more. One then saves the capital outlay, the purchase of the new machines associated with the more radical modernization needed to attain the 50 per cent increase in productivity. This capital outlay is then delayed to the time one expects to need an additional increase in production capacity. And, unfortunately, the whole process of modernization in general is slowed down, because no experience with new methods of production is gained.

The expectations of future income and price developments are interrelated with present* economic conditions, and with the situation in the past.

Firstly, the credibility of a future increase in production is seriously undermined if there is a surplus of production capacity over effective demand in the present. The point can be illustrated by comparing figures of growth rates and unemployment in selected industrial countries.

The computations were based on Tables 176 and 22 of the 1969 *Statistical Yearbook* of the United Nations. The relation between high growth rate and low unemployment is not really as clear-cut as would appear from this selected list, because some countries were left out in order to enhance the main tendency. In many cases one could find some special reason why a particular country did not conform to the

* The postulated negative relation between the level of unemployment and the rate of growth of productivity appears to contradict the notion that the threat of unemployment stimulates personal effort. One has to consider what is more important, technical efficiency or personal effort.

	Percentage increase in per capita *gross national product at constant prices 1960–8*	*Average percentage unemployment of labour 1960–8*
Japan	110	1·0
Norway	36	1·3
Austria	33	2·8
Belgium	33	3·5
United States	30	4·9
Canada	28	5·2

main tendency of high rates of growth for countries with low unemployment. For example, Italy, with a growth fraction of 44 per cent and an unemployment percentage of 3·4, possesses a marked lack of regional balance. One could argue that only half of Italy is really industrialized and that the rural, relatively underdeveloped south is responsible for most of the unemployment. Again, the United Kingdom, with a growth fraction of only 17 per cent and an unemployment percentage of 1·9, is well known for the conservative and restrictive anti-modernization attitude of its trade unions. There is, so to say, more unemployment than the figures indicate, because industry is over-staffed and people are artificially kept in unproductive work. Given the fact that U.K. growth is curtailed by recurring balance-of-payments problems, that is, of course, a logical attitude on the part of British trade unions.

Pressure of demand, backed by purchasing power, on the supply of goods and services is not in itself sufficient to ensure economic growth. First of all it is the volume of demand, the number of the various articles sold, which is critical for the expansion of production capacity, not the money value of income.

A fiscal and monetary policy aimed at stimulating domestic demand and purchasing power should therefore be accompanied by administrative controls on nominal incomes and prices to prevent cost-push inflation. Otherwise the volume of demand may remain the same, or even less because of higher cost relative to foreign competitors, while prices rise. The authority charged with implementing an incomes and prices policy should consider first the desirability of maintaining a semi-stationary level of the average price level and, secondly, should allow for some degree of adaptation in the price structure.

Anticipating the results of the rest of this and the sixth chapter, we may outline an incomes and prices policy which favours economic growth.

Wage increases in the major export-orientated sectors of the economy can be related directly to productivity increases. Wage increases in the rest of the economy are to follow the same general trend, but detailed adjustment may be judged either on considerations of parity with other sectors or on the labour-market situation in the sector concerned. Prices in the sectors which are subject to international competition are best left free, while increases in other prices may be limited to increases in costs, less an assessment for possible increases in productivity. Such a price control implies a productivity target and its desirability is doubtful, except in cases where the type of reorganization and modernization in the industry in question can be indicated, i.e. when there are reasonable grounds for assuming that the productivity target can be met. In all cases the controls are intended to guide the market to the price structure assumed to be similar to the one which would arise eventually as a result of competition (if there was competition), rather than one forcing the economy into an arbitrary course planned without regard to market factors.

The regulating functions of the price structure come under two main headings. The function to be discussed presently is the penalization of inefficient and wasteful use of resources. The other function is to equate supply and demand and will be discussed in more detail in the next section. If all firms were keen on increasing their profit, whatever their financial position, both functions would work together in a way different from what they actually do. Prices indicate which resources are the most urgent to economize on. They also enable accountants and production managers to separate the possible efficient from the clearly inefficient methods of production, because the latter operate at a financial loss.

At this point we recall the analysis in section 1.10. If, under conditions of perfect competition, all firms always maximize profit and all purchasers always buy from the producers who offer at the lowest price, there would be a clear separation between the inefficient and the efficient methods of production and only firms using the most efficient methods could stay in business.

All market prices would be equal to their efficiency prices, and this means that all inefficient production methods cause losses. This is not actually so; instead, market prices distinguish between the clearly inefficient* methods of production, which do cause losses, and a variety of possible efficient methods of production, some of which are more profitable than others.

In such a situation it is possible for the existing income- and price-structure to be substantially maintained and carried forward into the future, with a continuation of substantially the same, traditional methods of production. These methods of production are profitable at the prevailing prices, hence possibly efficient, even if in actual fact some are inefficient and would be revealed as such if all firms behaved competitively. There may be a moderate increase in production, although it would have been possible to increase production much more with the help of relatively little investment and the introduction of more efficient methods of production.

Possible obstacles to modernization are threefold:

(i) *Lack of information.* Certain production processes are known to technical experts, and they are more efficient than the ones in use, but firms' managers either do not know them at all or they do not realize their economic usefulness.

(ii) *Lack of market.* Increased production cannot be sold. There is already less than full utilization of the existing capacity. Therefore, increased productivity means less employment and not more production.

A firm might increase its profit through modernization, even when it cannot sell more, by reducing its cost of production. It could fire a part of its staff. That would only be efficient from the economy-wide point of view if the people who lost their jobs in one firm found something useful to do elsewhere. There is, however, one more obstacle to modernization, which is:

(iii) *Lack of disincentive towards doing nothing.* The typical firm is making a profit, as it has done for years, so why bother about modernization?

The remedy for the two last-mentioned obstacles to economic growth would therefore be a high and rising income of the purchasing public, combined with steadily rising costs. The rising cost of production

* This assumes that all production factors are fully employed. The costs of production factors not fully employed are no real costs to society at large.

factors—as well as, perhaps, the costs of some semi-finished products relative to the end-product of a particular sector—would shift the dividing line between the profitable (and hence possibly efficient) methods of production and the clearly inefficient ones. Some hitherto possibly efficient ones cease to be profitable, while other production methods—either actually employed by some firms producing the same article or else known about—are profitable at the same prices. This reveals the now unprofitable methods of production as clearly inefficient and they will have to be abandoned in favour of more efficient ones.

4.6 WHICH PRICE EQUATES SUPPLY AND DEMAND?

Which price enables an industry to supply, and continue to satisfy a growing demand? We do not refer, at present, to the 'ideal' or competitive market equilibrium, but to the requirement that in any exchange economy there has to be some approximate equilibrium between supply and demand at the prevailing prices. Otherwise the economy ceases to be an exchange economy, because the government is forced to resort to a system of allocation which is not based on financial payments for all essential products. We should distinguish here between the general case of the industrialized market economy and the more specific case of the capitalist economy. Presumably it would be possible—and rational—to run a socialist economy on the basis of decentralization and require individual production organizations, factories, shops, etc., at least to cover their current operating costs from the proceeds of sales and, if possible, give a specified return on investment as well. Major capital expenditure would, however, be financed by state or industry-wide organizations and would not be geared to the profitability of a firm, and hence of existing methods of production, but to that of a particular project, i.e. to the potential of the new, modern production facilities. Calculation of interest as a cost factor is just as logical* in a socialist economy as in a capitalist one, but no problems of market adjustment arise in this respect. The capital allocation to production sectors—as distinct from the allocation within a sector to different investment projects—can, if necessary, be geared to plan targets rather than to profitability. A discrepancy

* I have discussed this in more detail in my book *Allocation Models and their use in Economic Planning* [17].

between the rate of return on new investment in various sectors of the economy might indicate that actual prices were not equal to the theoretical efficiency prices, but planning agencies would still adjust the supply of production capacity to the demand for the product of each industry separately. In the rest of this section we will, however, discuss the relation between the supply of production capacity and the financing of new investment by the capital market on one side, and the demand for the product of various sectors of the economy on the other side.

According to the competitive model, the price-equilibrium function is instrumental to the penalization of inefficient use of resources. Technical innovation (according to the competitive model) is the initiative of a firm which sees profit in a new production process and installs new capacity based on the newer more efficient method of producing. That addition to the supply capacity causes a reduction in the prices of the end-product, which penalizes the other firms in so far as they do not at once follow the innovator's lead.

The majority of established firms do not themselves maximize profit relative to the scale of their own operations. Profit maximization in the limited oligopolistic sense determines the *structure* of the market. This mechanism operates, however, by the behaviour of *some* firms at certain points in time. An established firm will try to expand, regardless of profitability, as long as this can be done without serious price concession, i.e. if its market expands and if it can finance the new investment. This last consideration may imply that the firm must try to raise funds on the outside capital market. That outside capital market is accessible in two ways, by the attraction of general finance capital, and by the intermediary of banks and similar institutions. If a firm is making a satisfactory profit, as good as any alternative open to the general investor, the firm can raise money without having to convince investors of the profitability of the specific purposes for which the funds are needed. Otherwise a money-lending house, bank, etc., will demand detailed information and, as a rule, managerial control in the form of the appointment of one of its agents to the firm's board of directors.

General finance capital does try to maximize profit, and as a result the price regulates the supply of production capacity in an industry in two rather different sets of circumstances, namely:

(*a*) If there is a surplus profit, a surplus of the revenue from sales over all costs, including overheads and a 'normal' return on capital, obtained by means of the established methods of production. This surplus will then give rise to a particular high return to external capital, shareholders, etc. An industry with this type of surplus profit will draw the attention of financial institutions and may attract outside capital, either by new firms entering the industry or established firms raising additional capital from outside the industry. The rate of return on new investment in established methods of production will therefore not rise much above a certain economy-wide market norm, as a higher value causes competitive behaviour and price adjustment will be the result. In this connection 'competitive behaviour' does not mean perfect competition, but competitive behaviour in the limited oligopolistic sense. Nevertheless, in these most profitable sectors of the economy, the price serves as a regulator of the supply of new production capacity, at least in the long run.

(*b*) In the negative, the price restricts the supply of production capacity if there is no profit at all on the established methods of production, while at the existing prices investment towards modernization gives rise to a lower return than the normal rate of return for investment elsewhere. If an industry is really unprofitable the worst affected firms will close down and a reduction of the supply of the end-product will force an upward adjustment of the price.

Note that there is a wide margin between these two extreme positions. There are, in fact, still two qualitatively different positions between these two extremes, indicated by the terms 'moderately profitable' and 'least favourably positioned'.

A firm or even an entire industry may make a moderate profit, although not as much as could be obtained if the same amount of investment as this particular industry is still planning were to be invested elsewhere instead. An industry in this position will not easily attract outside capital. This is so partly because existing firms are reluctant to become dependent on outside money-lenders if they can avoid this, which they can. Also, reorganizations are unpopular as long as things appear to be going well, and investment for expansion without reorganization of the existing production facilities implies price concessions in order to increase the firm's market share. Quite possibly, in such a moderately profitable sector, there may be a theoretical possibility to obtain a substantial profit by modernization. The odds are, however, that the available more efficient methods of production will only be applied in additionally installed production capacity, following an expectation of increased sales.

The least favourable position arises, if existing traditional methods of production are not profitable, or are expected to become unprofitable in the near future, by a further adverse change in the price structure, while profitability can be restored by modernization, and investment to that purpose yields a satisfactory return. If that is the position, a firm will seek to obtain outside capital, if necessary at the cost of losing control to outside interests, as otherwise its very existence would be in danger.

For the economy as a whole, there is nevertheless a general market rate of return on investment, which operates in combination with other, non-price financial factors to equate the total demand for capital goods, arising from modernization and from the increase in demand for end-products, to the supply of finance capital. This 'normal' rate of return is, however, not effective everywhere, nor is it an average of the rates of return in different sectors. It is a maximum rate, demanded by profit-maximizing finance capital. It applies to the most profitable sectors of the economy (as the actually realized rate of return) and to the least favourably priced sectors of the economy (as the potential return on modernization). Note that there is an inversion of the usual direction of the slope of the demand function for capital goods, in the case of an unfavourably priced sector with potential possibilities towards a restoration of profitability by modernization. If the price of the end-product drops relative to the costs of labour and materials, then a hitherto moderately profitable sector (or firm) will need to modernize, and the demand for capital goods (and outside finance) rises.

For the moderately profitable firms the price is set either by extraneous factors, of which outside competition is the most likely example, or by the requirement that profit should be sufficient to finance new investment. Because of this investment finance restriction, the fastest growing sectors of the economy cannot be moderately profitable: they must be most profitable and attract outside finance capital.

The price of the product of a sector in which most firms are moderately profitable can be determined by the economy-wide finance-capital rate of return, if some of the better positioned firms in the industry are most profitable. If the sector is more homogeneous, however, the price is not an equilibrium price in any meaningful sense, except in the very long run. In the long run, the oligopolistic equilibrium determines the market structure. It is nevertheless quite possible for a different price to prevail for a longish period of time, until a change in the market structure becomes effective. In the meantime the price is determined either by custom, or by outside (international) competition, or by government control. The price must be at least sufficiently high to allow the financing of the sector's investment out of its profit, otherwise the supply of new production capacity will not keep up with the increase in demand. The residual profit will either be spent on shareholder capitalist's consumption, or be invested elsewhere, i.e. become part of general finance capital.

The viability of the least favourably positioned firms in the industry is *not* a price-determining factor on its own. These firms must either modernize or close down.

For the economy as a whole, the supply of finance capital (which includes savings from the profits of moderately profitable firms and from labour income, and new loans created by the banks) is equal to the realized demand, the purchase of new capital equipment. The idea that the two are equalized by the price, the rate of return demanded by finance capital, needs some qualification. The following points arise.

(i) If the rate of return on profit-maximizing finance capital is increased, but the social distribution of income does not change, i.e. the ratio between prices of products and the rate of pay of labour remains the same, some most profitable sectors become moderately profitable, but the total income from profit remains the same. The demand for new investment by the sectors which were most profitable, and became moderately profitable, is reduced, but the supply of finance capital is largely unaffected except if the higher quoted return prompts additional savings from labour income. An increased supply of finance capital out of a higher income from profits will emerge, only if prices are pushed upwards relative to wages and salaries.

(ii) If most profitable sectors do stay most profitable at the higher rate of return the increase in the prices of the products produced by the most profitable sectors means higher costs for the least favourably positioned sectors, and this causes an increase in the demand for capital goods instead of a reduction.

For these reasons, the usual supply-and-demand reactions towards the price of finance capital exist, i.e. a reduction in demand and an increase in the supply as a response to an increase in the rate of return demanded by finance capital; but these reactions are particularly weak. Against this there are major non-price influences, which are:

(*a*) On the demand side the technical demand for capital goods arising out of an increase in the demand for end-products.

(*b*) The creation of new loans by the banks (or the government, if it repays government bonds). If the physical limit on production capacity makes it necessary, loan creation must be compensated and this can be done by the public budget, since taxation is a form of forced saving.

(*c*) Inflation increases the immediate supply of finance capital, although it may well reduce its supply in the long run by discouraging saving. Suppose a firm financed the construction of a factory out of an interest-bearing loan. Further, suppose the price structure allows the loan just to be repaid out of operating profit. Then, if all prices rise proportionally by a factor two, the loan can be repaid out of half of the operating profit, and the other half is used to finance the purchase of new capital goods.

The last two factors, creation of additional finance capital by credit or by inflation, can be used by the government as a means of effecting price-adjusting market interference. In other words the government can control the social distribution of income between capital and labour without changing the rate of growth. It stands to reason that credit creation, either by the banks or directly by the state, is a more rational instrument than inflation. There are, however, some side effects to be considered, because of the rate of interest as a cost factor fails to indicate the true return to society of additional investment.

4.7 THE ROLE OF INDICATIVE PLANNING*

Indicative planning is meaningful both in a decentralized socialist

* *See also* Chapter XXII of E. M. Meade [30].

economy and in a monopoly-capitalistic (or, more precisely said, an oligopoly-capitalistic) economy. In both cases it is possible to treat prices as more or less exogenous.* This assumes a certain price structure, either the existing one or an amended forward projection of it, analyses the demand for various products, and confronts them with their supply. If supply and demand do not balance, an adjustment is sought, not by actual market-adjustment (trial and error†), but by calculations and consultations with people who know the various industries. Such an adjustment may, and probably will, involve a slightly different level of the economy as a whole, as represented by macro-economic aggregates like total consumption, total investment, gross national product, etc.

The exercise is *not* meaningful in a perfectly competitive economy, if it exists. With perfectly competitive behaviour there is a completely simultaneous interdependence between each price and each sales volume. Such a simultaneous interdependence would complicate the simulation of market adjustment, but even a complicated adjustment might be attempted if considered useful.

There is, however, a more fundamental objection, which is that a forecast of the level of production and sales in a particular sector of the economy or a particular industry is meaningful to a separate firm in that industry only if the firm expects a substantially unchanged market share. The assumption of an unchanged share of each firm in the total sales of an industry as a whole allows the individual firm to take the forecast for the industry prepared by a co-ordinating body, the planning agency, as a guideline for its own expected sales. That constant-share assumption implies, however, limited competition. The assumption of a strictly constant market-share may be over-restrictive. The share of individual firms can and does change over time, even under oligopolistic limited competition. Nevertheless, a firm which assumes that it will increase its own output by a factor two, despite the fact that the demand for its product in the economy as a whole is falling, will refuse to co-operate in a scheme of indicative planning.

* The exogenous treatment of prices in this section is conventional, i.e. existing published National Plans do not pay much attention to the simultaneous interdependence between prices and volumes. The fact that this interdependence is fairly weak is not an altogether logical reason for neglecting it completely. We shall come back on this point. *See* sections 4.8 and again 6.7.

† *See also* the concept of 'tâtonnement' discussed in section 9.6.

It wants to drive its competitors out of the market instead of framing its own expansion plans with reference to the general expansion of the market for its product.

Indicative planning is, by and large*, non-compulsory and one cannot solve any fundamental conflict of interests by non-compulsory methods. The economy is to be guided among lines of growth, which, one assumes, would eventually emerge as the result of 'pure' market forces in any case. One hopes, however, to attain an adaptation of supply to demand by an organized process of exchanging information. The same adaptation would eventually emerge from the unguided market process as well, but in the meantime there would be temporary discrepancies as a result of imperfect anticipation of future market conditions. These discrepancies would normally resolve themselves as a surplus of production capacity over realized production. Such a surplus capacity could arise either because the sector itself had over-invested or because there was insufficient supply of labour, raw materials or components elsewhere. This includes the case where, due to the lagging performance of export sectors, the government is forced to reduce the general level of economic activity, to reduce aggregate purchasing power, in order to reduce imports. It might then happen that in one sector of the economy a particular industry had spent a considerable amount of money on new investment, and generally had made an effort towards modernization, only to find that it could not utilize the increased production capacity. That is the situation one would hope to avoid and, as we saw in the previous section, this affects the long-term rate of growth as well.

There is, of course, no truly 'optimal' plan. What is aimed at is a market situation where the supply of goods and services, the production of any sector, operated at approximately its full technical production capacity, equals the demand at prices which allow each sector to maintain a normal rate of return on its investment. That equilibrium is, however, not a once-for-all situation, because under the influence of technical progress, the amount of product to be obtained from a given amount of inputs can be increased.

The assessment of how much increase in productivity is to be expected in a given sector contains a necessarily arbitrary element. In the first place one cannot hope to attain perfect efficiency and one must

* There is a possibility of implementing a productivity target by a price control operated at a level which drives the less efficient firms out of business.

assume that in the period to which the plan refers only some of the possibilities towards increasing productivity will be implemented. Furthermore, one does not even know what the potentially increased productivity really is. In other words, the increase in productivity is hoped for and encouraged, but the framing of a plan is more specifically concerned with equating production capacity to the future demand for the product.

The framing of a National Plan is started with a postulated overall rate of growth for the economy as a whole. This is broken down by the central co-ordinating body into sector targets. One assumes that the co-ordinating body will already consider at this stage the development of public expenditure in consultation with the various departments of the government, e.g. the building of roads, schools, etc., the number of civil servants, and so on. The 'translation' of an overall economy-wide rate of growth into specific rates of growth for the various sectors can be done with the help of fairly sophisticated and elaborate calculations, but the reader of this book can think just as well in terms of extrapolation of trends from the past. If industry x has in the past expanded its production at a rate which was just 1 per cent per year higher than the rate of growth of the total national product, then a postulated rate of growth of 5 per cent for gross national product means a rate of growth of 6 per cent for industry x. Thereafter, firms and industry committees on the basis of the production target (provisional sales forecast) will frame their plans for new investment and their anticipated requirements of labour, raw materials, and semi-finished products. Then comes the confrontation of the supply of the various products and production factors with the demand. In the case of a product the supply is the set target; for a domestic production factor (labour, land) it is the available supply, as determined by demographic and/or geographical conditions.

A special case arises with foreign currency in the confrontation of exports (supply) with imports (demand). The central co-ordinating body may have set separate export targets, or it may have left the assessment of export possibilities to the specialists in the sector committees. In an industry with substantial export the sector target represents an estimate of domestic demand, and the specialists in the industry itself can, if necessary, adjust the estimate (target) for their total production according to their own assessment of export possibilities. The estimate of the sector demand is the estimated final use by consumers and government, plus the estimated export, plus the required amounts of semi-finished products and capital goods listed by the various sector committees. The normal assumption about market adjustment is that a firm will know its market position through actual sales and orders placed, and it should somehow find an adaptation of its production plan to its market position. This may in turn affect the sales of other firms and there are bound to be certain inconsistencies, leading to an excess of production capacity over realized production. Under a system of indicative planning this adjustment is performed by calculation, so as to restore equilibrium between the planned supply and the projected demand arising from it without waiting for the actual supply-demand position to emerge. This adjustment may or may not require an adjustment of the macro-economic, total rate of growth as well. If the total demand for a macro-economic production factor (e.g. labour) turns out to be in excess of its supply, the assumed overall rate of growth is higher than can be achieved.

4.8 THE ADJUSTMENT OF INCOMES AND PRICES

Adjustment of a price and a rate of pay are decisions in favour of one group of people or other economic agents, firms, etc., at the cost of a similar group. If the price is raised the sellers benefit and the buyers pay more. For this reason, prices and incomes cannot be planned in the same 'indicative' way as can be done with amounts.

A central co-ordinating body, a planning agent, might make the statement: 'On the assumption of a 5 per cent per annum rate of growth of gross domestic product, we expect the demand for steel to increase at a rate of 7 per cent a year and the demand for petrochemical products at a rate of 11 per cent a year.' The likely result of such a statement by the central body is that firms in the steel sector will base their investment decisions on a growth rate of saleable output of 7 per cent a year, and firms in the petrochemical sector will assume 11 per cent a year. This is why only 'indicative' planning is needed. The finally agreed plan will be implemented as a result of the sales anticipations which arise from it.

If, however, the central co-ordinating body pronounces: 'given the expected deterioration of world trade and the increased international competition faced by our export industry, it is necessary that wages do not increase by more than 5 per cent', this statement is likely to be challenged or else ignored by trade unions, who will press for higher increases.

One of the precise advantages of the central forecast in indicative planning is its non-controversial nature. Even if the statistical basis of the forecast is perhaps not very strong *it is accepted as a frame of reference for sector plans.* This enables the central co-ordinating body to verify the internal consistency of the plan by aggregating the sector plans when they come back to it. The wisdom of introducing a controversial price-forecast in this framework is questionable, except if there is a firm statistical basis. The notion of 'constant prices' is hardly more than a fig-leaf, concealing the fact that the controversial subject of prices and incomes is avoided. If, however, for some reason it is desirable to introduce a price control, forbidding an increase in the price of a specific product or production factor above a certain figure, it is only logical to include an estimate of the future level of operation of this control in the central forecast. The controversial element cannot be avoided in that case.

There are two kinds of reason prompting a desire to control incomes and prices.

One purpose is to regulate the average level of prices, i.e. to curb inflation. This is related to the desirability of maintaining full employment of labour and installed production capacity. The government can regulate money income and purchasing power by means of fiscal and monetary instruments. Thus it can adjust spendable income by changes in taxation; it can adjust the money supply by means of the surplus or deficit on its budget and though credit control and loans on the stock exchange. The technical demand for labour and machine capacity is, however, related to the amount produced, the number of items, kilograms, metres, etc., of the various products. It is possible for the money value of sold output to rise at a normal rate while the amount stagnates, because the prices rise and limited competition results in a systematic tendency in this direction. Fiscal and monetary policies can curb the (rise in the) money value, but this may hit the amount sold rather than the price. Any curb on any price will, to some extent, relieve this problem. If prices are brought under control, an equal amount of money will buy a larger amount of products than would be the case at a higher price level. Even if the purchased quantity of the product which is subject to price control does not increase, its claim on buyers' income is reduced and this frees purchasing power for other products. In deciding which prices are to be the subject of controls we have to consider two types of argument, namely, enforceability and administrative convenience, and the possibility of distortion in the price structure.

The desirability of controlling the price *structure* can, in a way, be an argument in its own right, if one seeks to enforce modernization by making technologically backward methods of production unprofitable. But this way it is a much more questionable argument than maintaining a certain average price level. The strongest case for a price control as opposed to a forecast without administrative implementation arises if the two arguments interlock and point in the same direction. This is the case if, in an 'open' economy with international trade, there is actually or potentially a deficit on the external payments balance while there is unemployment of domestic labour at the same time. Then the desirability of containing domestic inflation (the absolute price level) and the competitive position relative to the outside world (the price structure) point in the same direction. A mature developed country is technically capable of producing a range of sophisticated industrial products. A mature industrially developed country's ability to compete effectively in the international market depends, therefore, mainly on the price at which it is able to offer certain products.

To maintain full employment in the presence of increasing labour productivity, total production must increase. A growing production requires an increasing amount of imported raw materials and semi-finished products, and the increasing income associated with growth also generates an increasing demand for foreign products. The relation between imports and exports is not, however, a purely technical one. A country which is still in the process of *becoming* an industrially developed country may introduce domestic production of products which were hitherto not produced at home, but imported. For a country which is still on the borderline of being an underdeveloped country, there are even good reasons for actively promoting import substitution, if necessary by means of restrictions on imports. On the other hand, a smaller mature developed country is likely to have *specialized* in certain export products, in which it has developed a technological lead even over other developed countries. Not everyone can be specialized in everything and if specialization is successful in some products, the likelihood is that the fabrication of some other products will be gradually phased-out in favour of imports. Imports may therefore rise actually faster than production. The precise relation between imports and activity level is a typical long-term problem. The immediate short-term problem is that more production implies more imports. Increasing imports can be paid for only if exports rise at a similar rate.

The control of nominal labour cost in the domestic economy will allow the export sectors to offer their products for sale at an internationally competitive price, and to make an acceptable return on their investment at the same time. This allows exports to increase, and thereby enables the economy as a whole to grow. In order to control the cost of exports it would be sufficient to control the nominal level of wages and salaries in the export sectors. The effectiveness of such controls depends mainly on two factors: on the state of the labour market and on the plausibility (or lack of plausibility) of any claims for higher nominal wages and salaries.

The likelihood of inflationary wage settlements, which could give rise to cost-push inflation, is at least as great in the sectors of the economy which mainly supply the domestic market as in the export-orientated sectors. The limited short-term mobility of labour between various sectors of the economy largely shields the labour supply of the export sectors from the direct influence of the income level in other sectors. People will by and large remain in the sectors where they work even if some sectors pay a few per cent more than others. Nevertheless, a pay rise in other sectors of the economy is bound to increase the plausibility of similar claims in the export sectors.

The other factor which systematically influences the labour market in any sector of the economy is the level of unemployment. There is, so to say a 'critical level' of frictional unemployment and, if unemployment drops below that level, any attempt to control nominal wages is bound to be ineffective. That threshold is higher if the controlled level is felt as unfair, and nearer to exact full employment if the controlled level is generally considered to be a fair one. Therefore an incomes policy must embrace the whole of the economy, even apart from any arguments about the intrinsic desirability of a more general, economy-wide incomes policy. The logical norm for the rate of increase in nominal income from employment is cost parity with foreign competitors. For most of the 1950s and 1960s the price level of internationally traded products was relatively stable: this meant that the norm 'cost parity with our foreign competitors' was approximately in line with 'the general wage level to follow the average increase in productivity in the export-orientated sectors of the economy'.

The distinction between world-market orientated sectors of the economy (chemicals, electronics) and home-market orientated sectors (construction, housing, personal services, haircutting, maintenance of domestic appliances, retail trade, internal transport) is to some extent—but by no means completely—also the distinction between the capital-intensive science-orientated sectors and the labour-orientated traditional sectors. Because of this prices inside a country can rise, and rise regularly over time, even if the prices of internationally traded products are stable. If, however, the general price level of internationally traded products should maintain a persistent rising trend, this is bound to result in more inflation inside individual countries, unless they adjust their exchange rates.

International trade transmits inflation from one country to another. Inflation has occurred at about the same time, and has persisted until now, in more or less every industrial market economy from the mid-1960s, accelerating, also on a worldwide scale, in the 1970s.

An individual country attempting to keep the rise in nominal earnings of its working population in line with productivity, while all its competitors practice inflation, would see its exports rise faster and faster and its imports stagnate, because foreign exporters would price themselves out of its internal market. The result would be a persistent situation of excess demand for labour; claims for higher nominal incomes could no longer effectively be resisted. Incomes policy—or for that matter any comprehensive price control in an exchange economy—is meant to be simple price regulation. The reader will recall that in section 1.3 we found that a simple price control, not backed by market intervention and/or rationing, can be effective only if the controlled price is not too far from the level at which that particular price would have settled if left free. Incomes policy is nevertheless of considerable importance and effectiveness, mainly because it breaks the wages and salaries versus prices *spiral* without resorting to deflation and unemployment. The following can now be observed concerning price controls.

Because of the presence of foreign competition there is no case for price controls in the main export sectors. The main purpose of incomes control, as a growth strategy, is to maintain a reasonable rate of profit in the export sectors. The level of the prices in these sectors is largely determined by international competition. There is a certain case for price control in sectors which are orientated on the domestic market. Tariffs of public utilities are an obvious case. Unfortunately there is no clear norm for the level at which these controls should be operated. If all increases in costs justify a corresponding increase in price, the control is probably superfluous, because prices would not rise faster without control. Also, a norm for price rises which allowed all increases in cost to be passed on to the buyer of the product would fail to fulfil a potential function of price control. The requirement to maintain a certain selling price, while costs of labour and materials rise, can be a stimulus towards the increase in productivity. On the other hand, a too rigid price control may in fact prevent desirable investment, because the means to finance it are not there. Or it may even drive some firms out of business, while no others enter, causing a drop in the supply of the product.

For this reason free imports, if possible, are to be preferred over price control. With free imports the price is set by international competition, as is the case in the export sectors. Either the domestic sector is capable of increasing its own productivity, and maintains its market position despite foreign competition, or it loses its market share. In that case, part of its labour force will eventually be re-allocated to other sectors of the economy. If there is no full employment, the alternative would, of course, be an increase in unemployment. Since maintaining full employment in general is dependent on an effective incomes policy, we come to a paradoxical-sounding conclusion. An incomes policy, involving restrictions on the free price formation of labour, is a pre-condition for allowing free competition in the markets for end-products without causing unemployment.

4.9 THE INFRASTRUCTURE COST OF GROWTH

An increase of national production requires sooner or later an increased capital stock, and this increase of capital stock is obtained by means of new investment. This is true for industrial capital, machines, buildings, etc., as well as for infrastructure, roads, ports, etc. It is also by and large true for 'social' infrastructure facilities like hospitals, schools, town halls, etc.

One reason why additional social infrastructure is required is that economic growth is usually associated with social mobility and migration; hence new social facilities in geographical areas with increasing population are needed. Also, services like theatres, social clubs, community centres, etc., to some extent have an income elasticity. It is possible—but not very wise—to direct growth purely in the direction of increased expenditure on personal consumer goods, like motor cars, television sets, etc. One makes on the whole a more sensible use of the proceeds of a higher national income, if in contrast this is associated with more leisure, shorter working hours and more holidays, and with increased use of such leisure facilities as swimming pools, sports grounds, theatres, holiday centres, etc. The increased demand for services generates demand for investment in buildings, and so on. (This is the accelerator principle, *see* section 1.16.) When facilities for leisure activities are provided by public authorities the accelerator demand for investment arises in the public sector and a higher rate of growth implies that a greater percentage of current production should be allocated to public investment. To plan for a high rate of growth implies planning high taxes and high public expenditure, even as a percentage of national income.

The above observations appear fairly obvious. It is after all logical that increased welfare should be associated with additional personal consumption as well as with more leisure and with more social consumption. Complications arise, however, in practical political terms when it comes to paying higher taxes.

It is possible to stimulate production by creating additional demand for it. The fact that this requires additional material capital in the form of firms' new investment in vehicles, machines, and buildings is obvious. We shall come back to this aspect of the problem in Chapter 6. We are now concerned with the demand for public expenditure.

A balance has to be found between the claims on the one hand for increased personal consumption, to be fulfilled by lowering taxes and by paying pensions and benefits to needy categories of private people, and increasing public consumption and public investment on the other. Examples of what may go wrong are:

(i) More packed food and technical gadgets for personal use are produced, and people find that public facilities cannot adequately cope with increased amounts of litter and more cars on the same streets and roads.

(ii) Leisure time is increased but social facilities for leisure activities are not and they become crowded.

(iii) Economic growth is associated with urbanization: employment in the cities increases, while employment in rural areas falls. People have to move from rural to urban areas. Housing is partly provided on a 'social' basis (publicly sponsored low-cost housing programmes), and the 'social' housing sector in the growing cities fails to keep pace with the increasing urban population. The result is a housing shortage and people have to live overcrowded, in 'bidonvilles', 'shanty towns', and the like.

(iv) After a housing shortage has developed, it is attacked by standardizing and mechanizing the building industry and the result is large numbers of dull, uniform system-built flats.

All these things have—wrongly—been presented as disadvantages of economic growth as such. They are, however, the result of society's refusal to recognize that a balanced growth of national income costs more than just factories and machines.

5

The position of an underdeveloped country

5.1 WHAT IS AN UNDERDEVELOPED COUNTRY?

An underdeveloped country is a country where industrial employment, although desired, is not available and cannot be made available except on a very limited scale. Usually the bulk of the population lives on subsistence farming, which yields a fairly low income. This distinguishes an underdeveloped country from certain developed, but predominantly agricultural, countries such as New Zealand, where there is a high-productive, high-income agriculture which works for export as well as for a domestic market and people have no wish to move out of agriculture into industry, at least not more than they are actually doing.

Low agricultural productivity is related to the lack of industrial employment. The point is that there is little purpose in increasing labour productivity in agriculture if there is no alternative employment. Producing television sets, refrigerators, steel sheet, computers, microscopes, aircraft, electric locomotives, etc., is not practicable in an underdeveloped country, because it lacks infrastructure, market for these products, technical skill, and capital. To be sure, there is usually a certain amount of local industry, mostly small-scale industry of a not too complicated technical nature, but this is too small relative to the supply of (mainly unskilled) labour.

There may be, and there usually is, a certain amount of export-orientated mineral extraction and high-productive plantation type agriculture also. These enterprises are usually, but not always, owned and managed by foreign business interests.

5.2 CAN AN UNDERDEVELOPED COUNTRY BECOME A DEVELOPED COUNTRY?

For most underdeveloped countries, particularly the smaller ones, becoming a developed country is only possible under certain special conditions. We repeat the four essential obstacles: lack of infrastructure, market, technical skill, and capital. Of these obstacles lack of market is the most difficult to overcome by conscious effort of planning, backed either by international aid or by savings from the revenues of the traditional mineral and agricultural exports.

Roads, railways, airfields, and ports can be built, people educated and trained, and imports of machines can be financed in this way from savings or foreign loans, and this will no doubt encourage local small-scale industry. Certain types of complicated and technically sophisticated products are, however, produced in industrially developed countries on a mass scale. A small developing country cannot hope to establish production facilities which are at all comparable with those of the leading foreign producers, simply because of the overheads of initial installation and the servicing of the equipment needed to produce these advanced-technology products. The only way out is to plan at once not only for the supply of the domestic market but for export as well.

The introduction of new methods of production, including new types of production organization, requires some form of co-operation from those engaged in similar activities elsewhere. Some element of continuity of tradition is inherent in all human activity. Therefore, to establish modern production facilities at all a developing country is dependent on technical assistance from established producers: this assistance will not be given if the intention is to compete with the established producers in their traditional markets.

In section 1.6 we discussed the fact that established manufacturers rarely build factories in low-income countries. It is true that, from the point of view of an industrial capitalist, there are some rational arguments for this reluctance, but they are not sufficient to explain the actual situation. We will now review these arguments. First, there is the point of exploitation in general. Large-scale unemployment in underdeveloped countries results in favourable terms of trade for the industrially developed countries. One could perhaps explain the attitude to development aid of right-wing political parties, which are associated with industrial capitalism in a Marxist sense, as the expression of their desire to see the supply of raw materials at low wage costs perpetuated. But can one expect an individual firm, even a large concern, to forego immediate profit because keeping underdeveloped countries underdeveloped is more in the interest of the capitalist class and of developed countries in general?

Next, we consider the possibility of loss of scale of production.

This is not really applicable; the realistic proposition is to establish an assembly plant, or a plant for making certain specific components or materials. The implication is that the new plant remains an integrated part of the parent-company's production organization and no loss of scale occurs.

Then consider the possibility of loss of the plant through nationalization, or the possibility that the government of the developing country may demand certain concessions, special payments, a greater employment of its own nationals at a senior level, etc., and threaten nationalization if these demands are not met. Some concession may indeed be obtained by the developing country from the company. However, the developing country's government cannot really afford to nationalize and neither can it afford to demand so much in the way of concessions that the venture ceases to be profitable for the parent company. A government which threatens nationalization has to assume that the parent company will at some stage call its bluff and refuse any further co-operation: the plant will come to a standstill through lack of certain components and through lack of a market, which is controlled by the parent company. Nevertheless, few industrialists do invest in developing countries. They fear that developing countries' governments will nationalize without compensation, despite the irrationality of such action from the developing countries' point of view. Or their non-action is the result of tradition, rather than of calculation.

For smaller developing countries the only way to develop large-scale advanced technology industry is to form regional common-market zones which together form a sufficiently large market, protected from open competition with the established producers. Only after the possibility of selling directly to a certain region is largely closed to the established producers will the latter be inclined to co-operate in the establishment of new, locally based production organizations.

5.3 ADAPTATION TO THE BALANCE OF PAYMENTS RESTRICTION

We take it that most underdeveloped countries have, for the foreseeable future, to resign themselves to the fact that the fabrication of at least certain types of technically sophisticated products is a monopoly of the industrially developed countries. Now if, as in ancient Tibet, people's preferences were for sober, locally produced food, locally made woollen clothes, huts or houses and temples from locally cut stones, and time to meditate, this would not be so much of a problem.

In actual fact, people's preferences are now to a large extent for watches, motor cycles, television sets, refrigerators, and the like. These things must be imported and cost foreign exchange. Again, some less sophisticated products like matches, soap, modern-type textiles and clothing, houses with proper sanitary equipment, china cups and saucers, can and often are produced locally, but still cost some foreign exchange in the form of imported materials and components.

Some developing countries are in a relatively favourable position in that they have substantial export earnings from ores or other raw materials or from agricultural export. Although this may not provide much employment, it allows considerable import, and this may lead to enough employment in local small-scale industry, urban handicraft, trade, etc., as the country can afford the import of some foreign-produced components and materials. It is also quite possible that, due to lack of export earnings, the money income of the population and the expenditure of the government have to be kept at a level which is too low from any other point of view. The demand for imported consumer goods like watches, motor cycles, etc., and the demand for imported materials and equipment, like dyes, chemicals, small tools, water taps, etc., may not exceed the available foreign currency earnings. It is this 'affordable' level of imports, which determines the level of internal income which the government can allow or generate.

If the country is fortunate, that level of economic activity is sufficient to secure a reasonable level of industrial employment in the local industry. The oil-producing countries in particular are in a relatively favourable position here. Unfortunately that level may also be fairly low; this is especially so for countries whose main export products are faced with competition from industrially produced synthetics, such as natural rubber which has to compete with both synthetic rubber and plastics.

5.4 THE NON-IMPORT POLICY OF A DEVELOPING COUNTRY

The attitude of the governments of underdeveloped countries towards imports often is, and always should be, totally different from the attitude of a government of a developed country towards the same problem.

It is good textbook economics to assume that the free flow of goods and services promotes the most efficient use of national resources. For an industrially developed country this is in a broad sense approximately true.

For an underdeveloped country free import without duties, import licences, etc., would cause unnecessary unemployment. The problem is that the true limits to the country's production are the supplies of certain mineral ores and what quantities foreign markets can absorb of its traditional export products. Accordingly, anything which saves more foreign exchange than it costs is efficient and should be encouraged. The fact that at the prevailing prices—and including a payment to the abundant local labour—many of these activities would make a loss is irrelevant from the point of view of efficiency.

For example, a farmer may want to buy a tractor. This will save him the cost of feeding oxen, also the wages of a man to do the ploughing, because with the greater horse-power of the tractor he can manage it alone. It does not produce additional crop. The cost of the tractor is its purchase cost (in foreign currency) plus the cost of imported fuel. On the other side, the only real saving may be the fodder which used to be given to the oxen. The labourer's wages would be a real saving in a full-employment economy, where the labourer would go somewhere else and do something useful—become a builder's labourer, a hotel assistant, or go to work in a factory. But if there is already unemployment, the saving of his wages is no real saving to the economy as a whole. Therefore, if the government either taxes the tractor and the imported fuel, or simply refuses an import licence, it is the government's intervention and not the free flow of trade which promotes the true efficiency. If the farmer does not buy the tractor, foreign exchange is saved. It can then be used to buy either some consumer good like a motor car, or else something like a stone-cutting machine, enabling the country to use locally cut stones for building instead of having to import building materials.

A second, quite different point is the so-called 'infant-industry' argument. So far we have taken a country's technological capability and efficiency as given data. It is reasonable to assume, however, that once production of a particular article has started in a country, it will be easier to bridge the gap in knowledge of the most efficient methods of producing that particular type of product, than it would be on the basis of formal instruction only.

The point has been made with some vigour by the German economist F. List [26]. In List's time, the early to middle part of the nineteenth century, Germany *was* a developing country.

5.5 INCOME FORMATION IN A THINLY POPULATED LOW-INCOME COUNTRY

Population density is a relative concept. For example, Egypt is rather thinly populated relative to its total territory. However, the bulk of that territory consists of deserts and nothing will grow there. What matters is the area of good-quality agricultural land relative to the population that has to eat the food grown on that land, and the Egyptian population is very dense in relation to the area of the fertile Nile valley. When arable land is abundant nobody needs to go hungry. Likewise, primitive huts made from local wood, leaves, baked mud or locally cut stones, will be available as well.

It is true that malnutrition occurs in thinly populated low-income countries, but this is not so much a problem of economic reform as of information, of helping the people to learn which foods are good to eat, which crops should be grown, and how they should be cultivated. The more strictly economic problems are concentrated around imported sophisticated products and the export products which have to be sold abroad in order to pay for imports. Where the first necessities of life are available in any case, the measure of additional prosperity is the availability of sophisticated consumer goods, like watches, refrigerators, motor cars, radios, houses with air-conditioning, larger urban-style houses, and so on. Some of the productive activities associated with these sophisticated products, like servicing and maintenance, have to be effected locally, and will give rise to employment in the local urban sector. Some activities like the fitting and assembling of certain parts or components can also be performed locally, even where import of the complete product is possible.

Following the argument of the previous section we maintain that, wherever this results in a reduction of the foreign-exchange cost relative to importing the complete product, the government should promote such local production. The comparison of the foreign-exchange cost should not include import duties, even if, once a domestic industry is set up, the government puts a tariff on imports. But even after this has been done one is left with the fact that only industrially developed countries can produce all the vital components of certain high technology products. Therefore, to obtain these sophisticated products at all, one has to spend some foreign exchange. The amount of sophisticated consumer goods which can be made available is therefore dependent on the amount of foreign exchange available.

5.6 THE MAIN EXPORT PRODUCTS OF UNDERDEVELOPED COUNTRIES

Foreign exchange is produced by the export sectors. It arises in two ways. Firstly, it comes from the traditional agricultural export products, like tea, cocoa, and rubber. The amounts of these products sold by all underdeveloped countries together is clearly determined by the demand for them, mainly in developed countries.

It so happens that the opportunity cost of producing an additional unit of coffee is virtually nil, involving the employment of an otherwise unemployed man and the cultivation of some otherwise uncultivated land. According to the market-adjustment principle coffee producers should therefore offer their coffee at a very low price indeed, so as to outbid each other. For each of them would gain from an increase of its own coffee export (at the cost of the others) as long as there was a market for the coffee at all. Furthermore, the demand for coffee is rather inelastic to its price, as the main coffee consumers can already consume all the coffee they wish, hence a drop in the price would result in a loss of income to the coffee producers collectively, not adequately compensated for by an increase in the volume of sales. The main result of this situation would be that the terms of trade would be unfairly favourable to the consuming countries, like North America and Western Europe.

Brazil and Liberia thought this was wrong and the International Coffee Agreement regulates the coffee market in order '. . . to assist in increasing the purchasing power of coffee-exporting countries by keeping prices at equitable levels . . . '*

The other main source of export revenue are industrial raw materials, like crude oil, iron ore, or bauxite. Their production is

* Extract from the preamble of the 1962 International Coffee Agreement.

pursued in industrially developed countries as well, and on a capital-intensive—rather than a labour-intensive—basis in developed and underdeveloped countries alike. The direct employment in these industry-geared export sectors is therefore relatively small. The main advantage to underdeveloped countries of possessing exportable oil or bauxite is the foreign-exchange earnings which arise from these exports. Because they are essential for industrial production in developed countries the demand for these products, especially oil, is rising.

5.7 RICARDO'S TERMS OF TRADE THEOREM

Underdeveloped countries may be dependent upon the export of certain products which other countries, including industrially developed countries, can produce by more efficient methods. The same situation, with very much the same result, may also arise when industrially developed countries produce synthetic substitutes for the traditional products of low-income countries. This is an application of Ricardo's theory of comparative costs in international trade which we illustrate by quoting from him (Chapter VII of [38]):

> 'England may be so circumstanced that to produce the cloth may require the labour of 100 men for one year; and if she attempted to make the wine, it might require the labour of 120 men for the same . . . To produce the wine in Portugal might require only the labour of 80 men for one year, and to produce the cloth in the same country might require the labour of 90 men for the same time. It would therefore be advantageous for her to export wine in exchange for cloth . . . notwithstanding that the commodity imported by Portugal could be produced there with less labour than in England . . . '

Note that in this (Ricardo's) example, Portugal, not England, has the higher labour productivity for both productive activities. The implication for the terms of trade is that they are unfavourable for the low-productive country: 'Thus England would give the produce of the labour of 100 men for the produce of the labour of 80 Portuguese . . . '

The reasons why this is so can be illustrated with the help of a more modern example: rubber and motor cars. The amount of labour, including the indirect labour cost, which is expended on the raw materials needed to produce 1 tonne of synthetic rubber in the United States is well below the amount of labour required to produce 1 tonne of rubber in Malaysia by bleeding rubber trees. Nevertheless, Malaysia has to export rubber to the United States in exchange for motor cars. The reason is simple: to offer the rubber on terms which are competitive with the synthetic rubber is the way in which Malaysia can obtain the largest number of motor cars. Suppose it takes the equivalent of one month's labour by one man to produce a certain amount of synthetic rubber in the United States, and it takes the equivalent of one month's labour by one man to produce one automobile in the United States. Then the price system equates that amount of rubber to an automobile. Malaysia will not get an automobile for less than that amount of rubber, despite the fact that it may take the equivalent of one month's labour by *five* men to produce that same amount of rubber by bleeding rubber trees in Malaysia. It explains why so few Malaysians can afford a motor car.

5.8 THE PLIGHT OF THE DENSELY POPULATED POOR COUNTRY

A poor country's population may be too numerous, not only relative to the level of employment which can be sustained by the level of imports the country can afford, but also relative to the amount of food that can be grown on the available agricultural land. In that case the population will not only have to go without things like transistors and watches, but even without sufficient food itself.

The problem is not only one of population density. Some advanced industrial countries are just as densely populated, but thrive on it, because it provides labour supply for their industrial export sectors; food is imported.

It is the combination of being technically backward, and hence being unable to produce and export sophisticated industrial products, with not being able to feed the population from the country's own land, which can force people to go hungry.

No country hitherto has been in the position that, with an average harvest over the country as a whole, it has been unable to afford the amount of food which, evenly distributed, was enough to prevent starvation. Nevertheless people have died from hunger, even in 'normal' circumstances, i.e. excluding war, blockade, etc. This is firstly because some countries do not have a substantial 'reserve' in their capacity to feed their population. They have to earmark part of the revenue from such export earnings as they have for the import of food. This reduces imports of industrial materials and consumer goods, and hence industrial employment. Secondly, the average nutritional standard of the population, although normally sufficient to stay alive, is low, and people are fed only just above the starvation level. Under these conditions it can happen that the poorest among the population (the aged, the sick, the fatherless family, the unemployed landless labourer) do indeed die from hunger, even under 'normal' conditions. And exceptionally bad harvests may cause famine.

Four possibilities for ameliorating the situation should be obvious:

(i) Increase the yield of domestic agriculture by irrigation, fertilizers, introduction of high-yield and disease-resistant varieties of existing types of crops or of more suitable types of crops.

(ii) Increase foreign-exchange earnings by more export, export at higher prices, or more foreign aid.

(iii) Restrict imports of non-food products in order to save foreign exchange to buy food.

(iv) Reduce the growth of population.

A fifth possibility is not so immediately obvious but is nevertheless of some importance, namely improve internal transport and construction of storage facilities for food. This makes it possible to use the surplus product of more favourable years or regions to overcome a local mishap in the harvest.

Except for new types of crops or reduction of population growth, most of these possibilities are directly related to a country's general economic position, because they require increased imports, or a re-allocation of imports, or new investment.

5.9 BALANCED OR UNBALANCED GROWTH

One of the crucial strategy decisions to be taken by a country wanting to industrialize concerns the extent to which it allows itself to depend on foreign trade. If the increase in domestic production is to rely solely on domestic resources and domestically produced capital goods, this can mean slow growth, as much capital will be needed and it will take time before it is bearing fruit.

Some of the sectors which will require substantial investment are: transport (railways, lorries); agriculture and its supporting industrial sectors (fertilizer factories, irrigation projects); electricity (power stations); and general industry requiring all sorts of tools and machines. If all these capital goods are to be produced in the country themselves it will take time and much work.

One can obtain much quicker results by buying some of the more sophisticated capital goods abroad. To be able to increase imports substantially it is necessary to export more as well. Suitable export products are: certain relatively labour-intensive products like toys, some textiles and, in the case of a thinly populated country, also food, either in its 'natural' state or as dried fruit, tinned vegetables, etc. Some foreign exchange has to be earmarked for investment in the export sectors themselves; but it may well be, and often is, possible to achieve a faster overall rate of growth if the building of railways and factories and power plants can start at once, without having to wait until the domestic steel mills produce rails and a domestic machine-building industry produces machines. Moreover, in this approach, no resources are earmarked for capital-intensive advanced technology projects like fertilizer factories, precision-instruments factories, and so on. The disadvantage of the alternative strategy of 'unbalanced' growth is that the country becomes more dependent on foreigners buying the domestic export and, if they do not, the whole strategy of expansion is in danger.

Now a small country may have no choice. The 'unbalanced' type of development, concentrating on the sectors of production which do not require much advanced technology and heavy capital equipment, may be the only way it can develop at all. However, a bigger country has a sufficient internal market for heavy industry, steelmaking, electronics, and machine building and if there is doubt about foreigners' willingness to buy the products of any proposed export sectors, the country can try to build the required capital goods itself instead of relying on export as a means of paying for them.

The disadvantage of this alternative strategy of 'balanced' growth is first, that it is slow relative to the amount of capital it requires and, second, that in the initial stage one builds steel mills, power stations, etc., without so far producing any additional consumer goods. Consumer goods will only become available to the population at large after the additional steel production has been used to build fertilizer plants, rails, and machine tools; the fertilizer has increased agricultural production and the machine tools have been used to make consumer goods; and both have been transported by the new transport facilities.

In the meantime the standard of living of the population will actually *fall*, as an increasing industrial labour force must be fed and clothed from a so-far unchanged production of consumer goods.

The two approaches can also be used in combination, one after the other. Initially, when there is a very narrow industrial base, there is no technical and industrial tradition and virtually no internal market for machinery and other capital goods. Once a certain amount of infrastructure and light industry are established, their further expansion provides an established domestic market for a capital-goods producing sector. The installations for this can be imported, the initial capital outlay being at least partially financed from the export earnings of the older light industry.

6
Regulating a growing full-employment economy

6.1 THE RATIONALE OF ECONOMIC REGULATION

How is an economic system to be organized? The purpose of economic activity is to obtain end-products. These end-products can be essential goods for personal consumption, such as food, they can be desirable products such as toys and motor cars, or they can be collective goods such as schools and hospitals.

The centrally planned economy, where the government sets out to organize the production of the desired products, has therefore an element of *a priori* logic. The main disadvantage of such a system is the information and co-ordination problem which it involves.

The first problem is simply to agree which end-products are desired. According to the novel, Robinson Crusoe and Man Friday formed a two-person island economy: they could agree by discussion and majority vote (Robinson Crusoe having the chairman's casting vote) on a collective plan for production and consumption. For a whole nation this is just not possible.

The composition of consumption is determined even in a fully centralized Soviet-type economy by means of a market system. People are paid money and the state produces products, which are offered for sale to the citizens; if some are not sold, while other products are sold out, this is an indication to the state producer that less of one product and more of something else should be produced. There may be delays in the administrative machinery before these adjustments are made, nevertheless consumers' choice plays a role, even in the nearest equivalent to a completely centralized planned economy that exists.

The other main problem is that of efficient planning and co-ordination of production. Which of several technically possible methods of production is to be used, how much of the intermediate semi-finished products is needed, and where is the production to be carried out?

The market economy has a solution for this problem and it is the contention of its advocates that it does the job more efficiently than the single-state-producer. It should be borne in mind that the concept of a single state-producer is an abstraction, and that actual decisions are taken by individual offices within the state's administrative apparatus.

Theoretically these individual offices are all subordinate to a central authority, but in practice they will have to take many decisions on their own. An official may be responsible for preparing the production plan for industry *X*. He may be ill informed, both about the specific advantages and problems of separate firms in the industry and about the requirements of client industries, users of the product of *X*.

The two essential characteristics of the market economy, which give rise to the claim that it is more efficient than the centrally planned economy are:

(i) The flexibility, the decentralization, which originates from freedom of an individual firm to decide how much to produce and which methods of production to use; and

(ii) The indication of the cost of a particular product or production factor by the paid exchange price.

The unregulated exchange economy, operating in an industrial or industrializing society, does not, however, function according to the behaviour pattern indicated by the competitive model. These discrepancies give rise to malfunctioning of the price as the indicator of the true social costs and to a restriction of production, by market limits, to a level below a national economy's technical capability to produce.

Oligopolistic elements arise naturally in an industrial market economy and one of their results is cost-push inflation. According to the 'perfect competition' model any inflationary tendency would stop as soon as there is the slightest bit of unemployment and surplus capacity. Unemployment would stop the rise in rates of pay, and surplus capacity the rise in the price of the industry concerned.

Massive unemployment and surplus capacity will indeed stop inflation, as long as there is any competition at all, but a little bit of it is not enough to stop inflation under conditions of limited competition. The possibility of finding a compromise, some unemployment and a little bit of inflation, is restricted further because in a half-open (national) economy there is no direct competition of production factors,* while there is competition of products, subject to a balance-of-payments restriction. It is, however, possible to introduce elements of regulation and control into the framework of an exchange economy.

The adjustment of prices, or at least some prices, by administrative control, instead of by free bargaining in an oligopolistic market allows the market to operate at the level of the economy's technical production capacity, rather than below it. The freedom of a firm to plan its production according to its own advantage, subject to certain well-defined requirements, is retained.

The economic and administrative logic of the resulting system of planning via the market is the same, irrespective of the social-political framework.

'Firms' can be privately owned enterprises; state-owned ones like the British Steel Corporation or the French automobile manufacturer Renault; or Yugoslav-type workers' co-operatives. A corollary of this view is that, if decentralization of a Soviet-type economy is taken seriously, the same problems which have been predominant in Western countries' economic policy—unemployment†, incomes regulation, price control, and foreign exchange policy—will arise in the East as well.

6.2 THE PERMANENT FULL-EMPLOYMENT STRATEGY

No one can hope to obtain an exact balance for each grade of labour and for each product in each submarket in each place and at each point in time. Perfect equilibrium will not be realized, either by completely free competition or by the most perfect system of planning; neither will it be achieved by any compromise between the two.

The unregulated market economy's solution to this problem is to have some surplus of supply in most submarkets, some 'frictional'

* I submit that an essential contribution to North Western Europe's economic stability has been provided by the flow of immigrant labour from Eastern Europe (refugees to West Germany), from southern Italy, and from North Africa. In two countries, Switzerland and the U.K., the acceleration of inflation in the 1970s was preceded by a politically motivated curb on immigration (of Italian and coloured Commonwealth Citizens respectively).

† In 1969 Yugoslavia had 8·2% unemployment (*Statistical Yearbook of the United Nations*, 1970, Table 24).

unemployment or surplus supply, in the hope that it is not too much. The full-employment strategy, on the other hand, aims at absorbing at least part of the unavoidable discrepancies by excess demand rather than by excess supply. The inflationary tendencies which result from this strategy are then to be contained by administrative controls, although the intention is to exercise these controls as far as possible at the 'equilibrium' level.

It would be futile to try to maintain a price control in the face of massive excess demand. It would be ineffective; worse, if it were successful the result would be a queueing economy. Products would be traded against money but a potential purchaser's obtaining the product he desired would depend on the time he was willing to stand in the queue, rather than on his ability to pay the set price, since that is no problem.

The versions of the permanent full-employment strategy, or more precisely the modes or systems of planning arising from it, discussed in the following sections of this chapter are specific to industrially developed countries. This is the case partly because of the administrative problems involved and partly because the reasons for the government's interference in the working of the economy are quite different in an underdeveloped country.

Full employment—and full utilization of other capacities as well—conceived as a balance between excess demand in some submarkets and excess supply in others, rather than as a single precise balance, implies that there are *gradations* of full employment. We will therefore discuss, in the remainder of this chapter, not just 'the' regulated exchange economy, but a number of conceivable systems or modes of planning. Although most of these modes of planning contain elements which correspond to actual practices and policies, the discussion will be centred on their intrinsic logic. 'Full employment', understood as a mix between frictional excess supply and frictional excess demand, can range from 'approximately full employment' where there is still a noticeable degree of unemployment, to predominance of excess demand. The more the balance is on the excess-demand side, the more instruments will be needed to contain the upward pressure on prices.

The reverse is also true; the more effectively price inflation is contained, the greater the amount of goods and services that can be bought by a given income.

6.3 CONTROLLED INCOMES AND INDICATIVE PLANNING

The purpose of the full-employment strategy is to help the free enterprise economy, as far as possible, realize the performance which is the supposed result from perfect competition working under approximately the same material and technical conditions. The conditions cannot be assumed to be exactly the same, because of the presence of economies of scale in capital equipment and technical innovation. These economies of scale, together with consumers' lack of competitive behaviour, are the reasons why the realistic alternative to state planning is not perfect competition, but oligopoly.

Furthermore, firms do not always maximize profit even in the oligopolistic sense of considering price and quantity simultaneously, and a further restriction of competition results from this.

I submit that, in the absence of substantial immigration, a controlled incomes policy is the minimum requirement for combining the free exchange of other goods and services, including free international trade, with permanent full employment throughout a country.

There is a conceivable intermediate situation: full employment in the sectors and regions of greatest expansion, and underemployment elsewhere. Pockets of regional unemployment or low-income underemployment could serve as a reserve labour supply which is never completely exhausted, and just possibly they could stabilize the nominal rate of pay throughout a country without formal control.

Immigration is the other possible cause of an elastic labour supply, as is the case in West Germany. The West German 'labour reserve' is to a considerable extent not in West Germany itself, but in Southern Italy, Turkey, and Eastern Europe. The thesis that free wage bargaining is incompatible with full employment presupposes a given national labour supply and leaves West Germany as an exception.

In a country without substantial immigration full employment and free income formation are incompatible.

Once there is genuine full employment, and quite possibly even before this is uniform throughout a country, cost-push inflation, made possible by limited competition, will sooner or later create a situation where balance-of-payments problems and/or an accelerating rate of inflation force the government to pursue policies which restrict domestic demand to a level corresponding to less than full employment of labour.

There is an element of asymmetry in the proposal to control only rates of pay for employment and no other prices. To be sure, there is a good case for controlling at least some prices as well; the case for controlling only incomes is mainly one of administrative expedience.

The two main criteria for assessing the appropriate level at which to operate the control—statistics of unemployment and productivity—are available without too many problems. And, most important of all, the control of incomes only is sufficient to maintain an approximate full employment of labour, provided there is a satisfactory rate of expansion of world trade, allowing exports to increase.

Now consider the question of anticipation, irrespective of limited or perfect competition.

If world trade grew at a smooth constant rate, and there were only the most gradual changes in technology, all sectors of the economy could adjust themselves to a constant rate of growth. In reality, actual variations in world trade and changes in technology require adjustments, and the anticipation of these is made easier by indicative planning.

We have discussed indicative planning at some length in section 4.7. The one point to be stressed here is the relation between planning and the full-employment strategy.

We accept as unavoidable some degree of disequilibrium, some frictional excess supply in some submarkets, side by side with equilibrium or even excess demand in other submarkets. That does not mean we should not try to minimize this measure of disequilibrium. If the separate submarkets are more in line with one another, there is less excess supply in total, without more excess demand.

If we assume that excess demand stimulates upward price adjustment, while excess supply does not to the same degree prompt price reduction, it follows that better co-ordination reduces inflationary pressures. Therefore, indicative planning allows a more outspoken pursuit of the full-employment strategy, than would otherwise be possible without additional controls.

6.4 THE BUSINESS CYCLE, THE LEVEL OF DEMAND, AND CREDIT CONTROL

The rather minimal amount of regulation described in the previous section is probably sufficient to maintain approximately full employment with some degree of business-cycle fluctuation that gives rise to temporary unemployment on a moderate scale during recessions.

The presence of full employment of labour, at the peaks of the cycle, does not mean that production is necessarily at its limit of technical capacity, only that there is no unemployment of labour in the socially relevant sense, i.e. people without jobs. There may be underemployment in the economic-technical sense that it would be technically possible to produce more by means of the same resources. There may be underemployment of labour in the already employed. People may have a job and be paid a salary, but the firm employing them may sell less that it can produce; as a result they are working only part of the time and for the remainder are just 'standing by' while the firm waits for orders.

There can also be underemployment of real capital, machines and buildings, for the same reason. A firm may have a surplus of capital over labour, so that some machines stand idle even though everybody is working at a particular time. Conversely, it could be that employees might have to wait for tools and machines.

We cannot really expect that all capacities are always precisely adjusted to each other and to the required quantity of their particular type of product. The main criterion to which the operation of macro-economic policy instruments is to be adjusted is that of full employment of labour in the social sense.

There is some degree of irregularity in the demand for labour as well as in the demand for the various products. It can arise either from imperfect anticipation of demand and/or technical change or from an unstable behaviour of demand itself, due to the so-called 'accelerator effect' arising from the technical demand for real capital. For example, a plan, and accordingly the norm for domestic income increase and for taxation, might be based on the assumption that world trade would rise by 7 per cent, whereas it turned out to rise by only 5 per cent. This would be imperfect anticipation.

The accelerator effect operates because the construction of capital goods requires the use of capital goods. For example, an additional order to build a big ship may be received from abroad. This results in additional demand for steel, and a steel manufacturing firm may find that demand approaches the maximum technical capacity of the available furnaces and rolling mills. The steel manufacturing firm now places orders for additional furnaces and other equipment, which is demand for the machine-building industry. The machine-building industry has already received additional orders from the shipbuilding industry, and now decides to build a new plant requiring, among other things, steel bars and steel for reinforced concrete. This increases the demand for steel even more; the increased steel production leads to increased demand for iron ore and coking coal, which has to be transported by ship. This means that a domestic shipping company reacts on the increased demand for shipping by ordering an additional ship. At this point the spiral stops, because the shipbuilding industry has its order book full and cannot or does not want to recruit more labour. So it makes the shipping company wait for its ship until the ship ordered from abroad is finished.

This accelerator effect is one of the major causes of 'the business cycle'. At the peak of the cycle the capital-goods producing sectors of the economy, and some related supporting sectors are over-expanded relative to others.

The process then starts to work the other way. As soon as demand for end-products ceases to increase, the demand for capital goods could in theory cease completely. This extreme case does not actually occur. Unless there is an actual fall in the demand for end-products, consumption goods, exports, etc., some firms will invest and order new capital goods because they are now able to finance investments which they had been considering for some time.

Nevertheless, it is well known that the capital-goods producing sectors of the economy, like shipbuilding, construction, machine tools, are particularly prone to cyclical fluctuation. Cyclical fluctuation is augmented by the multiplier effects, that is, variations in employment and paid wages giving rise to a corresponding cyclical fluctuation in consumption.

There are two versions of the accelerator principle. One version, described, for example, by Harvey and Johnson [15], assumes that firms adapt their production capacity fully to realized sales, as recorded in the previous time period. It is the *fixed* accelerator. 'Production capacity' is understood as the amount of equipment which is necessary to produce a given amount of output by means of normal operating procedures. It does allow for a certain amount of 'extra output' by such measures as overtime working, etc. The fixed-accelerator model assumes firms as investing only when realized production (sales) is more than normal production capacity and then enough to equate the following period's normal production capacity to the previous period's realized production. This version is criticized by Harvey and Johnson (loc. cit. [15], p. 95), and rightly so. Indeed, one more point of critique of the fixed accelerator, not explicitly listed as such by Harvey and Johnson, is possible. The fixed accelerator 'accelerates' too much. If that was the way an industrial economy worked, it would be completely uncontrollable. It would oscillate from deep depression with no investment at all, to violent expansion, and vice versa. There is, however, a refined version, the *flexible* accelerator.

I now follow my ex-colleagues in the Dutch Government's Central Planning Bureau [4], who use a linear version of Goodwin's more general non-linear accelerator [13]. *See also* a later application by van der Werf [51] and my own *Forecasting Models* [16]. In the flexible version of the accelerator, firms aim for a technical production capacity which is actually greater than current production. The difference between production and the production capacity aimed at depends on previously experienced variations in demand. In any single time period, adjustment of production capacity to output is partial. One postulates a desired surplus capacity (reserve capacity) and an adjustment percentage. Say the desired surplus capacity is 10 million and the adjustment percentage is 25 per cent. While realized output is only 6 million below full-capacity production, firms will find that their standby capacity is 4 million below the desired level and will order new equipment to adjust production capacity by 25 per cent of that difference, i.e. 1 million.

If output is persistently erratic firms will gradually aim for a larger standby capacity and a lower adjustment percentage.

This version of the accelerator is much more realistic than the cruder fixed accelerator. It leads to the conclusion that it is normally possible to produce some additional output out of normal production capacity, and it does not result in a too violent business cycle.

At this point it is useful to mention that the business cycle has been less pronounced in the post-World War II period than it used to be. For most of the period it would be more accurate to speak of mild recessions, alternating with short periods of full employment, than of a well-developed cyclical variation in the level of economic activity. Several factors have contributed to this flattening of the business cycle.

The notorious Great Depression of the 1930s was to a certain extent due to special factors, which we would hope not repeat* themselves. The overriding systematic factor is the higher average level of demand, at least in industrial countries.

This means, firstly, that a given fluctuation in demand results in less fluctuation in production and employment and to excess demand at peak periods instead.

Secondly, the fluctuation in demand is less pronounced, because unsatisfied demand and orders waiting for completion do not lead to secondary demand in other sectors of the economy. The so-far unfulfilled order for a ship waiting in the order book while the wharf is working at full capacity does not lead to additional demand for steel, but to a continuation of the high level of demand for steel, corresponding to the wharf's full-capacity production.

Thirdly, social security legislation and progressive taxation have reduced the magnitude of the multiplier†, and the augmentation of the business cycle with it.

There is, nevertheless, a residual cycle‡, and the question arises what can or has been done to curb this residual cycle. Consider an attempt to achieve this by means of another dose of the medicine already taken, a further increase of the average level of demand. All the remaining variation in demand would then be accommodated either as variation in the 'standby' capacity inside the existing production organizations, or would lead to temporary peaks of excess demand which would simply not be satisfied.

A substantial amount of excess demand is, however, contrary to the nature of a money-exchange economy. The function of money income is to limit demand to just about the quantity which can be produced

* There is an uncanny analogy between the collapsed (private) international loan-structure, following the stock exchange crisis of 1929, and the international indebtedness of central banks, which led to the dollar crises of 1971–2. Fortunately, there are indications that the authorities will not allow the situation to follow its 'natural' fatal course, and complete collapse has not followed so far. (*See also* Chapter 8.)

† *See* section 1.15.

‡ Contrary to what we would like to believe, the autonomous part of the government's budget (i.e. public expenditure and changes in tax rates) has not significantly contributed towards eliminating the business cycle. Worse, there has been to some extent an 'election cycle'. At the time of a national election the government ensures full employment, if necessary at the cost of a balance-of-payments deficit, and this is corrected in the first two years of office of the succeeding (or re-elected) government, if necessary at the cost of unemployment

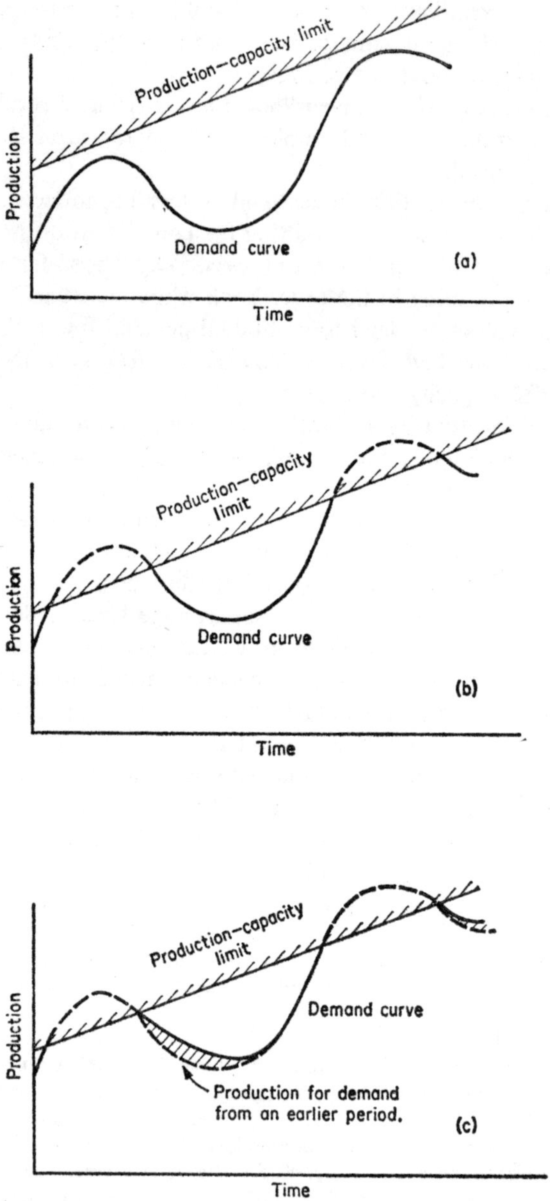

FIGURE 2 Demand curve and production capacity

and, if demand is much more, prices will be pushed upwards, irrespective of any attempts to restrain them. In particular, the effectiveness of an incomes policy presupposes the absence of a substantial excess demand for labour.

It is none the less possible to prescribe a small dose of the same medicine of excess demand, and to suppress the resulting inflationary tendencies at peak periods by credit restrictions and temporary increases in the rate of interest.

The idea may be illustrated graphically by examining the curve of realized production we would assume to arise from various levels of total demand. First, let us assume that there is still some unused production capacity, even at the peaks of the cycle. This relation between realized production and the physical production capacity might be illustrated as in Figure 2(*a*).

Now suppose the whole level of the demand curve is pushed upwards and that 'excess demand' is lost forever as demand. Then the same graph would look somewhat as Figure 2(*b*).

In fact, demand is not lost but held up in a queue, and at least part of it is postponed and supplied at a later stage. This results in a further flattening of the curve of realized production, as in Figure 2(*c*).

It is useful to distinguish here between primary and secondary demand for goods and services. This distinction relates the demand for capital equipment and inventories needed in the distribution channels of trade to the corresponding demand for end-products. Primary demand is the public demand for goods and services, e.g. heating of public buildings, expenditure on road building, etc., as well as consumption and export. Secondary demand is investment by firms in fixed assets, machines, vehicles, buildings, and in inventories (stock-building). The technical demand-relation between the total and the secondary demand is of the 'stock-flow' type. An increased level of the flow of total demand, primary as well as secondary, calls for a higher level of the corresponding stock-variables, the stocks of machines, buildings, etc., needed to produce the flow.

Similarly, the desired equilibrium level of stocks in the trade channels which must supply a given level of demand is increased according to the trade flow which passes through. The increase in any stock can be achieved only by a once-for-all purchase, often greater than the increase in the flow. The planning strategy is now to control primary demand at such a level that there is just room for a secondary demand corresponding to a normal rate of growth, at the equilibrium amount of investment corresponding to this primary demand, and not for accelerator-type peaks in the secondary demand.

For example, let us assume that 5 per cent is considered a normal rate of growth, that the capital–output ratio is 3 and the inventory–output ratio is 0·5. Then, on the average, in a year in which growth was indeed 5 per cent, investment in fixed assets would amount to 15 per cent of gross national product and inventory building would be 2½ per cent.

Public expenditure and consumption would then be planned to claim together 82½ per cent of the maximum producible gross national product. (Equilibrium balance of payments is assumed, exports would cancel out imports.)

Suppose, furthermore, that the import fraction is the same for all types of expenditure and that the overall import fraction is 30 per cent of gross national product. Then, if the full-employment production capacity is estimated to be 100, this means that nominal labour income and the exchange rate are set at a level permitting 30 units of exports.

If public expenditure is planned at 10 units, with a planned increase of 5 per cent per year, transfer payments and taxes are geared towards leaving a private spendable income likely to result in 72½ units of consumption in the current year and expanding at 5 per cent as well. If the banking system is assumed neutral, i.e. private investment equals private savings, financial equilibrium at full employment requires that net taxes from full-employment income equal public expenditure. For example, a tax of one-third of all income in excess of 70 units would match the 10 units of public expenditure, at the full-employment income of 100.

This would by and large stabilize consumption effectively at its planned amount of 72½. For a change in demand, the change in production would be 70 per cent of the change in total turnover, the remaining 30 per cent going to imports; of the 70 per cent a third would go to increased taxation, leaving 46·6 per cent as private spendable income. At a marginal propensity to consume out of private income of, let us say, 80 per cent this would leave an increase in consumption equal to 37·3 per cent of the total increase in expenditure.

Expressed as a multiple of the initial non-consumption expenditure impulse, this means that the multiplier is $1{:}(1-0{\cdot}373) = 1{\cdot}59$, so that an initial increase of non-consumption expenditure of one full unit leads to 0·59 units of additional consumption. Hence, if the fluctuation of secondary demand (investment and stock formation) is controlled within reasonable limits, the amplification of the cycle by the consumption multiplier is no major problem.

The control of cyclical variation in the secondary demand is brought about, in real terms, partly by avoiding uneven growth in primary demand, and partly by the production-capacity limit. If production is already at its full capacity no further increase (and hence no accelerator effect) will occur.

Some irregularities in the growth trend are quite unavoidable and a certain degree of accelerator-type fluctuation in demand will arise, though not to the same extent in production. Actual queueing of orders and excess demand on individual firms is prevented by monetary controls. Thus the banking system is required to refrain from financing any investment demand in excess of the planned 30 units, except if for some reason the demand from other types of expenditure has slackened.

Credit control is, however, not a particularly effective instrument for controlling capital expenditure, at least not in a free exchange economy with free money relations with the outside world (*see also* section 3.6). For this reason cyclical credit control is, at best, a help in reducing the cycle a bit further; its complete elimination is not possible and mild recessions will occur from time to time, even in the well-run free exchange economy.

6.5 THE REGULATED EXCHANGE ECONOMY WITH CENTRAL ALLOCATION OF CAPITAL

Under this heading we discuss an 'ideal' mode of planning, which cannot actually be implemented in its pure form, because national governments cannot plan international trade with any degree of reliability. We will, however, postpone a discussion of this complication till later.

From an economic and administrative point of view, central allocation of capital is a logical extension of the anti-cycle control system discussed in the previous section. At a still higher level of overall demand there is a permanent excess demand for finance capital—or at least demand for capital goods and for loan capital to finance their purchase is never less than the supply of real capital, the production capacity of the capital-goods producing sectors.

If the government is able to use the banking system as an instrument of economic policy in this way, we must assume that at least the banks themselves are publicly owned and controlled.

Borrowing and lending of finance capital, and the issuing and acquisition of interest-bearing titles, other than to and from the state-controlled banking system, will be illegal.

The supply, as well as the price, of finance capital is firmly under the control of the government. It sets the price and the rate of interest by administrative decision; it controls the supply, by means of rationing, at a point below supply/demand equilibrium, or possibly at the equilibrium point at the lowest levels of demand. The purpose of the central allocation of finance capital is not primarily to decide on individual investment projects. The initiative towards investment is assumed to come from individual production organizations and, just as in a free, unregulated exchange economy, the main responsibility for the financial outcome of an investment project is the firm's. Capital rationing is intended to adjust the total level and the timing of the flow demand for capital goods, in order to avoid any overstraining of the production capacity of the capital-goods producing sectors. Control over labour and products is limited to simple price control, without rationing, and production firms are free to maximize profit within the limitations of price control. This assumes that there is approximate equilibrium between supply and demand for both labour and products. Otherwise the government's control over prices and incomes will break down or, worse, the market system will cease to function altogether, prices and incomes becoming irrelevant, because obtaining products will depend exclusively on their physical availability.

Nevertheless, some degree of pressure from demand on the available production capacities is necessary, otherwise the assumed excess demand for investment will not arise—at least not under the conditions assumed so far, with a price structure and objective economic conditions resembling the industrial capitalist full-employment economy and a free market.

The attempt to utilize capacity more or less to the full is therefore in practice an excess-demand strategy, even if the excess demand for products is limited to relatively small, marginal amounts.

The presence of a more or less evenly spread pressure of demand upon supply throughout the economy then leads to a strong technical demand for capital goods, *and* to an upward pressure on prices. The technical demand for investment leads to rationing of finance capital, and the upward pressure on prices is to be resisted by price controls.

Regulation is, by and large, 'according to the market'. The controls are as far as possible operated at levels supposedly attained also by the 'perfect' free market. This implies that no special benefits from economies of scale are obtained, at least not under this mode of planning. As far as there are any gains in economic performance and efficiency, these are a greater degree of utilization of capacity, the elimination of the business cycle, and the induced technical progress which may arise from these two primary results. I assume the practical way to implement this idea to be not unlike the process described in section 4.7 as 'indicative' planning. The plan is, however, no longer purely indicative: on the one hand, the expansion of the various sectors of the economy is limited by the central allocation of finance capital and, on the other hand, the excess-demand strategy means that industrialists can safely assume that, if they produce the planned amounts, they will be able to sell at least the domestic-market part of the product, with a possible exception of some marginal amounts of poor quality. In other words, they can go ahead and produce the planned amounts without too much worry about whether they can sell the product. Framing the plan under conditions of central allocation of capital is therefore more like a collectively organized exchange of provisional orders, with the state acting as arbiter, instead of 'only' organized market research, as is the case with indicative planning in an economic system without central allocation of capital.

In a market economy prices are just as important as the amounts, and volumes and prices are interdependent. This is the dividing line between a regulated market economy and a decentralized planning system, in which prices are not related to costs, despite the outward forms of market exchange. (*See also* P. J. D. Wiles [52].) Also, in a genuine exchange economy there is approximate equilibrium between supply and demand even if, in a regulated exchange economy, there is (more often than in the unregulated exchange economy) marginal excess demand rather than marginal excess supply, and the price is a controlled price.

The method of preparing a plan for a regulated exchange economy is to some extent the same as the preparation of an 'indicative' plan for a free exchange economy, i.e. by organized exchange of information. Firms would, in their own interest, plan to sell more or less their share of the forecast production of their product at the set price, and to produce it at the lowest possible cost, again calculated at the given prices.

The central planning agency would initiate each round in plan preparation with a provisional forecast of the macro-economic variables—consumption, investment, total export and import, etc.—both in volume *and* in value, with an expected volume of production and a corresponding price adjustment for each sector of the economy. The agency would, of course, ensure that the macro-economic figures and the provisional sector forecasts were consistent with one another.

Furthermore, because price controls play an essential rôle in implementing this version of the permanent full-employment strategy, it is logical that prices should be integrated with the plan. The forecasts should take substitution, i.e. adjustment of the composition of demand on the indication of relative prices, properly into account. Precisely because prices are no longer free to adjust themselves, it becomes more important to anticipate their effects so as to be able to control them at the correct approximate equilibrium levels.

One would first of all assume a total for domestic consumption and a complete allocation of public expenditure, together with a set of forecast prices. These prices, and the price of labour as cost factor, would be used to assess the comparative cost position relative to foreign competitors. One would then apply appropriate cost elasticities* to assess any variations in the export of each sector relative to the trend of foreign demand. Domestic consumption would be distributed over the sectors of origin (including import) and one has thus obtained total primary domestic demand. To obtain total production one needs secondary demand, investment in fixed assets and inventories. This is a simultaneous relationship taking into account capital–output ratios, to assess the investment needed, and substitution elasticities, to assess the distribution of demand. (*See also* my *Forecasting Models* [16], section 4.5.)

While the actual economic system in its day-to-day operation will

* The proposition that costs, rather than the domestic price, determine exports can be defended for the regulated as well as the free exchange economy. The exporter is assumed to offer in any case at the internationally competitive price. If that price is well above his costs he has an incentive to export. Price controls are directly relevant as determinants of export costs, however, because they influence the costs of the exporting sectors when they refer to intermediate products.

contain a considerable element of limitation of demand by supply bottlenecks, the plan is largely based on anticipation of demand, including the technical demand for capital goods, in order to be able to anticipate the required supply.

6.6 THE REGULATED EXCHANGE ECONOMY WITH CAPITAL ALLOCATION AND GOVERNMENT-CONTROLLED FOREIGN TRADE

The economic conditions experienced by an individual firm or person working or living under the planning and control system envisaged in the previous section can be described, in the main, as a market economy with marginal excess demand rather than excess supply.

If such a situation actually existed it would tend to influence the country's international trade in a systematic way. The reason is that a factory manager who believes he can sell everything he can possibly produce will not make any special effort to sell. He will limit himself to printing a catalogue of the products fabricated, with their technical specifications and prices. The task of actually communicating these details to the end-users, consumers in the case of consumer goods and other factory managers in the case of capital goods, would be left to purchasing agents of the users, that is, trade organizations, shops, and agents of investing firms, rather than to sales representatives.

If a firm, used to operating under conditions of excess demand, is confronted with the competition of a firm operating in its own (foreign) home market under conditions of excess supply (surplus capacity), then, at equal costs, the latter firm has the edge and will be the successful competitor simply because it is keener to sell. This tendency is strengthened by the fact that a firm which works under conditions of excess supply will also be the prompter supplier. Delivery time is a point in competing for orders.

For this reason, free international trade is compatible with an excess-demand strategy for the internal market, only if domestic costs are kept at a level well *below* the cost of those foreign competitors who operate under conditions of surplus capacity.

This is most apparent in the case where domestic sales are subject to price control, while export prices can be higher. Then a manufacturer will be eager to sell abroad, provided his costs of production (and the domestic price) are actually lower than the price which his foreign competitor has to charge in view of the latter's own cost of production.

Similarly, a difference between the domestic and foreign price will dissuade the domestic buyer from buying the imported product, despite the importer's active sales promotion, because it is more expensive than its domestically produced counterpart.

Such a situation of positive cost differential is, however, not easily maintained for a largish number of products.

The problem is further complicated by uncertainty and random fluctuation. In the domestic market this is to some extent overcome, firstly, by anticipating demand by planning, and secondly by the regulation of demand, keeping it in line with actual production capacity at a certain moment.

Therefore, foreign trade, if not planned right from the start in co-operation with foreign trade partners, is a source of uncertainty when the plan is being implemented. Foreigners may choose to buy less than the amounts planned for export, and their demand cannot be regulated in the same way as can be done with the domestic demand.

A further dose of the excess-demand recipe of controlled domestic costs does not solve this problem satisfactorily, as an acute queueing problem would develop and the supply of the product to the domestic economy would be affected unfavourably, should the uncertain foreign demand turn out to be extra-strong.

A remedy for this problem may be sought in two directions.

(i) By compromising the excess-demand strategy, thereby making industry sales-conscious. I suppose it is quite possible to find a balance here: one allows marginal and temporary surplus capacities so that industrialists are stimulated to sell, without losing interest in the further increase in their technical production capacity. In effect, we are back—perhaps not in name and form, but at least in substance—to the mode of planning described in section 6.4, with the addition of price controls. Rationing of finance capital is permanent as a system but it is really needed only to 'chop off' peaks of excess demand for capital goods. At other times, firms may find requests for credit easily granted.

(ii) Alternatively, one can shield the domestic economy from foreign market conditions by restricting foreign trade, curbing exports at times of high foreign demand and curbing imports if foreign and/or domestic demand is slack.

In so far as this is a system at all, and not the incidental use of control to counteract isolated individual crisis situations, the introduction of a licensing system in international trade as opposed to internal trade is a barrier to international trade as such and we have to consider its possible allocative effects. The controls may well prevent and delay a more efficient use of resources.

The problem is mitigated if trade is to a considerable extent with other countries running their own economies on similar lines. This takes the systematic bias out of the relative competitive position, but it leaves the problem that foreign demand is not in the control of the national government. However, a country can negotiate guaranteed import quota.

Country *A* can approach the government of country *B*, asking it to commit itself not to place any restrictions on the import of a certain product *X* from country *A* into country *B* before a specified level of this trade flow has been achieved, and offer similar guarantees for *B*'s export in return.

If both *A* and *B* run a planned economy then the industry *X* in country *A* can base its planning on this export figure, more or less as it would do in the case of an estimate of domestic demand, assuming country *B* undertook this commitment in co-ordination with its own domestic plan.

Actual orders would have to be obtained from individual firms in the importing country, and industry *Z* in country *B* could only obtain a guaranteed supply of a specified amount of product *X* from country *A* by direct negotiations with *A*'s industry *X*.

6.7 PRICE CONTROL IN THE REGULATED EXCHANGE ECONOMY

The 'regulated exchange economy' is an 'ideal' type of economy, thought out in the process of writing this book, rather than a historically existing system. Elements of it are present in both Western European and Soviet-type economies, notably the procedure of plan preparation, capital allocation, and excess demand. Price control is also present or has been present both in the war economies of Western Europe and in the Soviet-type economy. What is so far largely non-existent is a logical theoretical framework, from which one can infer norms for particular price adaptations.

One cannot, however, control a global price level without at the same time controlling a large number of prices of individual articles.

One could, of course, control only nominal factor-rents (e.g. labour incomes and land rents) and leave prices of products free. Rents on exhaustible mineral resources and, where appropriate, other natural availabilities like fresh water and clean air, are in any case within the control of the government. Public charges on amenities (say to combat pollution) need not be geared towards the 'full employment', i.e. exhaustion of these resources. Then product prices would establish themselves in the 'normal' way as the prices which 'equate supply and demand'. This means in fact that the control over the price of labour ensures full employment of labour (absence of unemployment in the social sense), but surplus capacity within production organizations will persist. This is not the excess-demand strategy.

Any control on any price will help to underpin the excess-demand strategy, but if price controls are arbitrary and haphazard there will be a loss of allocative efficiency. We met an example of this problem in the historic case of low-cost housing. If the government controls the price of housing at a level below its 'free' market level and wishes to avoid rationing, queueing, housing shortage, etc., it must ensure a corresponding supply of new housing. The result is that a large sum of finance capital is drawn into the building of houses and flats, at a financial return well below the potential return in industry.

More generally, if product *A* is controlled at an exceptionally low price level and product *B* is sold at a free price or at a controlled price which is not exceptionally low, the return on investment for new production capacity to produce *A* is less than on building a factory for *B*. This would not be a major problem on its own because the plan would in any case ensure an adequate supply of both products: the central allocation of capital would ensure adequate investment in industry *A*, regardless of its lower financial return. The inefficiency arises when *A* and *B* compete as alternatives towards the cheapest way to produce another product, say *C*.

For example, if *A* is steel and *B* is plastic, the use of glass-fibre reinforced plastic as a construction material for ships, boats, and motor cars is discouraged; the increased demand for these end-products results in additional demand for steel, requiring the construction of steel mills with a low return on their capital.

The loss to the economy at large is not the lost financial return on the steel mill, which would have been built in any case, and is compensated for by the gain of obtaining steel bars for engineering at an extra-low price. The real loss is the capital invested in the second steel mill, when a plastics factory, requiring less real resources, should have been built instead.

Unfortunately, there are serious problems to be faced before one can establish in a realistic context what precisely *is* the 'correct' price of a specific product.

The following line of argument possesses the appeal of elegance and logic. The regulated exchange economy seeks to attain the allocation which would be attained under conditions of perfect competition, if it existed. Therefore the norm for proper price calculation, for which we are looking, is the one perfect competition is supposed to attain, i.e. zero return on any additional investment, earning its cost—including interest on the invested capital—but no profit on top of that.

In practice one has to consider under conditions of regulation (just as much as without it) the factors preventing this 'pure' competitive price from prevailing in the unregulated exchange economy.

Recall sections 1.7, 1.8, and 1.12. The main factors which raise the price above the cost of the most efficient producer in the free, unregulated market economy, and which likewise force a regulating government to allow the same in a regulated market economy, are threefold:

Lack of Profit-maximizing Behaviour, and of Knowledge, in the Production Organizations

Not all firms use the most efficient methods of production. The proposal to force all sluggish and traditional firms out of business, by establishing a price at which only the efficient ones could earn the cost of the necessary labour and materials is, in fact, a revolutionary and disruptive proposal: large numbers of firms would inevitably be forced out of business. It is wiser to recognize that knowledge of the most efficient methods of production and the will and ability to implement them is very much a scarce resource, which, quite rightly, earns some rent in the form of a profit over and above the costs of production and return on capital as such.

Fixed Costs and Increasing Returns to Scale

The true cost to society of an *additional* unit of product X is the cost of labour and materials in the newest type of an X-product factory, plus the additional capital costs incurred by building the newest X-product factory on a larger scale to produce an additional unit.

This marginal full production cost does not include the cost of central administration and research, borne by industry X as a whole*, nor the initial fixed cost incurred in order to build a new X-factory at all.

A further point arises in connection with establishing 'correct' prices by computation, by the government, rather than by free competition and market adjustment. It is as follows.

Lack of Knowledge in a Particular Government Office

Theoretically the government is better informed about all the new developments in an industry than an individual firm, which is only concerned with its own innovation. The government can audit the accounts of all the firms and the costings of all projects for new investment. In practice, however, decisions about price adjustment would be taken by offices other than the ones evaluating new investment projects; as a result, prices will have to be related by and large to actual profitability, and not to the potential profitability implied in the costings of new investment projects.

This brings us to a second-best alternative which is not unlike the arrangement one assumes to exist in an unregulated exchange economy except that, in the unregulated economy, inflationary pressures are kept in check by the presence of surplus capacity, rather than by price control.

The realized cost per unit in the least efficient firm in the industry gives a norm for the price level in the whole industry. Other, more efficient firms have a 'premium', a 'bonus', a profit to the owners,† which is the rental on their superior efficiency.

The price must also establish approximate equilibrium between supply and demand in the long run, and this means that increased costs would justify an increase in the price only if there were no surplus capacity in the industry. Hence, regulated price-formation in the regulated exchange economy is roughly similar to the 'free' market in

* There is the possibility of avoiding duplication of research under planning by concentrating research in special industry-wide research institutes, whereas under conditions of private oligopoly each firm maintains its own research organization.

† For cost calculation it is irrelevant whether these owners are the state, the workers in the firm or private capitalists.

the unregulated exchange economy. The systematic difference is the level of surplus capacity in the industry. In the unregulated exchange economy there is normally some surplus capacity. A firm will be able to pass increased costs, less the productivity increase in the least efficient firm in the industry, on to its customers except in certain somewhat special conditions. The non-price-increasing conditions in the unregulated exchange economy are the presence of at least one competitor while *substantial* surplus capacity exists in the industry.

At this point the purely economic question of cost calculation interlocks with problems of social and political organization. Somehow there must be provision made for the fate of a firm which does not manage to cover its costs, that is, is it to be wound up, either immediately or after a certain cumulation of deficit, and, if so, on whose authority this is to happen; if it is not wound up, how is the deficit to be financed? It would be undesirable for a price to be adjusted at short notice, dependent on the productivity or the closing down of a single firm which happened to be the least efficient one.

By itself, this is a problem common to both the regulated and the unregulated market economy and there is a complication which is specific to price control. In deciding which cost increases are to be passed on to the customer, and which should be recovered out of increases in productivity, the price-setting authority implicitly decides which firms are to be able to continue operation.

The price forecast to be included in the plan would combine all the relevant elements. They are:

(*a*) The industry's long-term productivity trend.
(*b*) The cost-proceeds position of the least efficient firms in the industry.
(*c*) The demand/supply position, i.e. whether the firms which are at present the least efficient should be encouraged to close, in which case the cost of the next most efficient group becomes decisive.
(*d*) The expected rise in the industry's costs.

A further point concerning cost prices in the regulated exchange economy is that calculating zero-profit prices assumes a fairly sophisticated information framework. Accounts of the various firms have to be in existence together with a government department competent to audit and interpret them. If this is not the case, one has to choose between no price control—abandoning or at least compromising the excess demand strategy—or control of some prices at more or less arbitrary levels.

It might be thought that the required minimal rate of return on capital, the capital charge to be included in the calculation of cost prices, would largely determine the income distribution.

This is, however, only one aspect of the question. The demand for new investment is determined primarily by the expected increase in the demand for end-products. In a regulated oligopolistic or in a regulated mixed economy the resulting demand for finance capital is one of the factors determining the financial rate of return. Even there the government can intervene in the capital market on the supply side, by providing alternative sources of finance, public investment, and bank loans, and can restore macro-economic equilibrium in the economy at large by compensating taxation.

For example, let us assume a postulated rate of growth of 5 per cent a year, a capital–output ratio of 4. Then, irrespective of the method of regulation by which the 5 per cent rate of growth is to be achieved, 20 per cent of production should on the average over the years be allocated to investment, so as to keep the growth of production capacity in line with the actual production determined by either demand or supply as the case may be.

Let us assume that 10 per cent of production is earmarked for public expenditure. Then pricing policy and fiscal policy together should somehow ensure that 70 per cent of the potential (or normal) production capacity is demanded by other outlets for production. For the sake of simplicity we will assume that the only remaining production outlet is consumption, neglecting the complication of international trade.

Let us furthermore assume that the propensities to consume of the two income categories are 90 per cent of the after-tax income from employment and 30 per cent of profits after tax. The macro-economic equilibrium condition that total demand equals current production capacity is then satisfied by, for example, after-tax shares of 71·6 per cent for labour and 18·4 per cent for capital together with a financially neutral state and banking system.

The same total demand for consumption is also generated by a 74·4 per cent after-tax labour income and a 10 per cent after-tax capital income. This is a total private spendable income of only 84·4 per cent of the available production capacity. The resulting consumption is, however, 70 per cent of the available production capacity, as before, except for the distribution between capital and labour, which is somewhat more favourable for labour. The planned investment (20 per cent of the available production capacity) should now be financed with the help of a direct contribution from either the state or the banking system equal to the gap in the private sector's savings, i.e. 5·6 per cent. The fiscal intervention in income formation by means of taxation, and the intervention on the capital market, do not have to be exactly co-ordinated.

For example, if under conditions of controlled rates of pay to labour, the government injects 'too much' capital and finances a full 7 per cent new investment, 'overfinancing' will result in a rise in the volume of investment, a reduced volume of consumption and a drop in the income share of labour, because of rising prices leading to higher profits.

Under conditions of oligopoly the equilibrium establishes itself—with in fact some surplus capacity—by market adjustment.

The one overriding requirement of equilibrium is that aggregate demand in money terms equals the total cost of full-capacity production, and that may require intervention on the income side as well as controls on the cost side. Under a regime of more comprehensive price control the problem presents itself from a different angle. To be sure, there is still an income distribution problem even in a decentralized socialist economy based on workers' co-operatives. Profits, in so far as not used for reinvestment, would lead to benefits paid by particular firms on top of regular wages, causing unequal distribution of income over the economy above the nationally controlled basic wages. Interest charges paid to the state banker could be used to finance public consumption.

Under a regime of price control, irrespective of its social-political flavour, which could include a corporative or fascist type of economy with private capitalism being regulated by the state, income distribution is determined by the way the price controls are operated. The amount of fiscal and monetary intervention needed to maintain macro-economic equilibrium follows *as a result of the price structure.*

In a partially regulated market economy (incomes control only) the relationship is the other way round: the fiscal and monetary intervention comes first, the income distribution is the result. The equilibrium conditions are the same, except that the point of equilibrium is moved from marginal excess supply to marginal excess demand.

There is also an allocative aspect i.e. the efficient use of capital, which cannot, however, be pursued to its logical conclusion by any form of market economy, regulated or not, for the reasons discussed in section 1.12.

6.8 THE PRICE AS A PRODUCTIVITY TARGET

We have assumed till now that price regulation is 'according to the market'; that the (controlled) price structure is similar to the one arising in an unregulated exchange economy when that unregulated economy uses comparable production capacities and other availabilities but operated at a somewhat lower level.

What would happen if the government contained the price of a particular sector of the economy, a particular product, below this assumed equilibrium level? For example, the government might refuse permission to increase the price in response to rising costs, even if there was only a quite marginal surplus capacity or none at all.

If there is no increase in productivity, the financially weakest firms will leave the industry, and the result will be excess demand for the remaining firms. If, however, there is a possibility of further increase in productivity, the price stop may stimulate its realization.

The effectiveness of (the expectation of) rising costs as a means of implementing a productivity target depends greatly on the existing lack of homogeneity in the industry. If there is a wide difference between the efficiency performance of different firms within the industry, demand and production may be shifted towards the more efficient firms, which expand their production capacity, either entirely by their own new investment, or by taking over the assets of the liquidated firms and reorganizing them.

Increased average productivity of the industry as a whole then arises, firstly because the most efficient firms increase their market share and, secondly, because new expansion contains the latest and most modern methods of production.

That a process of this kind is not impossible may be illustrated by the following extract from a report of the former Prices and Incomes Board [34] concerning the brick industry:

'. . . The brick industry is divided into two sectors, fletton and non-fletton. The fletton sector, which is based on a particular clay known as Oxford clay, enjoys a natural cost advantage because this clay . . . requires less fuel for firing. . . .

In contrast to the non-fletton sector, which is made up of about 400 mainly small producers, the fletton sector comprises four firms only. . . .

About 90 per cent of all fletton bricks are made by LBC*, which therefore has a dominant position in the industry. The four companies in the fletton sector between them employ about 7,800 manual workers. Of these 85 per cent are employed† by LBC. . . .

The brick making capacity in Great Britain is estimated by MPBW‡ to be adequate to meet demands in the foreseeable future. . . .

The agreement reached in August last year between the Pressed Brick Makers Association, representing the four fletton brick makers, and the trade unions to raise wages by an estimated 4·9 per cent on average contained no provision for improved efficiency. LBC's consequential request for a price increase also sought compensation for declining profit margins. . . .

Since the completion of our studies in the field, a new agreement was concluded giving process and maintenance workers an average increase of 20 per cent as from 6th July. . . .

if the expectation were that the low level of brick sales were to continue for some time ahead . . . a price increase would not be justified, since it would be desirable in those circumstances to encourage surplus high-cost brick making capacity to go out of production. . . .

if LBC . . . can at once pass on wage increases to its customers, then it is under no pressure to resist wage demands. . . .

In the event . . . the Government informed the company that it had no objection . . . and no recommendation on our part is called for.'

The extract illustrates most effectively the workings of unregulated price formation under limited competition.

One assumes that, under the conditions of surplus capacity actually

Notes by A.R.G.H.

* London Brick Company.

† Note that the three remaining companies employ 15 per cent of the labour force, but produce only 10 per cent of the bricks!

‡ I assume this abbreviation means: 'Ministry of Public Buildings and Works'.

existing, a price stop—which the government failed to order—would have forced some of the smaller, less efficient companies out of business and increased the market share of the more efficient company, LBC.

The presence of surplus capacity in the brickmaking industry implied that a withdrawal of some of the least efficient production units would have been possible, without any disruption of the supply of bricks to the building trade.

Setting a maximum price, which compels the more efficient producer to offer at the true cost of production and the customer not to pay more than he needs, is, quite generally, a contribution to efficiency* whenever the market structure is one of limited competition and different standards of productivity. This includes the monopoly-capitalistic market and, indeed, from one point of view it is more appropriate in an otherwise unregulated monopoly-capitalistic market, with surplus capacity, than it is in a planned economy with full employment of both labour and capital.

Under conditions of full employment, the adjustment, the reallocation of demand to the more efficient firms (or alternatively the modernization of the less efficient ones) is only possible over a period of time, as in both cases it requires additional investment. In an economy with surplus capacity on the other hand, it can be implemented at once by closing down some of the least efficient production units, and operating the more efficient ones at or nearer to full capacity.

Price control 'against the market', as a positive instrument towards the increase of productivity by a specified percentage, and not merely as a facet of the general control of the price level, should be incorporated in the plan. The presence of full employment prevents immediate adjustments, hence industry needs time to anticipate the consequences of planned price-adjustments. These consequences might be less drastic than actual failure of some of the less efficient firms.

The less efficient firms might try to become more efficient, either on their own or with the co-operation of the more efficient ones.

Now consider the less obvious case where an industry is relatively homogeneous. If there is a possible, more efficient, method of production, a potential productivity which is higher than the actual, then a planned cost-increase without compensating price increase can still be used as a productivity target, set before all firms in the industry alike.

* *See also* section 1.9.

Two problems need considering if such a strategy is contemplated. The first is how to assess the magnitude of this potential productivity. Performance of similar firms engaged in the same industry in another country is one possibility, engineering estimates are another.

This is an example of a much more general relation between information and planning. The wisdom of creating or not creating a particular control depends, among other things, on the availability of the information needed to establish the level at which the control should preferably be operated.

The second problem is the limited enforceability of a productivity target. If, for whatever reason, the planned productivity increase is not realized, the government has little choice but to concede price increases it did not initially intend to concede, or else to finance the deficit of the firms lagging behind. Forcing firms out of business if there is already excess demand in the industry is not a practical proposition.

The point is most salient if the national economy comprises only one or two firms in a particular sector. Forcing a substantial part of a domestic industry out of business would have unacceptable consequences, both for the employment of people with skills and training geared to that particular industry—and to the balance of payments, because the product would have to be imported.

With a somewhat larger number of firms, it might still be possible that the planned cost-increase would create a situation where, despite initial homogeneity some modernizing firms become more efficient than others, some of which could be forced out of business. The very fact that this is a possibility would be an incentive to all firms in the industry.

A small-size economic region, where major industries have a market large enough for only one or a few firms, is therefore at a disadvantage.

7

Planning under conditions of structural unemployment

7.1 LABOUR SUPPLY, RESOURCES, KNOWLEDGE, AND MARKET

In an industrially developed economy, it is possible to regulate the income level and the price structure in such a way that the available nominal income and the current price structure result in an effective demand for labour, about equal to its available supply, and in a demand for imported products, of approximately equal value to the proceeds from exports.

The adjustment of the income- and price-structure to the requirement of equilibrium on both the labour market and the external balance of payments is more or less the minimum requirement of successful economic policy in an industrially developed country.

Now consider the other limitations, scarcity of physical resources and lack of knowledge of more efficient methods of production.

Concerning physical resources, land, minerals, etc., one presumes that here too the price system, in the form of rents on land and royalties charged on the exploitation of mineral deposits, limits the productive activities which make an intensive use of these resources. In fact, the future balance between the supply of exploitable mineral deposits by additional prospecting, and its demand by the production methods of the next generation, is in no way guaranteed by a present price-structure combined with a rapid increase in labour productivity.

For many minerals the present rate of increase in demand, if continued, would exhaust known reserves in the not-too-distant future.

We anticipate on the results of more intensive prospecting and the development of substitutes.

Concerning limits to production, caused by lack of knowledge, there is a large and probably increasing discrepancy between 'potential' and realized productivity. This amounts to underemployment of knowledge. Under these conditions it is logical that an investing firm which taps knowledge so far unused by other firms receives a generous return on its investment, providing it can also sell the increased output. The full-employment strategy aims at accelerating growth, by moving the market limit progressively outwards.

This strategy depends crucially on the assumptions that (*a*) full employment of labour is possible, and that (*b*) there is a still-untapped reserve of technical knowledge and potential productivity. The negative of either of these two assumptions is factually possible; the negative of assumption (*b*) is, however, most unlikely.

Theoretically, it is possible that the limited availability of physical resources within a domestic economy, and the limited possibility to import because of external market limits on exports, can limit production even with *full utilization of all known methods of production*, and that maximum production does not result in full employment.

The real-life case of unavoidable structural unemployment is the one where the *traditionally established* methods of production, operated at levels which are within the appropriate resource limits and the balance-of-payments restriction, do not provide full employment of labour. This means that the full-employment strategy in its widest sense—the removal of resistance to the introduction of new productive activities, arising from the market limit—is still valid.

The presumption that paid costs are a reasonably approximate indicator of the true costs of a product to society at large does not, however, hold under conditions of severe unemployment.

7.2 THE ROLE OF IMPORT DUTIES IN AN UNDERDEVELOPED COUNTRY

The factors which limit the level of economic activity in an underdeveloped country are the lack of operative knowledge of certain production processes and the limited availability of foreign currency.

For certain technically specialized products, domestic production is altogether out of the question and this gives rise to a relatively high import fraction. For the same reason, the export market is relatively weak, export being concentrated on a few, often traditional, products.

For certain other slightly less sophisticated products the position is not basically different from the situation in a developed country. The information on how to produce is present but this does not mean that a product is actually made, except if there is a ready market for it, and, in the case of a private firm, the incentive of a profit. In an underdeveloped country profitability is, however, not always a correct indicator of the desirability to produce.

Under conditions of structural unemployment the prices of production factors do not give a valid indication of the true cost of their use to society at large. The employment of someone who would otherwise be unemployed is not a cost to society, as no alternative product of his labour is lost (although an employer has to pay wages).

With structural unemployment there is a fundamental contradiction between the social (income-distribution) function of the price of labour and the allocative function. The normal allocative function of a price as a cost item is to discourage the use of a particular resource: this is not necessary, indeed may be undesirable, in the case of unemployed labour.

One theoretically possible solution to this problem is to subsidize the employment of labour, but there are social-political, administrative, and financial disadvantages to be considered. A payment which is seen as not related to work done does not give the same satisfaction as a normal wage or salary. That is the social-political consideration. The administration of a subsidy with reference to every single employee is about the largest administrative operation one might consider, and gives rise to the possibility of fraud. That is the administrative consideration. The financial consideration is simply that, without adequate revenue, the state does not have the means to finance the subsidy without creating a vast increase in the demand for the true scarce resource, foreign currency.

This leaves, as the second-best alternative, the introduction of an import duty which raises the price of an imported product, as well as of its domestically produced substitute.

Consider, let us say, the costing of the domestic production and of the import of transistor radios.

Let us assume that the price of an imported radio is £2·00 in foreign currency. The cost of domestic assembly of a similar radio might be £2·50, consisting of £1·50 direct and indirect labour cost, and £1·00 direct and indirect costs for imported products. At these prices the import is in the stronger market position and there will be no domestic production.

However, say the government levies an import duty of 50 per cent on raw materials and semi-finished products and 100 per cent on finished products. The sales price of the imported radio then becomes £4·00. Its cost of production becomes £1·50 direct and indirect labour cost and £1·50 direct and indirect imports, including import duty on imported components. So the total cost of domestic production is £3·00, compared with £4·00 for the imported radio. These are the prices that are relevant to a domestic firm considering whether or not to produce the radio. The true cost to the national economy is £1·00 imported components for the domestically produced radio or £2·00 for imported radio, both before and after the introduction of the import duty.

The import duty serves to compensate an inherent inconsistency in the price structure by means of another distortion.

The same result, as far as the cost of imports is concerned, could be obtained by devaluing the national currency. This would mean that to pay £2·00 for the radio in foreign currency (international money), £4·00 of domestic money would be required from now on.

The disadvantage of such a proposal is its impact on export revenue, if export is inelastic relative to its price. If the currency is devalued by a factor 2, this means domestic producers will be able to sell in foreign markets at half the former price yet receive the same payment in domestic currency. Competition between different domestic producers in foreign markets may well prevent any sizeable rise in the export price in domestic currency. Devaluation will in any case imply a drop in the amount of foreign currency charged by domestic exporters for their products, although the reduction may be less than the devaluation when exporters take advantage of it and increase their prices in the domestic currency.

If the volume of exports remains substantially the same or increases by less than the drop in the (foreign currency) price, we say that demand is inelastic, and the country's foreign exchange earnings drop, because a lower price is charged. (The earnings are the product of a reduced price and a not much increased quantity.) If the volume of exports rises by a greater percentage than the price drops, we say that demand is elastic, and earnings of foreign currency increase, because the amount sold increases by more than the price drops.

The amount sold may also be inelastic because of an inelastic supply. Here the foreign demand for domestic exports increases, but the country cannot supply because it is physically unable to produce more. Under conditions of unemployment of labour this would imply either a limit to a national resource or a short-term bottleneck arising out of lack of productive facilities. Such cases might involve trees and crops planted (in agriculture), shafts sunk (in mining), or machines installed (in industry).

There might well be a difference between the short-term elasticity of supply, which is small, and the long-term elasticity of supply, which is much greater; more favourable prices might stimulate the planting of additional trees and crops, the sinking of additional shafts, and the installations of additional machines.

On the other hand the long-term elasticity of demand might well be much lower than the short-term elasticity of demand. Initially a price concession leads to increased sales at the cost of other countries' market shares, but eventually the latter adjust their prices as well, and the much lower elasticity of demand for the product prevails.

Such a price response by competitors is much more likely for a raw material than for a more specialized industrial product. The competitors of underdeveloped countries are, by and large, other underdeveloped countries dependent on the earnings from a relatively low number of traditional export products. They cannot afford to lose their market.

There is an essential difference with industrial products. Owing to the greater diversification of its export production, a developed industrial country can afford to lose its market for a particular product.

The combination of a low short-term elasticity of the supply of exports with a low long-term elasticity of demand for exports can make devaluation altogether unattractive, and an import duty will be resorted to instead.

7.3 THE REGULATING ROLE OF PUBLIC EXPENDITURE

One of the results of a high import duty is a high level of public revenue. The prime purpose of the tariff is to stimulate the domestic production of substitutes. Suppose this is completely effective in the sense that there is no remaining import at all for a particular group of products for which the policy was intended. The result is an initial surplus on the external balance of payments. At an unchanged level of exports this allows an increase in the level of domestic expenditure, leading to additional imports.

The hitherto unemployed, who obtain work, say in the radio factory discussed in the previous section, will indeed increase their consumption. This is the multiplier effect of the increase in import-substituting production. However, the real value of an unchanged income is reduced by the import duty, because the same money buys less radios, television sets, watches, and so on.

To restore external equilibrium the government has to increase its internal expenditure up to the point where its expenditure matches its income. Public revenue will increase at a higher level of production and expenditure, not only by the duty on radios imported despite the tariff, but also by the duty on increased imports of all sorts of products which are not produced domestically thus far. The eventual result is that imports are back at their original value, equal to exports, and the tariff revenue is not much less than the full tariff proceeds from the initially imported batch of products. The revenue from the tariff is not, however, fully equal to the one which would be obtained if the tariff was paid over the initially imported collection of products. Imports of high-taxed end-products will be reduced, and part of the compensation following the increased level of internal economic activity will consist of relatively low-taxed semi-finished products and capital goods.

Note the inversion of what one would consider the normal, logical theory of public finance in a developed, full-employment country. (*See*, for example, R. A. Musgrave [33].) With full employment one would start by asking what public expenditure is needed to satisfy collective wants and other desiderata. Then one would establish the level of taxation required to maintain macro-economic equilibrium at that predetermined level of public expenditure; only thereafter would one enquire by what types of taxes the required public revenue is to be obtained.

In the presence of structural unemployment we decide first of all, on the basis of non-market cost indications, which productive activities are efficient and ought to be made profitable. Then we decide the price and tariff structure needed to make the predetermined productive activities financially viable in a market-economy context, despite the fact that a money wage (not a genuine cost) is to be paid to labour.

The tariff structure then determines a public revenue to be obtained from a level of import matching the available export. Only then, at the end of the ride, does one decide which level of public expenditure is needed to sustain the level of internal activity from which the equilibrium balance-of-payments import will arise.

That expenditure level is broadly equal to the duty income from the maximum (export-balancing) level of import. Note, however, that macro-economic equilibrium is defined in an underdeveloped country in terms of an external balance-of-payments equilibrium rather than as equilibrium of the labour market. Once a position of genuine full employment of labour has been reached, we are no longer speaking of a truly underdeveloped country.

There is, presumably, a position between the underdeveloped country, where full employment of labour in any strict sense is simply not attainable, and a fully developed country where it can be attained without protective import duties. This would be a country which could attain full employment only with the help of protective import duties.

7.4 REASONS FOR PUBLIC INVESTMENT

One reason for the government financing productive investment is that the revenue obtained from import duties, the primary function of which is to protect the domestic industry, may be more than is needed to finance traditional public functions like administration of justice, the police, etc. This argument arises even more pointedly if the government obtains revenue not only from import duties, but also from royalties on the exploitation of mineral deposits, oil, metal ores, and so on.

The 'surplus revenue' should be transmitted back into the private sector of the economy. It can be used to finance private consumption by such means as transfer payments, unemployment benefit, and old-age benefit.

It may be used to finance productive investment in the private sector. The government can have a useful role in acting as banker for the private sector, financing the purchase and construction of local co-operative irrigation schemes, the building of houses for personal occupation, and of shops and workplaces for shopkeepers and artisans. However, when it comes to larger projects, cement factories, fertilizer factories, steel mills, etc., a government as banker will have to verify the technical and commercial viability of the proposed project in some detail. This means that the 'decentralization' argument for market production as opposed to public production simply does not apply to that particular project, at least not at the moment of its inception.

There remains the incentive argument. Clearly there is room for various schemes of profit-sharing as an incentive for efficient performance, rather than a rigid division between a state and a private sector. This applies to industrially developed and underdeveloped countries alike.

Current production of cement, fertilizer, and steel would naturally be for the market. The reasons for state finance and state initiative in the field of production, as listed so far, in no way contradict the existence of market relations between producers, including state-financed and state-owned factories and the purchasers of their products. The more fundamental problem, the discrepancy between social and private cost, has been taken into consideration for import-substituting products, by imposing protective import duties. Hence production and investment, publicly sponsored as well as private, should normally be required to be profitable or at least cost-recovering.

Special cases for public investment projects which do *not* recover their cost in the commercial sense can, nevertheless, be made. There are, first of all, *infrastructure investments.* As we saw in section 2.2, adequate infrastructure is one of the conditions for a large market, and hence a pre-condition for large-scale specialized industry. The one major difference between a developed and an underdeveloped country in the desirability of infrastructure investments is one of perspective. A developed country will want to consolidate and expand its position as a developed country and its infrastructure with it. An underdeveloped country desires to establish that condition in the first place.

One other reason, discussed already in section 2.2 in connection with regional unemployment, is the desirability to compensate labour-costs (paid without being a true cost to society) by transport costs, which are a true cost, but are not charged.

Furthermore, constructing certain infrastructure projects at minimal *foreign-currency* cost may well provide considerable local employment for construction workers, and this is no true social cost, since the construction workers would otherwise be unemployed.

The construction of roads, canals, irrigation works, etc., understood as a means of recycling funds from import duties back into the private sector of the economy is less costly than it appears.

The next special case concerns *export production at a loss in domestic currency*. Suppose an iron ore mine, with blast-furnace and steel mill annexed, is costed as follows:

(*a*) *Capital outlay*:
Local building labour and local labour-component of locally produced materials 100; imported materials and equipment, plus imports contained in locally produced semi-finished products 100.

(*b*) *Running costs per year*:
Local labour 100 per year; foreign-currency bonus to foreign technical specialists 2; imported special ingredients and tooling 5.

(*c*) *Production value per year*:
True import cost of substituted import products 50, plus 25 import duty, allows sale at 75; export 35.

At the prevailing prices, current production valued at 110 is barely covering operating costs, which are 107. An operating profit of 3 per year is clearly not worth the capital outlay.

The picture is, however, different if we consider only the foreign-exchange costs, also valuing the production on the basis of its foreign-currency earnings. In that case the production value is 50 plus 35, or 85 per year, and operating costs are only 7. The net foreign-currency earnings of 78 per year are, in fact, well worth the foreign-currency component of the initial capital outlay.

The scheme assumes that the government has indeed the funds available to finance the local part of the initial capital outlay.

Note that it is the export bit which causes the commercial unprofitability, because output is evaluated at the unprotected world market price and costs are evaluated at internal prices which include labour costs.

Unless the diseconomies of small-scale production were to be very substantial indeed, it would be possible to cut the project to just under 60 per cent of its size and sell, at a profit, in the protected home market only. That would still save the country valuable foreign currency by import substitution, but it would nevertheless be an unnecessary loss of export earnings.

7.5 WIDENING THE MARKET

Since full employment of labour is not an attainable target for an underdeveloped country, until it ceases to be so, the term 'full-employment strategy' is inappropriate. The underlying idea—the continuous expansion of the domestic market thereby creating the expectation of further expansion—is, however, the same.

The term 'widening the market' is, to my knowledge, due to Merhav [32]. There is a more specific point which makes the *absolute* size of the market a consideration of some importance, quite apart from the psychological effects of its rate of expansion on induced technical progress, and the import of new technical ideas in the case of a developing country.

Capital goods, as normally produced by the capital-goods producing sectors in industrial countries, are suitable for a plant size which is normal for a developed country.

An underdeveloped country wanting to become a developed country must therefore either be a *large* country, with an internal market of some size despite its state of underdevelopment, or it must order or have constructed special, extra-small capital goods. It is clear under those conditions that the first introduction of a new capital-intensive production process should be in the form of one single national firm, and that it should supply more or less all of the domestic demand, with preferably some export as well.

The introduction of a few large import-saving projects does, of course, allow a higher general level of economic activity, because the available export earnings can serve a smaller relative import fraction.

If, by producing steel at home instead of importing it, the import fraction is reduced from 20 per cent to 15 per cent of production, it becomes possible to raise the level of domestic economic activity by one-third, since 15 per cent of $1\frac{1}{3}$ times the former level is equal to 20 per cent of the former level, the available foreign-currency earnings. The resulting larger internal market will then allow domestic production of other products for which the earlier smaller internal market did not justify the investment.

7.6 THE LIVING ALLOWANCE

Suppose the objective economic reality is that the quantity of various products, consumer goods, food, clothing, washing machines, as well as public goods, buildings, roads etc., which a nation can afford, is *not* limited by the amount of work which the people are able and willing to perform, but by some other objective circumstance, causing unemployment at the highest possible level of production.

The circumstance likely to arise for an individual country is the combination of import requirements with market limits on export revenue. The point will be discussed again in the next chapter, but the essentials of the relation between employment and external limits are reviewed here.

No country is capable of producing, within its own territory, all products. If other countries are interested in buying the specialized export products of country *A* only to the value of *x* million, no matter how much of them country *A* is capable of producing, there is an objective limit on the amount of imported products which *A* can afford. It will also limit to a certain extent the amount of internal production which country *A* can afford. Under mid-twentieth century economic conditions it is conventional to associate this situation with underdevelopment. Lack of knowledge, skill, national infrastructure capital, and internal market are, and are likely to remain, the main factors determining the fate of a particular country. At the same time we must face the fact that the amount of industrial products which can be produced from the raw materials the world as a whole can afford, is much less than the amount corresponding to employment of all the world's population or at least that part of it which can be considered as potential labour supply.

Say there is enough wood to make two chairs, and to make one chair employs one carpenter; if three carpenters apply, one of them will remain unemployed. The odds are that the unemployed one will be the least efficient one. And, in the context of development policy, it is useful to mention that a fourth person, who wishes to be trained to become a carpenter, will not be any help towards producing more chairs. Even if perchance he were successful in obtaining a commission to make one of the two chairs, it means that two instead of one of the established carpenters will be unemployed.

Unemployment in a particular country can arise because a specific national mineral deposit runs out, while the same mineral is still produced at substantially the same price in other countries. A general shortage of a mineral resource will, however, have its main effect on the users rather than on the producers of that particular mineral. The producers will spend an equal amount of national labour on mining less mineral out of thinner and sparser deposits and will obtain a higher price for it. Unemployment will then arise in the consumer countries.

If a nation can afford a reasonably acceptable standard of living for all its nationals, but not a sufficient level of economic activity to allow full employment for all, it becomes necessary to create financial provisions for those who cannot do useful work. We have been accustomed to think of such an unemployment provision as a special provision to cover an abnormal condition. We will have to re-think our attitude.

As we shall discuss in more detail in the next chapter, it is possible to regulate the level of global production to a certain extent, but the world can ill afford a substantial increase in global production because of the raw material requirements to which it gives rise. Therefore, unemployment somewhere in the world is unavoidable.

Should an increase in the relative price of raw materials be realized, it is possible that we will see a new category of less-developed countries. Established industrial countries failing to adapt their technology to the changing price structure, while others are more successful in doing so, will find their raw-material-wasting industries obsolete. At the new relative prices they will lose their export markets and become technologically backward countries.

Many of our observations about underdeveloped countries will be valid for this new category of less-developed countries as well. Then, if unemployment is a normal condition, people should be in a position to opt for it, and have some degree of status in society nevertheless. Some minimum income should be guaranteed to all, even if those who hold a job earn more. Since employment of labour is not a true cost to society under these conditions, it would be desirable that the living allowance should be given to all. It would be financed out of public charges on raw material extraction and industrial production. Those who wished could, of course, still attempt to find a job to earn themselves some money on top of their living allowance.

Furthermore, the ratio between the living allowance and the earnings from employment would determine the cost of hiring labour, to be paid by industry. This ratio should therefore be considered as an instrument for regulating the supply, as well as the demand, for labour at a level which is consistent with the material and external (international) limits to national production.

8
The World

8.1 WHAT LIMITS THE WORLD'S PRODUCTION?

In 1969 the world's total population was about 3·5 billion people.* Of these, 315 million, or just under 9 per cent, lived in North America. These 9 per cent of the world's population produced 34 per cent of all the world's energy, 25 per cent of all the passenger cars, 16 per cent of all the cement, and 55 per cent of all the newsprint. They also flew 81 per cent of all the airmail and used 56 per cent of all the world's telephones.

This unequal distribution of production and consumption over the world's population is partly due to an unequal absorption of the world's supply of natural resources, made possible by the Americans' superior industrial technology and the market dominance which stems from that technological dominance.

Nevertheless, the American performance strongly suggests that it should be possible to increase the total of the world's production, by improving the productivity of the other 91 per cent of the world's population.

It is, unfortunately, not possible to establish with any degree of scientific rigour what the real limits to global production capacity are. One can, however, formulate a proposition, a hypothesis, and discuss its implications, which will be done in this chapter. This proposition consists of two main points. Firstly, there is the resource-allocation aspect. On a global scale, the technical limit to increasing production stems from technological failure: material resources are limited and technology fails to provide the most efficient methods of production. The failure is aggravated because these methods are likewise inadequate for absorbing the waste products in our living space.

* The figures in this section are all obtained from the first summary table of the 1970 *Statistical Yearbook of the United Nations*, either directly or by dividing the North American figure by the world's total. Note that the 'billions' are U.S. style, i.e. one thousand million (the Continental 'milliard').

Secondly, the level of the world's production is limited by market factors. Most notable is the regulation of world trade by the global supply of international liquidity at a level which corresponds, at best, to full employment of labour in the dominant industrial centres rather than to global production capacity.

Looked at purely technically it would be possible to regulate global demand for products at a higher level than is actually realized at present, or is likely to be realized in the near future. There is an analogy between the problem of regional unemployment and unequal development inside developed countries, and that of developed versus underdeveloped countries.

Our discussion of the implications of this problem in a world-wide context is unavoidably somewhat speculative, because of the absence of an effective planning agency equipped with the necessary powers. We will pursue this discussion, nevertheless, so as to identify the main bottlenecks.

Suppose, for a moment, that we could overcome all these problems and regulate the level of the world's economy in the direction of global full employment of labour. We would then soon find that the 20–40 per cent return from additional investment in labour-saving equipment, as at present applicable in countries with a full-employment economy, seriously overstates the true benefits of this type of investment. We cannot have global full employment of labour unless we invent new technical processes which are more resource-efficient and environment-sparing, rather than being just labour-efficient.

Individual firms and countries can only realize this return on increased labour productivity if, and for as long as, they can increase their consumption of raw materials from imports. This is only possible if not too many other countries do the same. The spread of industrialization beyond the established developed countries is restricted by the limited possibilities for developing countries to import capital goods and export the products to be obtained by means of these capital goods. This factor has so far contained the demand for raw materials to a certain extent.

8.2 WORLD INFLATION AND WORLD ECONOMIC REGULATION

For the major trading countries inflation is a world-wide phenomenon, rather than a domestic problem of a particular country. A single country, which contained its domestic price-level for a decade or more, would create a situation where its export industries were cheaper than almost any other supplier of the corresponding product anywhere in the world. Foreign demand for its exports would therefore rise out of all proportion to the country's own need for imports. Moreover, importers who were importing foreign products in competition with domestically produced similar products, would increasingly find that the imported product was more expensive than the domestically produced one. Increased exports, and increased domestic consumption out of a higher income, would generate an increased demand for production and for production factors. Although these production factors include imported raw materials, the net result would nevertheless be a surplus on the balance of payments and excess demand in the domestic labour market at the same time.

The knowledge, or the presumption, that higher wages will eventually lead to unemployment is a main disciplining factor for trade unions not to press for higher wages, and for the government to resist domestic inflation. Conversely, the combination of an over-tight labour market with a surplus on the balance of payments makes it very difficult for the government to resist inflationary pressures in the domestic economy.

Unless there is a very serious reduction in the rate of growth of the real volume of world trade, and a corresponding increase in unemployment throughout the world, the problem of world-wide inflation is likely to get worse. The reason is that the era of implicit regulation of the world's liquidity supply by the United States' economy has come to an end. It has been followed by conscious regulation by international agreement. The alternative, a stabilization of international liquidity at substantially its present level under a regime of floating exchange rates, seems somewhat unlikely since the creation of I.M.F. Special Drawing Rights. Nevertheless, the inability of the available stocks of internationally accepted tokens of payment to keep a sufficiently fast-growing value of trade flowing, is a factor which limits the total value of world trade.

Consider the figures apposite, assembled from various issues of the International Monetary Fund's *International Financial Statistics.* We will analyse these figures as representing a closed system, in which the balance-of-payments restriction and the associated requirement to remain competitive in the international market do not exist.

The closed economy presents the quantity-of-money theory in its

WORLD TRADE AND STOCKS OF INTERNATIONAL LIQUIDITY BY TYPE
(in billions of $)

	1950	*1960*	*1970*
Gold	35	38	37
US $	6	12	24
English £	10	7	7
I.M.F. Drawing Rights*	—	4	11
Total of these types	51	61	79
World imports	57	112	294
Average number of months' import-reserve†	11	7	3

'pure' form. The value of goods and services traded is the product of its average price and the amount traded. At the same time, the value of the turnover must be paid in money tokens, and each trader will deem it necessary to keep a certain stock of money in reserve. This 'required money-stock' (for circulation purposes) is by and large a function of the sum of money which is circulated per time period. This relation is expressed by the concept 'velocity of circulation'; the required money-stock is the value of trade, multiplied by a parameter, the velocity of circulation.

If that restriction is indeed binding, we would have

$$P \times T = M \times V$$

where P is the average price-level,
T the amount of goods and services traded,
M the stock of money, and
V the velocity of circulation.

If V is held to be a technical parameter, hence constant, then it is clear that for most of the post-World War II period the inequality relationship

$$P \times T < M \times V$$

was true.

The 'velocity of circulation' is not a purely technical constant. In particular we have to consider the Keynesian theory of interest, which holds that at a relatively higher rate of interest people (and central

* Ordinary account and Special Drawing Rights taken together.

† Quotient of liquidity and world trade, multiplied by 12. The 'velocity of circulation' would, of course, be the other quotient, trade divided by liquidity.

banks as well?) will exchange part of their cash holdings for interest-bearing titles. (*See also* sections 3.4 and 9.4.)

For international trade it is clear that the 1950 United States holding was not needed for purposes of circulation. US imports in that year amounted to $8·95 billion* and its gold reserves alone $24 billion, i.e. sufficient to finance nearly three full years of import. For most of the post-World War II period, the rest of the world has been supplied with international liquidity by the US balance-of-payments deficit.

The US contribution to the rest of the world's money supply has been even greater than its direct banker's role, granting long-term loans, buying shares, etc. The US has also reduced its gold holdings (from $24 billion in 1950, to 18 billion in 1960, and 11 billion in 1970), thereby increasing other countries' gold holdings.

This US balance-of-payments deficit was, at least up to 1970, purely a deficit on capital account, arising from overseas loans given by the US and purchase of European, Canadian, and Japanese shares by US investors. The supply of dollars by the US to the rest of the world cannot, however, be continued much longer, irrespective of its origin.† Otherwise there is a real danger that the dollar will no longer be generally accepted as international liquidity.

The first result of the distrust of the US dollar has been an increase in its supply. Private holders of dollars (i.e. US internal money) have started to buy German marks, Swiss francs, and Japanese yen. By buying marks, francs, and yen speculators have automatically increased the official dollar reserves of the central banks of Germany, Switzerland, and Japan. The stock of dollars held as official reserves in the rest of the world increased from $24 billion in 1970 to $61 billion in 1972. This extra supply of US dollars has in all probability caused a temporary reversal of the downward trend in the reserve/import ratio. But this reversal cannot persist, at least not in the present climate of inflation. If the US stays in deficit on this scale, other major trading nations will start to refuse dollars and the dollar simply ceases to be a liquid reserve in any meaningful sense. On the other hand, if the US balance of payments returns to anything like equilibrium, the reserve/import ratio for the rest of the world will start to drop again, on account of the rising costs of imports.

* United Nations *Yearbook of International Trade Statistics* (1952), p. 12.

† In later years there was a deficit on the current account as well. One assumes this to be due mainly to the Vietnam War.

It is possible to supply international liquidity nowadays by the I.M.F.'s creating more Special Drawing Rights. This assumes that one conceives the task of the I.M.F. as that of a *world central bank*, adapting its issuing policy to specific purposes of global economic regulation.

Fortunately, the indications are that the creation of new international liquidity by international agreement, in the form of I.M.F. Drawing Rights, will remain and increase. However, the very fact that this is, with good reason, *seen* as a regulation, rather than as a process controlled by nobody in particular, creates a radically new situation.

The total amount of new creation of international liquidity becomes a matter of discussion between international organizations and national governments.

This concept of the I.M.F. as a world central bank is precisely the rationale of the 1969 version of the Fund's Articles of Agreement, by which the novel institution of Special Drawing Rights was created. A few words about the way Special Drawing Rights are effectively created may be useful here. The essential concepts about Special Drawing Rights are *allocations* and *designations.*

Drawing rights on a national central bank (i.e. banknotes) are legal tender throughout the country of issue by authority of the national government. This is not so in the case of I.M.F. Drawing Rights. Instead, member countries have taken upon themselves the commitment to act as part of the collective world central bank, until a member's designation is exhausted.

If country *A* has been designated a sum *X* this means that it is required to supply convertible currency (which may be country *A*'s own) in exchange for Special Drawing Rights; the S.D.R.s are booked over from some other country *B*'s account with the I.M.F. up to the sum *X*. As long as the system works, there is no particular burden on countries which the I.M.F. has designated, because Special Drawing Rights are obtained in exchange. Indeed, some central banks may well accept S.D.R.s without being designated.

The other concept, 'allocation', indicates a method of bringing new liquidity into circulation. A 'normal' central bank does this by lending money to its national government, to finance its expenditure, or to commercial banks, or by buying bonds, shares, etc.

The international equivalent of this method of bringing money into circulation would be that I.M.F. was to finance World Bank loans to developing countries, possibly also intergovernmental projects of general world economic significance and United Nations peacekeeping operations. That is not the 'allocations' principle. Allocations are on the basis of members' quota. The national economic equivalent to this procedure would be for the state to send a sum of money to all its citizens, in proportion to their last tax assessment!

There are, it is true, some restrictions on the use of an S.D.R. allocation, of which the major one is to keep on the average over a number of years an S.D.R. holding equal to at least 30 per cent of a country's cumulated allocations. That obligation can, however, be discharged by supplying the country's own national currency to other countries in exchange for S.D.R.s. Hence, even this 30 per cent obligation hardly limits the free-grant properties of an S.D.R. allocation, if that allocation is to a country with a convertible national currency.

Moreover, I.M.F. is more or less committed to salvage any country which runs into serious balance-of-payments problems, in order to prevent the national government resorting to unilateral measures harmful for the rest of the world; such would be the 'forbidden instruments' discussed in section 3.7 above.

I.M.F.'s Articles of Agreement [20], p. 279, stipulate in Article I(v) one of its purposes to be:

> 'To give confidence to members by making the Fund's resources temporarily available to them under adequate safeguards, thus providing them with opportunity to correct maladjustments in their balance of payments without resorting to measures destructive of national or international prosperity.'

The situation, which has arisen several times and is likely to arise again in the future, is the following. A developed member country, say *A*, has failed to contain domestic inflation. This has the following results:

(*a*) Its international competitive position has deteriorated, and a balance-of-payments crisis has resulted from this.

(*b*) Its clients, faced with the rising price of imports from *A*, have the prospect of a deterioration of their terms of trade. A client-country, say *B*, can shift part of its imports to one of *A*'s competitors, say *C*. However, unless *B* reduces the total volume of its imports, or increases its exports (for example to *A*), *B*'s balance of payments will suffer as well. *C* will of course be in surplus, and so will be *A*'s supplier, let us say country *D*.

Now if *A* is already short of reserves, this situation may force *A* to restrict the level of activity of its internal economy. By so doing *A* restores its external balance, which is the purpose of the stop, but the side-effects are likely to be: unemployment in *A*'s domestic economy, and conversion of the initial surplus of *A*'s supplier, *D*, into a deficit. The new equilibrium on *A*'s external balance is at a lower level, therefore *D* has lost export revenue.

If we assume that *C* has continued to supply at the old price level, *C*'s gain in export earnings (its surplus) equals the volume of *A*'s loss in export, and is less than *A*'s loss in export revenue, which is partially compensated by the rise in *A*'s export price.

The drop in *A*'s export-revenue in value is, via *A*'s restored balance of payments, also *D*'s loss in export revenue, irrespective of any price adjustment in the flow from *D* to *A*. Therefore the end result for *C* and *D* is that *C* is in surplus and *D* is in deficit (but not so much as *C*'s surplus). Since imports of *A*, *B*, *C*, and *D* together are equal to the same flows classified by origin, i.e. total exports, the four balances must add up to zero. Therefore if *D*'s deficit is smaller than *C*'s surplus, *B* must be in deficit as well, despite the fact that no change in the amount of *B*'s exports and imports was assumed. The reason is the rise in *A*'s export price, for which *B* could find only a partial relief by switching some of its imports to *C*. *B* has suffered deterioration of its terms of trade.

There is no doubt that *A*'s action, restoring its external balance by reducing the level of internal economic activity, is 'destructive of national and international prosperity'. The United Kingdom in the 1960s is the most obvious example.

There is yet another reason why I.M.F. has little option but to salvage *A* by granting a standby loan.

If international liquidity is generally scarce, then *C* (read: West Germany) will, for a while, be only too glad at its surplus, and do nothing to eliminate it. *B* and *D*, however (read: low-income countries and the United States), will sooner or later be compelled to restore their balances, unless this is brought about by external forces.

The result is that I.M.F. is committed to keeping world trade flowing, if necessary *even at an accelerating rate of inflation.*

We are, in fact, dealing with a global equivalent of the familiar problem of regulating the volume of demand. To regulate the amount of production one needs to regulate the value of the available income and the cost of full employment (or full-capacity) production, in order to keep the two in line with each other. If costs rise, then the income can be increased as well and the result is inflation. If the income is increased by less than the cost per unit of product, then the volume of demand will be reduced. However, once inflation is there, one has no rational criterion for judging what is a tolerable rate.

As long as world trade was seen as an uncontrolled phenomenon, a national government had a norm, namely the country's competitive position relative to the rest of the world. For the world as a whole, this criterion does not exist.

Somehow we must return to rational economic calculation, but preferably without the painful adjustment likely to arise if price stabilization is achieved from the monetary side only, e.g. after a substantial increase in unemployment. There are, to be sure, several yardsticks of the rate of inflation depending on which price or weighted average (index) of prices is kept constant. Rational calculation would be re-established if the world returned to zero inflation—on no matter which yardstick, provided it was a generally agreed one.

Unfortunately, the international community's only genuine world-wide and global instrument of regulation, the creation of new Special Drawing Rights, works on the value side only. The nearest to any effective power on the cost side is the possibility of making balance-of-payments standby conditional on effective control of the internal price level. This works only for as long as a particular country is in deficit.

8.3 DEVELOPMENT AND DEVELOPED COUNTRIES

There is some doubt whether large-scale capital aid is the best solution for the problem of underdevelopment and, indeed, if there is a solution to this problem at all. We are, however, concerned here with the more limited question of the financing of such aid as is desirable.

The conventional argument among those concerned with aid to developing countries is as follows. Developing countries are poor. They need foreign aid to be able to hire agricultural, medical, and technical experts from developed countries and to buy capital goods, tractors, factories, railway equipment, etc., also from these countries. Because they are poor, developing countries do not earn enough money to pay for these imports. Thus, if developed countries are concerned with the lot of low-income countries, they should send money to finance these imports. Therefore, developed countries should reduce or contain their own expenditure. They must somehow find a balance between their own expenditure and aid to low-income countries.

This argument is often invoked in connection with a developed country's balance-of-payments problems. For example, in the British *National Plan* [35] was the observation at p. 6: '. . . the amount of aid we give must be subject to restraint while our balance of payments difficulties persist . . . ' This is an erroneous philosophy. The real costs of supplying capital goods to developing countries are the alternative uses, the opportunity costs, of either the capital goods themselves, or of the labour, materials, etc., needed for their production in the donor-countries' own economies. If, for some reason, production is restricted by demand factors and not by any material obstacle, the product, the capital goods needed by developing countries, might still be made and supplied without immediate payment to those who need them but cannot pay.

Precisely the same argument applies to agricultural surpluses.

Low-income countries want to increase their imports from industrially developed countries. They want machines, railway track and rolling stock, fertilizer plants, etc., and possibly food as well. The production of these things in industrially developed countries is limited by the relevant producing sectors' installed capacity and the supply of labour and raw materials, or by effective demand for the products in question, or by a combination of physical supply limits and financial limits on demand.

A credit grant by a developed country to a developing country, in order to finance the import of capital equipment, creates additional demand for export of capital equipment from industrially developed countries in general. Restriction of internal demand in the developed countries themselves is only called for if the increase in demand cannot be met out of surplus production capacity. If we finance a loan for some developing country to build a railway, and our own steel industry is already working at full capacity, we should restrict domestic investment so as to re-allocate steel from use in the domestic economy to rolling the rails for the developing country. However, if our steel industry is working below its technical capacity, we might as well produce the rails and supply the same level of domestic demand also.

That is true irrespective of the balance of payments. Exports which are not currently paid for do not strengthen the country's balance of payments, but neither do they weaken it. The complication is that few aid-giving countries are capable of supplying every product a developing country needs. Furthermore, the products which are produced in a particular donor-country may contain imported materials. As a result, a developed country may finance a project, of which the full cost is say $100 million, find that only 60 million of that sum is spent on its own export products, and that those 60 million contain a further 10 million of imported materials. The aid-giving country is then 50 million out of cash, of which 40 million is spent by the developing country on other countries' exports, plus another 10 million import component in the donor-country's own contribution. The solution to this problem is to lend $50 million to the low-income country, on the condition that it finds the remaining 50 million from some other source—its own reserves, from another developed country or from an international organization.

The correct policy in the case of a developed country with a national balance-of-payments problem could thus be stated:

> Our industry has surplus capacity available for the production of capital goods which are urgently needed by developing countries. We therefore plan to increase our export of capital goods to developing countries. Since our own balance of payments is not very strong at the moment, we are negotiating with other developed countries having surpluses on their balances. We hope these other developed countries will join us in a consortium. We expect our own share in this consortium to be about equal to or smaller than our share in the actual export of capital goods to developing countries which the consortium intends to finance. If no agreement on such international co-ordination of development aid can be reached we intend to restrict our direct credits to underdeveloped countries to 'tied' loans which can only be spent on equipment purchased in this country. In both cases the programme will not cost us any foreign exchange, and does not call for a restriction of our internal expenditure.

Although illogical, the 'budget limit' philosophy is a fact to be reckoned with in international as well as in national public economics,

For this reason the international liquidity problem is bound to affect development aid.

8.4 RAW MATERIALS AND NATURAL RESOURCES

The earth contains limited quantities of various ores, minerals, and so on. Therefore, it is good classical economic theory to require that the prices of various raw materials contain an element of pure 'rent', imputed to the availability of scarce materials, as distinct from the cost of their extraction from the earth. According to the model of competitive market adjustment, this rent is appropriated by whoever owns or controls these natural resources.

The question arises of what the appropriate price of this 'rent' element in the price of raw materials should be, relative to the other main cost factor, labour, and to the end-product.

For a single firm and even a single country this question does not arise because raw materials are transported to where they are required for industrial production, often to another country. For many raw materials the price is a world-market price.

This price reflects the short-term desire for profits of the owners of mineral resources and of the industrial companies who wish to exploit them, rather than the long-term interests of the world as a whole. The mineral resource limit is essentially different from a currently binding resource limit, as for example the limited availability of land of a certain description. There is no more than a certain quantity of that particular quality of land available. Thus, unless there is an actual excess demand leading to rationing or queueing, the demand for that particular quality of land is forced to be less than the available supply and the income and price structure will adjust themselves accordingly.

This does not apply to a mineral resource limit. There is no strict limit on the consumption of raw materials or of any particular raw material in a given year or other time period, but only on their total availability for all time to come. If the current price structure fails to discourage, but on the contrary encourages, the wasteful use of raw materials, then they will be used in a wasteful way at the expense of later generations.

So as to discuss and analyse this problem, we will, for the sake of argument, make some sweeping simplifications.

We assume there is a homogeneous product, called 'world production', which somehow aggregates together such varied articles as motor cars, visits to Honolulu, coconuts, houses, and coats.

We consider two methods of producing the product: one is labour intensive and the other is raw material intensive. This would presumably refer, partially but not exclusively, to the composition of 'world production'.

To produce motor cars is material intensive, but not particularly labour intensive, because of automation. On the other hand, to organize a trip to Honolulu can be done quite economically as far as materials are concerned, although some of the most material-efficient production methods, like sailing with the wind by clipper, have fallen into disuse. But the Honolulu trip is quite labour intensive, particularly if a certain standard of passenger comfort and entertainment is desired.

Another example of a choice between a material- and a labour-intensive production method is the choice between public transport and the use of private motor cars. The private motor car is efficient in terms of labour cost, because it is driven by the transport user himself. Self-service is economical in the use of labour. It is, however, a much more material-intensive method of transport.

The production of motor cars, jet flights, etc., could well be limited, by the available supply of raw materials, to less than the amount corresponding to full employment of labour. If that were found to be the case, we might as well employ the remaining labour by organizing trips by clipper to Honolulu. Some people might like to see Honolulu, even preferring that slow means of transport, half of them crewing the ship instead of being out of work at home, and the other half having a two months' holiday instead of a fortnight's by plane for the same price.

The usefulness of a further increase in labour productivity is restricted by the supply of raw materials. Conversely, an increase in labour productivity enhances the scarcity value of raw materials. Total production is the sum of the product obtained by labour-intensive and material-intensive processes. We may simplify and illustrate the interdependence by means of a system of equations. The aggregated labour-intensive process ('sailing with the wind') is material efficient, and the material-intensive process ('mechanized production') is labour efficient.

We indicate the labour-efficient but material-intensive process as p_1, and the material-efficient but labour-intensive process as p_2; the total is p.

$$p = p_1 + p_2$$

The total required labour supply is indicated by a and a_1 and a_2 stand for the labour required to produce one unit of product by the processes p_1 and p_2.

The labour-supply restriction is therefore

$$a_1 p_1 + a_2 p_2 \leq a$$

The total required material supply is indicated by m and m_1 and m_2 are the materials required for one unit of production. Assuming that the supply restrictions on both production factors are binding, we can 'solve' the three equations and express the levels of the two processes, and the total production, in terms of the available supplies of the two production factors.

For the level of the labour-efficient process we obtain the expression:

$$p_1 = \frac{-m_2}{m_1 a_2 - m_2 a_1} a + \frac{a_2}{m_1 a_2 - m_2 a_1} m$$

and for the material-efficient (labour-intensive) process:

$$p_2 = \frac{m_1}{m_1 a_2 - m_2 a_1} a - \frac{a_1}{m_1 a_2 - m_2 a_1} m$$

The total of the two is

$$p = \frac{m_1 - m_2}{m_1 a_2 - m_2 a_1} a + \frac{a_2 - a_1}{m_1 a_2 - m_2 a_1} m$$

The expressions

$$\frac{m_1 - m_2}{m_1 a_2 - m_2 a_1} \text{ and } \frac{a_2 - a_1}{m_1 a_2 - m_2 a_1}$$

are the efficiency prices or perfect-competition prices of the two production factors.

The concept of a price is only significant *relative* to the price of something else. In this case it is convenient to express the prices of labour and resource availability relative to the price of the end-product. This means that the price of the product is set at the number one, by requirement. The price of everything else is expressed as so many units of product, and the price of a unit of product can only be one unit of product. We then see from the above expression for p that

$$\frac{m_1-m_2}{m_1a_2-m_2a_1} \text{ and } \frac{a_2-a_1}{m_1a_2-m_2a_1}$$

are the amounts of product to be obtained by the employment of an additional unit of labour or of material resources.

That these expressions are indeed the perfect-competition prices can also be seen from the perfect-competition requirement that the proceeds (one unit of product) are equal to the costs for both processes.

The price of labour is indicated as w and the rental of the resource limit is indicated as r.

The perfect-competition requirements are then

$$a_1w+m_1r = 1 \quad (= \text{one unit of } p),$$

for the cost of one unit of product produced by means of p_1, and

$$a_2w+m_2r = 1 \quad (= \text{one unit of } p),$$

for the corresponding requirement for p_2.

From these two equations w and r are solved as

$$w = \frac{m_1-m_2}{m_1a_2-m_2a_1}$$

and

$$r = \frac{a_2-a_1}{m_1a_2-m_2a_1}$$

Since these expressions are prices, they should both be positive. This is indeed the case, because of our interpretation of the first process as relatively material intensive, i.e. $m_1>m_2$, and of the second process as the labour intensive, i.e. $a_2>a_1$. The denominator expression is then automatically positive as well: $m_1a_2>m_2a_1$.

Note that both prices evaluate, in effect, the difference in productivity of the two processes with respect to the other production factor. For example, if both processes are equally material intensive ($m_1 = m_2$), production is determined exclusively by the supply of raw materials and the supply of labour is irrelevant, resulting in a zero efficiency-price of labour.

In the 'normal' case ($a_1<a_2$; $m_1>m_2$), a further dose of automation and mechanization reduces a_1, thereby increasing the denominator and results in a *drop* in the price of labour relative to the product. All the increase in the evaluated return to production factors, and more than that, goes to material resources.

Denote a new, lower labour-coefficient for p_2 as a_2^*, the other technical coefficients a_1, m_1, and m_2 remaining the same. The new efficiency prices will be indicated as w^* and r^*.

We see that

$$w^* = \frac{m_1 - m_2}{m_1 a_2^* - m_2 a_1} < w = \frac{m_1 - m_2}{m_1 a_2 - m_2 a_1}$$

is true, since the assumed $a_2 > a_2^*$ implies

$$m_1 a_2^* - m_2 a_1 > m_1 a_2 - m_2 a_1$$

and the numerator remains unchanged (and was positive).

The simplest proof for the compensating relationship $r^* > r$ is indirect. The total production value is greater because of the increased labour productivity. Indicating the new, increased level of total production as p^*, we have

$$p^* = w^* a + r^* m > p = wa + rm$$

Since w^* is actually reduced, $r^* > r$ must be true.

Actual prices are not, of course, exact efficiency prices. Also there is a serious aggregation problem which limits the possibility of reallocating resources from one productive activity to another in the real world. Nevertheless, one would suspect that if prices were broadly related to efficiency prices in the sense that they encouraged the efficient use of resources, and penalized their wasteful use, there would be some rough correspondence between efficiency prices and actual prices. One would hope that investment in new types of equipment and the introduction of new techniques would be most profitable, if those techniques were more economical in terms of the scarcest and most exhaustible resources.

There is some degree of uncertainty about how the world's economy actually works. Our analysis is based on the assumption that there is a given supply of labour and of natural resources, and that increases in productivity are predominantly in the form of further mechanization and automation in the already mechanized part of the world's economy.

The outcome of the analysis is that the evaluated return on labour, as a result of further mechanization, will *fall*, due to a rising share of rents on natural resources.

This outcome is flatly contradictory to the development in the real world during most of the post-World War II period.

The contradiction primarily refers to the supply of production factors, rather than to the technical data. There is no actual limit on the supply of minerals in the period to which we refer. The development of a number of man-made substitutes for raw materials (synthetic rubber, plastic, rayon, etc.) is in fact a confirmation rather than a denial of the main trend in technology which is to substitute machines for human labour.

The point is that the raw materials which have been substituted are, by and large, materials which require a fair amount of processing labour. This applies particularly to agricultural products and activities, like the bleeding of rubber trees and the picking of cotton.

Production of earth-extracted raw materials has increased at a phenomenal rate,* because ore extraction can be mechanized but agriculture cannot be mechanized to the same degree. So far, the mining industries have been able to satisfy the ever-increasing demand by more intensive prospecting and by deeper and more efficient mining. Even where one earth-extracted material is substituted for another, the reason may well be the processing cost rather than the natural limit. Oil has been extracted instead of coal, not because there is more oil than coal in the earth (there is not), but because the mining of coal is too labour intensive.

The price structure, and the way it has developed in time, stimulates labour efficiency rather than material efficiency. Compare the following figures, drawn from Tables 8 and 144 of the 1970 *Statistical Yearbook* of the United Nations:

	1958	*1963*	*1970*
Export price of minerals	108	100	109
From developed countries	101	100	122
From developing countries	111	100	104
Production price of manufactured goods (unit value)	80	100	132

The amount of end-product, purchased for the proceeds of a unit of minerals, has actually fallen.

* I converted some absolute figures as given in the 1954 and 1970 *Statistical Yearbook* of the United Nations into 1953–69 percentage increments. The increase in world production was 146 per cent of the 1953 level for iron ore, 253 per cent for bauxite (aluminium ore), and 242 per cent for crude oil.

Moreover, the difference in price trend between the export of minerals from developed and underdeveloped countries suggests that the (fairly moderate) rise in the prices of minerals produced in industrially developed countries represents labour costs, rather than the rental on mineral resources.

Such a development of the price structure is bound to guide technology in the direction of increased efficiency in the use of labour, not towards the more economical use of minerals. It makes sense only if one assumes that labour, not mineral resources, is the main restriction on the further expansion of production.

All the same the demand for minerals has increased at a rate which is about two-thirds of the increase in the demand for the manufactured products made from it.

	1958	*1963*	*1970*
Quantity of manufactured products	70	100	151
Quantity of minerals produced	74	100	132

Despite the lack of price incentive, technical innovation has not been exclusively labour-saving. Presumably the difference in the two rates of increase represents the greater degree of complexity of the various products made. On the assumption that such greater complexity corresponds to a greater service from the products, this greater service of more refined products is a production increase for which no additional mineral input was needed.

Nevertheless, if the demand for various mineral resources continues to increase, roughly doubling every fifteen years, there will come a moment when all the reserves within men's reach are exhausted. The main reason why this has not so far actually happened for any important mineral is that our knowledge of where to find ore deposits, and how to mine them, has increased as well. More efficient and systematic prospecting and improved mining technology have allowed a more intensive exploitation of the earth but not, of course, increased the total of all existing—but not yet completely known—resources.

According to the assumption of market adjustment by price, the prospect of a future shortage of mineral resources should result in speculative purchases of suitable pieces of land and mining concessions, in anticipation of higher prices in the future, thus forcing up their present price. Perfect competition would in this case include speculation with perfect foresight.

Someone who knew that a particular plot of land was likely to contain an important oil deposit, or, for that matter, would be clean and pollution-free in the future, should be willing to pay a small fortune for it now, so as to reserve it for himself and his heirs and prevent any alternative use. His children or grandchildren would then sell it for a much bigger sum, for exploitation or residential development.

In reality one cannot expect such long-term speculation. Even if one were prepared to put up with the social–political implication that the full scarcity value of future mineral resources would be appropriated by the successful among today's speculators, it just wouldn't happen like that. Speculators are not prepared to pay in the present the full price for future scarcity less the cost of interest, and present consumption of minerals is not contained, but keeps increasing.

What should be done to preserve a sufficient stock of mineral resources—and its counterpart, a non-polluted environment—for future generations?

In principle the problem can be attacked from both sides. Governments of industrial countries can control the disposal of waste products. I suspect this will be done, if at all, mainly by administrative control and prohibition rather than by pricing.

'Clean' industry and agriculture which do not produce obnoxious waste products to be thrown away and carried into the air and water are also material efficient. If one cannot throw away obnoxious products one must either produce less of them or reprocess them after use. Reprocessing can be purely a question of burning or otherwise destroying some of the more obnoxious wastes. It is, however, equally possible that substances which used to be thrown away, thereby polluting the environment, can be put to an economically useful purpose.

Pollution control will therefore help to economize on minerals but it will not be sufficient in this respect.

There are some asymmetric points where the two problems, the depletion of the earth and the saturation of the seas and the atmosphere, fail to correspond to each other. Firstly, some of the most obnoxious materials are of organo-chemical composition and do not require scarce minerals for their production. Secondly, two important groups of relatively scarce raw materials probably can be processed in such a way that their eventual waste products are not detrimental to the environment, even if some of the present processing methods cause pollution. Metallic ores will eventually turn into scrap metal. That scrap metal can be reprocessed, but from an environmental point of view it is not particularly objectionable to bury it instead and eventually to build a new residential area on top of the scrap tip.

Fuels can be burned 'clean'. Many of the present pollution complaints concerning industrial fumes stem from incomplete burning. More complete burning will presumably increase thermal efficiency, but the environmental aspect does not provide an incentive to economize on energy as such. It is conceivable but so far not very likely that the symmetry property might reassert itself at a higher level, in the form of an increasing concentration of carbon dioxide in the atmosphere, so that even the 'clean' end-product of the burning of a fuel may become a nuisance.

At all events, if we are to avoid any further squandering of the earth's mineral resources at the cost of later generations, the downward trend in the relative prices of mineral resources will have to be reversed.

8.5 MONDIAL INCOME DISTRIBUTION AND THE RAW MATERIAL PROBLEM

Established industrial countries, as a group, import substantial quantities of raw materials from the rest of the world. For this reason the relative price-ratio between raw materials on the one hand and industrial end-products on the other is an important determinant of mondial income distribution. The question arises of what determines this price ratio.

As we saw in the previous section, there is no requirement for this price ratio to represent a genuine equilibrium in any period of time. The 'normal' classical assumption is that the price adjusts itself in such a way that the demand, at the prevailing price, equals the available supply.

However, since there is no strict limit on the supply of raw materials in any separate time period, the relationship can be inverted. The price is determined by exogenous factors, monetary and institutional factors, etc., and the realized supply is simply the demand at that prevailing price structure.

The following set of relations is offered here as a terms-of-trade determining mechanism, as long as there are no binding geological supply limits. In reality this is always a half-truth because expectations of a possible future exhausting of the geological supply affect the present price, only not sufficiently to ensure non-exhaustion.

By way of mental exercise we can separate completely the short-term demand from the geological supply limit. This amounts to assuming a completely demand-determined model which operates until at some future date we crash against the supply wall and have exhausted all natural resources. An attempt will now be made to spell out this demand-determined model.

The demand for raw materials, in terms of quantity is, in the short and medium term, largely complementary to the level of industrial production: so many cars made, so many tonnes of iron ore required, so much electric power generated, so much fuel needed.

World demand for raw materials is therefore equal to the raw material requirement of the level of industrial production corresponding to the available employment of labour in industrially developed countries.

In the short term that production level is virtually exogenous, except for cyclical variations of the level of employment in industrial countries. At a given state of technology the full-employment demand for raw materials is for all practical purposes a determinate figure. Actual demand can, of course, be less if industrial economies are working below their full-employment (capacity) levels. In the medium term, however, labour productivity in industrial countries is increased by new investment, automation, and mechanization.

The pace of this process is set by the pressure of demand for industrial products, and the demand for raw materials will increase more or less *pro rata.* The distribution of the benefits of this productivity increase is indeterminate. A necessary condition for the consumption of a particular exhaustible material continuing at its present level for, say, 200 years is that its price limits its demand to not more than 0·5 per cent of its geological availability.

That requirement would give rise to an income-distribution equilibrium between labour income and consumption of industrial products inside industrially developed countries, on the one hand, and raw-material producing countries on the other.

Owing to the absence of a definite supply limit in any single time period, the income distribution is determined by a complex of political and institutional factors, rather than by any objective technical requirement.

An individual industrial country cannot allow its internal price and incomes level to deviate too much from that of the rest of the world, as otherwise it could not simultaneously maintain full employment of labour and equilibrium balance of payments. For industrial countries as a group there is no such restriction. If there were a strict limit on the supply of raw materials, the economic policies of developed countries would have to adjust themselves to that supply limit. Instead, the demand for raw materials adjusts itself to economic conditions as shaped by political factors.

Raw-material producing countries will supply whatever industrial countries care to buy, and spend the revenue on industrial products. How much industrial product they will get in exchange depends on the industrial countries' internal price structure and the way this is influenced by developed countries' internal economic policies, rather than on any objective equilibrium conditions. It is reasonable to assume that there are, nevertheless, some systematic factors which shape the internal price structure of the industrially developed part of the world.

My guess is that the rising trend in the price of industrial products relative to raw materials (as actually observed in the post-World War II period) can be interpreted as the result of rising labour costs, under the influence of approximate full employment of labour in industrially developed countries.

If this is the correct explanation, the conclusion is that any increase in the general level of economic activity throughout the world will strengthen the rising tendency of the prices of industrial products relative to raw materials. Conversely, any slackening in world trade and industrial production will tend to increase competition between industrial producers and industrial countries, and the relative price of raw materials will rise or at least cease to fall. One assumes that raw material prices are relatively more sluggish and less responsive to change in demand, because they are to some extent 'pegged' by long-term contracts or tradition.

If this interpretation is indeed correct, the income-distribution result is that, of any increase in world production, raw-material producing countries will have some share, in the form of increased sales of raw materials, but that they will lose a part of the gain on their volume of export, by way of an adverse change in their terms of trade with industrial countries. The two are positively related to each other: the higher the demand for raw materials the higher the price of industrial end-products, because both are associated with a high level of total demand for industrial end-products.

Our evaluation of this mechanism depends on our assessment of the relative scarcity of industrial labour and raw materials. If the labour supply inside industrially developed countries is indeed the major scarce production factor limiting global production, this reaction of the price system to a demand impulse would generate broadly the correct incentive effect. Labour-efficient processes would be stimulated even if they are not particularly material efficient. If, however, raw materials are the true limiting factor, this is a perverse situation. If we move faster in the direction of exhausting major raw material supplies we should anticipate their future scarcity, instead of stimulating their increased use by a higher degree of mechanization.

There are more components and more sources of income which can change income distribution than just the terms of trade between industrial end-products and raw materials.

The position of food is slightly ambiguous. There is a resource limit (the amount of land) which limits food production in some of the more densely populated countries. And, unlike the geological limit on minerals, a land restriction limits food production in each separate time period.

I submit, however, that at present the position for the world economy as a whole is still that food production is limited by effective demand and purchasing power, rather than by a natural supply limit. Additional food production will require additional fertilizer, irrigation works, and transport facilities to bring it to those who need it. This means in fact that food is a relatively labour-intensive 'industrial' product, and that its cost price depends on labour costs rather than on the availability of land. If world population continues to grow, we shall eventually hit the land limit, hence the growth of world population must sooner or later be stopped. The position is not nearly as critical as with mineral resources, where even a stationary population, combined with continued industrialization in its present labour-saving and material-intensive form, means an increased rate of depletion of a non-replenishable set of resources.

Furthermore, food consumption is more evenly spread between rich and poor, and as a result the international trade in food is not the one-way poor to rich flow which we see in the case of mineral raw materials. For this reason the price of food does not have such a strong mondial income-distribution effect as is the case with mineral raw materials.

There is also a certain amount of industrialization in low-income countries. The young industries of developing countries are, however, favoured by roughly the same conditions as those in the already established industrial countries—the general level of international mondial demand, as represented by world trade. One assumes that the prices of developing countries' young industries will follow approximately those of established industrial countries. In other words, low-income countries which develop industrially belong for a small part of their economy to the industrially developed sector of the world.

8.6 A WORLD ECONOMIC POLICY

The concept of economic policy, market regulation by a single mondial authority, is necessarily speculative. Even so, the only rational way to approach some of the urgent problems of our time is by at least *thinking* in terms of a mondial economic policy.

This does not necessarily require the existence of a genuine supranational authority, equipped with those powers to regulate the world's economy which its officers might find desirable.

I assume we will eventually find it necessary to establish institutions to regulate the world's economy from a central point of view. There are, however, obvious political obstacles to such a proposal and some solution to present problems is required now. They can, to a considerable extent, be implemented by means of international negotiation and agreement. The objective reality is that there *is* a global economy and that one international economic agreement influences the results aimed for by another set of negotiations.

Therefore the rational way to analyse any attempt to regulate any aspect of the world's economy is to see it as an aspect of a co-ordinated world-wide economic policy. This section is devoted to a discussion of such a policy.

The three main problems by which the world's economy is plagued are: the present poverty and unemployment of a large part of the world's population, the danger of exhausting natural resources, and the accelerating rate of inflation.

Unfortunately, there are at best only two main instruments of world-wide regulating effect available. I refer to Special Drawing Rights and to the control over the prices of certain raw materials exercised by various commodity agreements and the international bodies which administer them. With some goodwill and a slight stretching of our imagination, we could consider the controls over raw material prices as facets of a general system of price controls. One would have to assume that more 'commodity councils' equipped with price-regulating powers would be set up.

What is totally missing so far is international control over incomes in industrially developed countries.

It is possible to stimulate the level of world production by creating more S.D.R.s, provided the resulting increase in the value of world trade does indeed lead to an increase in the volume of demand, instead of becoming dissipated in inflationary price rises.

The stimulation of world trade by financial conditions was most effectively illustrated in 1950 after the outbreak of the Korean war. That political event activated the then prevailing mechanism of implicit regulation of world trade by the United States' balance of payments, discussed earlier in this chapter. The then F.A.O. director, Norris E. Dodd, wrote at p. 1 of his 1950 annual report [45]:

> 'The crisis in Korea has had an impact on the economy of many nations which has brought about a number of fundamental changes in the outlook for food and agriculture. Demand for agricultural products will be stronger than had been anticipated . . . ; some of the currency impediments to international trade will be reduced . . . the threat of unmarketable surpluses will fade . . '

A roughly similar effect may be expected under conditions of conscious regulation, if increased issue of S.D.R.s is combined with a policy of stabilizing (i.e. restraining increases of) commodity prices. Developed industrial countries could then combine full employment at home with a surplus on their balance of payments, or at least a sufficient stock of foreign exchange reserves.

Low-income countries will profit from the increased demand for raw materials, and food-producing low-income countries (exporters of rice, soya, etc.) will find themselves exporting more food to other, more densely populated low-income countries.

Developing countries might also find that established industrial countries would display a more liberal attitude with respect to international capital aid, because they would no longer be worried about their own payments balances, at least not to the extent that they have been recently. The same argument is also valid for the attitude of developed countries to imports from low-income countries. The consumption of raw materials would, however, increase.

Conversely, one could give priority to the preservation of minerals. Various commodity commissions would increase the prices of mineral raw materials in the hope of containing their consumption, prices of agricultural materials not being similarly augmented. In fact, some existing commodity councils have powers to restrict the amounts to be produced. These powers are primarily meant to underpin the agreed price, in the presence of excess supply, rather than as an independent instrument. It should be borne in mind that many of the commodity councils are officially backed marketing boards and represent producers' interests.

It is most unlikely that a quota system will be used to restrict extraction from the earth by refusing to serve users who are prepared to pay the set price.

A rise in the price level of raw materials, occurring in combination with an unchanged supply of international liquidity, might well lead to balance-of-payments problems for a number of industrial countries and set in motion a recessionary mechanism. Countries with a deficit on their balance of payments would restrict public expenditure, increase taxes, and reduce their internal level of economic activity. This would hit the export earnings of other countries, including raw-material producing countries.

The result would up to a point be the opposite of the development which characterized the 1950s and 1960s. It would not, of course, be quite the reverse. The increased labour productivity in industrially developed countries would not be reversed and the terms of trade would be more in favour of raw-material producing countries.

High-income industrial countries would be worse off, as would those low-income countries which depend for their export earnings on such agricultural raw materials as rubber and cotton, than in the situation which would arise without increases in the prices of mineral raw materials.

Balance-of-payments problems of densely populated low-income countries would force them to economize on food as well, and for this reason food-producing countries would be hit too. Raw material consumption would, in fact, be reduced together with the general level of world-wide economic activity.

On the other hand, if the supply of international liquidity were to be increased simultaneously, no such contraction of world-wide economic activity would arise. Then, however, any reduction or containment of the increase in consumption of raw materials which might arise would have to come from a change in the input composition of production, i.e. industry would have to use fewer raw materials per unit of product.

A change in the factor proportions between the inputs of labour and raw materials can be expected only if the relative price ratio between the two is adjusted, if incomes from employment in industrial countries do not rise by the same percentage as the raw material prices. Or at least if the change in the present trend is a rise in raw material costs *without* a corresponding rise in labour costs. Unfortunately, it is quite conceivable that a policy of rising raw-material prices, combined with a continuation of expanding world trade and full employment, will simply result in more inflation. Labour costs, i.e. income from employment in industrial countries, can rise just as well, following rising prices of end-products.

What is necessary is for national governments to contain labour costs in industrial countries, following some form of international agreement for this purpose, coupled with a rise in raw material prices at the same time. It is at present not easy to see how this can come about. The problem is not so much the enforceability of a generally agreed policy, as the reluctance to co-operate in the first place. One possibility of enforcement would be to make balance-of-payments standby conditional on co-operation with an internationally agreed policy. Another possibility would be for international authorities—rather than national governments—to have the power to adjust the rates of exchange at which national currencies can be exchanged against one another. In that event national economies could be subject to as much inflation as the national government and the people chose, but there would be automatic stabilization of prices of internationally traded products at the levels decided upon by international agreement. The main problem is, however, whether rich countries would be willing to co-operate.

The alternative is a choice between stagnation and recession in world trade and industrial production or continuation of the depletion of the world's natural resources at an accelerating rate.

There are superficial indications, assuming a continuation of present policies, that the last course will prevail: resources will continue to be depleted at an accelerating rate until we more or less crash into the wall, having virtually exhausted one or more important natural resources world-wide. If that happens, or a situation arises that certain materials can only be obtained at considerably increased costs, by mining deposits of lower quality and at greater depth in the earth, market forces will enforce a price structure which reflects the scarcity of these resources. In that case it is quite possible that some established industrial countries will find their material-intensive technology has become obsolete. Industrial production will then be forced to contract, and much of the previous chapter will become applicable to a new group of low-income countries.

We will, however, attempt to outline the results of what would appear to be the more optimistic assumption. We will assume regulation of the world's economy, the main lines of that regulation being continued expansion of world trade, limitation of income increments in industrial countries to increases in productivity, and upward adjustment of the prices of raw materials. We will then see that the optimistic nature of our assumptions is a qualified optimism.

The first obvious result of the assumed policy is a considerable income benefit for those countries whose exports consist mainly of oil or other mineral raw materials, ores, etc. It would be desirable to redistribute a part of this additional revenue to raw-material and food-importing countries that are densely populated. The criteria for redistributing the additional earth rental and raw-material income which does not remain with the raw-material exporting countries would be:

(*a*) Compensation of the extra import costs arising from an act of deliberate international regulation to increase the price of certain raw materials so as to preserve them for future generations.
(*b*) Need.

This redistribution should be on a lump-sum basis, rather than being directly related to imports. The beneficiaries should include those established industrial countries which are most directly hit by the increase in raw material prices, unless they are in a strong balance-of-payments position nevertheless. The reason is not just to 'buy' their agreement to a price control system which is disadvantageous to them. This is a good argument, but it is not the only reason. Balance-of-payments problems of important industrial countries would make mondial economic regulation unpopular. Such balance-of-payments problems would also endanger the other main aim, maintaining the expansion of world trade, because the governments of these countries would reduce the activity levels of their internal economies as well as cut imports by other, more direct ways. Recessionary tendencies could, presumably, be compensated by the creation of additional international liquidity, but it is undesirable to put too much 'strain' on a particular instrument.

Concerning low-income countries, one desirable effect of a redistribution of income in favour of densely populated low-income countries would be to stimulate the demand for food and agricultural specialties like coffee, tea, and cocoa in the world-wide market. There is, therefore, a case for giving them a better relative share in the redistribution of mineral earth-rentals than would correspond to their terms-of-trade loss from the increased costs of imported raw materials. Thinly populated low-income countries would then be in a position to increase their export revenue by increasing the production and export of foodstuffs. Some increase in the relative price of food would result from the increase in demand. Thinly populated countries would then find it possible to increase food production for export.

The position with industrial production and its geographical distribution is less clear. There would be a certain increase in the demand for industrial products in low-income countries. The unknowns are the degree of industrialization of present low-income countries, and the employment position in both the established industrial countries and in present low-income countries. Unless we can economize on raw materials in a dramatic way, it is not at all certain if industrialization of the present underdeveloped countries, on a scale which would result in anything resembling full employment of labour throughout the world, is a feasible, or indeed a desirable, policy.

Suppose industrialization of less-developed countries was stimulated, say, by the World Bank providing capital grants out of newly created Special Drawing Rights. These funds would be used to finance the building of fertilizer plants, railways, cement factories, hydro-electric dams and power stations, in low-income countries. We assume that the operation of the projects would be on the basis of local domestic resources. That means that some of the earth's natural resources, which are at present 'protected' or 'locked away' in poorly accessible parts of underdeveloped countries, were to be tapped. Additional imports of the industrializing low-income countries which would nevertheless arise are assumed to be compensated by import substitution. For example, the resulting higher level of employment would be associated with more imports of consumer goods, but less cement would be imported.

There would therefore be no particular balance-of-payments problem for developing countries. Now consider the effect on established industrial countries. A sizeable part of the initial grant to developing countries would be spent on the import of chemical retorts, valves and control equipment, rolling stock, grinding mills, draglines, and generating equipment, etc. These are by and large the sophisticated capital goods of which, so far, established industrial countries are the exclusive producers. Established industrial countries would be glad to produce these capital goods at their normal prices. The additional internal income (and export revenue) in established industrial countries would stimulate internal expenditure and production for the internal market. A new equilibrium position would be reached, once the additional import of raw materials restored the external balance of payments at a higher level.

The higher income of raw-material exporting countries would stimulate the world's economy even farther. This is all very fine, but the end result is that the secondary (multiplier) effects of an increase in demand, anywhere in the world, and of a demand for investment in particular, accrue to a considerable extent to established industrial countries. Their economies are, so to say, the 'centre of gravity' of the world's economy. Therefore, the total increase in industrial production needed to achieve world-wide full employment is much more than the production of the hitherto unemployed in the underdeveloped countries.

At a rather low labour productivity the underdeveloped countries' additional production might not require all that much in terms of raw materials. The additional industrial production of established industrial countries, however, requires much more in raw materials, because a greater quantity of output is involved.

One possible counter-argument to this line of analysis is worth discussing. Would not the limit on the labour supply in established industrial countries restrain their possibility of producing more, and result in internal excess demand spilling over into imports, including imports of labour-intensive products from low-income countries? And would not the increase in the price of raw materials stimulate such a development? The argument is logical in itself, but not consistent with the assumptions we made earlier (in Chapter 4) about demand-induced technical progress.

Raising the cost of raw materials relative to the cost of labour does indeed stimulate the demand for labour. The resulting full employment of labour in industrial countries is itself a stimulus to labour productivity. In other words at an unchanged level of demand for industrial products, the same amount of industrial products will be made, by the domestic industry of the established industrial countries, from almost the same amount of labour and a somewhat lower amount of raw materials. The desired increase in employment in underdeveloped countries requires an increased industrial production and this will again raise the consumption of raw materials.

The effects of economic growth in the global market on the allocation of labour are different from the direct analogy of the national market, because of the political restrictions on migration. The 'centre of gravity' effect applies in both cases. As we saw in section 2.6 the result of increased demand for end-products in a national economy in the absence of a conscious regional policy is increased employment in the metropolitan and industrialized part of the country.

I suppose it would be possible, from a strictly technical point of view, to stimulate world-wide economic growth to a compound rate of say 9 per cent per annum, with the world as a single unified market. It would, however, assume among other things that the rate of expansion of production in the industrialized part of the world was even more, say 10 per cent a year. At such a rate of increase of production, labour productivity would rise fairly fast as well. Nevertheless employment and population in the developed part of the world would increase, largely by immigration from the underdeveloped part, by something like 5 per cent a year, or double in approximately fifteen years' time. Some sectors of the economy associated with accommodating an increasing population, like for example building, would attract even more people of whom a large percentage would be immigrants. We cannot, however, afford such a rate of growth, because of the raw material requirements, nor can we actually realize it from a social–political point of view.

Rich countries will just not allow immigration on the scale which would be needed. Should we attempt to increase the global rate of growth nevertheless, the result could be, up to a point, an overspill of demand for products from developed countries' established industries, which are already fully employed, to developing countries' young industries. Simultaneously, however, the result would also be that labour productivity in established industrial countries would increase by more than the modest 3 to 4 per cent a year to which we have grown accustomed. And that, unfortunately, still implies an increase in raw material consumption we can ill afford.

Theoretically it would be possible actually to *reduce* the level of internal expenditure in established industrial countries and produce capital goods for developing countries instead of motor cars, speed-boats, etc., without increasing industrial production. This would mean, in fact and substance even if not necessarily in form, that capital grants for developing countries were financed out of the taxation of established industrial countries. This corresponds to the reality that we need to contain industrial production within what we consider an affordable raw material consumption, but it is decidedly unlikely that rich countries would be prepared to co-operate in an international scheme which was directly to their cost and on a scale offering a real hope of full employment in low-income countries.

Such improvement of the employment position in densely populated low-income countries as is at all possible is more likely to be the result of an increased level of world industrial production as a whole, preferably compensated for by a more economical use of raw materials.

8.7 POLLUTION, MINERALS, AND THE WORLD RENTIER STATE

The concept of a *rentier state* was introduced into economic literature by E. Mahdavi [27*a*].

When a sizeable part of a country's income arises from natural resources' rents rather than from the labour and industry of its citizens, such a country may be called a rentier state.

Mahdavi's emphasis is on rents by (expatriate) extractors of oil and other minerals, and the Middle East oil-producing countries are the obvious examples. The state, assuming the prerogatives of the owner or at least the custodian of the resource, charges royalties, i.e. sells the resource and can distribute the proceeds among the citizens as it sees fit or use the revenue for its own purposes.

One of the peculiar aspects of the lack of well-defined priorities actually existing in Middle Eastern rentier states is the disproportionate growth of government bureaucracy. It would be a perfectly rational policy to hand out a certain share of the resource rent to all citizens as a kind of national dividend without any requirement to do work for it. (*See also* section 7.6 concerning the living allowance.) Instead, the aspirations of the educated minority are satisfied by civil service 'jobs' out of all proportion to the government's genuine requirements for civil service labour.

Similarly, Nigeria maintains an army the size of which can hardly be justified on security grounds alone, now that the civil war is over, except for the one particular security ground that dismissing large numbers of men who have been uprooted from their traditional background and trained to handle weapons might be dangerous, because they might become robbers. There are certain analogies between the Middle Eastern rentier states and the economy of the world, notably an undetermined income distribution and the substitution of one type of income for another. This is so, despite the fact that the situation of the world economy as a whole is not explicitly recognized as that of a rentier state.

When I speak of a *world rentier state* this introduces two new elements.

Firstly, there can be no question of external payments of rent. If an imputed rent for a scarce resource is charged and paid at all, it is paid by some economic agent or institution within the closed world economy.

Secondly, important scarce resources have no defined ownership status, and hence no price. Natural resources which are physically and legally accessible to all major trading nations may be indicated as *world natural resources*. The legal aspect is as equally relevant as the physical-technical one.

For example, the carving-up of the continental shelves among the coastal states has changed the mineral deposits under the shallow seas of these shelves from world resources into national resources. The coastal states can now demand royalties for the exploitation of mineral deposits under their coastal seas in the same way as they can for mineral deposits under land.

In a world in which the nation state is the dominant legal framework for economic institutions to operate in, such national appropriation of world resources is a likely thing to happen. This leaves only certain parts of the environment as *the* major world resources, because they cannot be carved up among nation states.

It is becoming increasingly clear that some of the remaining non-price world resources, like 'clean' ocean water, are in real danger of being exhausted. If there *were* a world economic authority equipped with appropriate powers, the disposal of materials and liquids into the sea would either be subject to stringent administrative restrictions (the use of the ocean would be rationed), or a disposal charge would have to be paid, so that the use of the ocean as a sink would have a price just like an 'ordinary' production factor.

As we saw in section 1.5 the equilibrium price of a production factor is the price which limits the demand for the production factor to the available supply. In the case of environmental factors like seas and the atmosphere, the 'available' supply would be the *acceptable* level of pollution.

If there were no other physical-technical limit to global production, the demand for world production factors would increase proportionally to world income. On the other hand, at any given state of technology, production is limited by the internal labour supply in the dominant industrial countries.

The interaction between two production factors, resource rentals and labour supply, is a well-known economic concept.

We may now reinterpret the results from Chapter 4 of this book as follows. At any set of relative prices there is a tendency towards introducing those production processes which result in the lowest costs per unit of end-product, the relevant costs being the costs at the prevailing set of relative prices.

The concept of induced technical progress means that the speed of adjustment of technology in the direction of increased labour productivity is influenced by a non-price market factor, i.e. the balance between marginal excess supply or marginal excess demand.

The asymmetrical element that induced technical progress favours labour productivity rather than material productivity arises because the supply of materials is much more elastic in the short run.

This asymmetry is not always present: stench and other environmental discomforts are helpful in stimulating environment-sparing production methods, but this is precisely what we would like to avoid. In a world of imperfect competition it is meaningful to distinguish between the long-term equilibrium between supply and demand and the short-term position. The long-term position is based on potentially known technology. It assumes that production makes use only of those of the scientifically known production processes giving rise to the lowest costs per unit of end-product. The short-term position assumes the use of those production methods which are currently traditional in industry.

I submit the following to be a valid description of the long-term equilibrium between supply and demand on a world-wide scale. If 'short-term' and non-resource restrictions like the technological backwardness of underdeveloped countries and the monetary limit on international trade are removed, the demand for world production factors would far outstrip their available supply capacity. Under these conditions rentals on world natural resources would be needed to contain the demand on these resources, and such rentals would be a sizeable fraction of the total value of world income.

The concept of an implied rental on a world production factor is not completely limited to pollution charges. Mineral deposits under the ocean floors and, even more topical in 1973, fishing rights are other possible examples.

It is also conceivable that certain congested international sea-routes can at some stage become bottlenecks in the cheapest shipping routes. The Straits of Dover and Gibraltar seem to be likely candidates, and sea-lane pricing would give rise to another resource rental.

In short, the world is a *rentier state* or is likely to become one, except for the fact that, in the absence of a world economic authority, the rent is not collected.

In actual fact the environment-protecting measures which *can* be taken are mainly the following two:

(*a*) Complete prohibition of certain well-defined types of pollution, either in the whole world or in specific geographic regions, by international agreement.

(*b*) Regulation of the *general* level of world production by means of the monetary limit on international trade.

If total production is contained, the demands on the environment are contained *pro rata.*

This is, up to a point, the situation in which we are living except that the 'regulation' is unplanned and that there is already more pollution than many people, including myself, find wholly acceptable from an environmental point of view.

Note that the distribution of the income imputed to world resources is indeterminate, as it always is in a rentier state. This is quite clear in the (hypothetical) 'explicit' case where it is assumed that this income is paid by producers to a world economic authority. In that case the authority can spend this income as it sees fit, in the same way as the governments of Kuwait and Saudi Arabia can do with oil revenues.

It might be argued that at least the proceeds of pollution charges should be distributed among those who suffer from the pollution. This argument is not generally tenable. In the first place, many environments have to some extent a threshold. If no more than a certain quantity of sewage is poured into a river or into a sea, the result is more plankton and more fish rather than dirty beaches, and no one has to be compensated. Secondly, the equity of paying money to someone living near a polluted beach and not to someone who cannot get to a beach at all is unclear. Thirdly, pollution is to a considerable extent the destruction of the environment of future generations and they cannot be compensated out of present income, except possibly by the roundabout method of investment.

Hence, if we ever seriously consider tackling the problem of global pollution by using the price mechanism, we will need more than just instruments of regulation. We will need rules of equity concerning the distribution of the imputed income.

The same indeterminateness exists in the 'implicit' case when the demand for world resources is contained not by the prices of the resources themselves, but at zero price by the level of global production as regulated by world trade. Note that imperfect competition is here in a sense beneficial, at least from an environmental viewpoint.

Under perfect competition the monetary limit on the value of world trade would not restrict the physical volume of world production. Prices would be adjusted downwards, and more products would be traded for an unchanged sum of money, until global full employment of labour was reached, and this would imply a catastrophically high demand on world natural resources.

Under the regime of imperfect competition actually existing the share of individual countries in the total demand arising from a given level of world imports is determined by the effectiveness of the marketing of national exports and the growth of labour productivity to which this gives rise. From a purely technical point of view it is more or less indeterminate. The more successful among the industrial exporting countries attain domestic full employment, and even high wages, despite the fact that unskilled human labour is not a scarce factor on a world-wide scale.

Substitution of the payment of salary for what is in reality an appropriation of a share in the value of a natural resource is also an analogy with the Middle Eastern rentier states. This second analogy is, however, less complete than the indeterminate distribution of the resource rental itself. The oil countries would function no worse than they do now if they cut out some of their bureaucracy and allowed half their civil servants to sit in their offices and play bridge. Here, salaries are but thinly disguised transfer payments.

The successful industrial countries do not, however, appropriate themselves a share of the value of the world resources; they take a disproportionate share of the resources. This allows their domestic industries to pay salaries well above the remuneration paid for similar work done in less fortunate countries, but the work has to be done. The Middle Eastern analogy would be the government handing out oil concessions to various tribes and towns, and the people would have to do the drilling now done by the expatriate oil companies.

The substitution of a marketing rent booked as an internal labour income, for what is in substance a resource rental, is not confined to world resources in the strict sense.

I have argued earlier in this chapter that the earth rentals to be included in the costs of mined mineral deposits depend on the relative priorities attached to present and future production.

To the extent that actually paid prices in a liquidity-restricted world economy undervalue the rents on nationally controlled mineral deposits, the successful industrial countries also appropriate themselves a disproportionately high share of scarce minerals. And, just as in the case of world resources, we can interpret the associated high incomes as marketing rents which displace the rental value on scarce mineral deposits.

The income distribution is further affected by internal taxes on the minerals or the products into which they are processed in the consuming countries. Petrol duty is the obvious example.

The reader should, however, realize that the analysis in this section depends crucially on the assumptions made in Chapter 4, i.e. the 'elastic' nature of the restriction on production which arises from a limited supply of suitably trained labour and the concept of induced technical progress.

9

The regulated economy and established economic theory

9.1 THE NEO-CLASSICAL MODEL

The term 'neo-classical' is a somewhat curious one. Keynes, in his *General Theory* [21], p. 3 says the term 'classical economist' was invented by Marx and covered Ricardo, James Mill, and their predecessors. Crouch ([9], section 7.1) states that the term 'neo-classical' emerged after the publication of Keynes's *General Theory* and referred to those economists who stuck to the older pre-Keynesian economics, while adjusting their terminology and the concepts in which the theory is formulated, to the dialogue with the Keynesian school. I rate the factual assumptions as the more important distinction, and I shall use the term neo-classical for all adherents of the same assumptions, irrespective of whether they wrote before or after 1936.

The 'classics' like Smith, Malthus, Ricardo, and Say did *not* create a single uniform body of economic theory. Their chief claim to the term 'classical' arises from the fact that they were the people who established economics, or political economy as they would call it, as a recognized subject of study. In so far as there ever was a logically consistent and generally accepted body of theory, this has been formulated by later authors like John Stuart Mill, Wicksell, and Alfred Marshall. In other words we can to a certain extent identify 'the' neo-classical economic theory, but not 'the' classical economic theory.

Our concern here is not with the contribution of particular people but with the logical relation between different economic theories, and the points where they differ.

As the title of this section indicates, we start this comparison by surveying the oldest complete* theory, which is the neo-classical one.

* The reader will note that I imply that any theory older than neo-classical theory is *not* a complete and logically consistent system. However, two theories may *appear* to be different because they are framed in terms of a different set of concepts. I do nevertheless hold that the most well-known 'oppositionist' theory, the Marxist one, is not a complete self-contained theory free of self-contradiction, though not everybody will agree with me on this point. At least one author,

There could, of course, be some doubt about what precisely *is* the content of the neo-classical theory and what is the dividing line between classical and neo-classical theory, if that distinction is made.

Personally I would classify as neo-classical any theory which adheres to the classical postulates of divisibility and competitive behaviour and arrives at a theory of money and interest as an integral part of the theory of value on the basis of these classical assumptions. Classical theory is then, in a sense, incomplete neo-classical theory, because monetary theory, and indeed, monetary institutions were not very well developed in the classical period. This is, however, not a generally accepted classification.

For example, Aschheim and Ching Yao Hsieh [3] make an intrinsic distinction between classical and neo-classical theory. This distinction is that the classics concentrated on production and growth and the neo-classics on value and distribution theory. They then state a 'reconstructed neo-classical model' (pp. 53–5 of their book) in which production is solely a function of employment.

By that reckoning the renewed emphasis on economic growth and its causes, by such authors as Solow using mathematical models, is a resurgence of classicism. I beg to differ. Solow and others have introduced mathematical models; this is their innovation. There is, however, a direct relation between economic growth and new investment on the one hand, and the imputation of a return to capital on the other. As far as I have been able to trace the sequence of ideas, it was Alfred Marshall ([28], Ch. IX, para. 4), who coined the term *quasi-rent* in this respect. *See also* my own *Allocation Models* [17].

The assumed result of perfect competition is that, at the perfect-competition prices, all income is imputed to production factors and none to productive activities. The return to the efficient productive activities is just equal to their costs, and inefficient activities are penalized by losses. It is, however, possible to produce more future products than present products from the same supply of labour and

---

Vickrey [48*a*], has made an attempt to reconcile Marx's theory with Keynes and modern income and expenditure analysis. The German protectionist school (Friedrich List) is another matter. Indeed, there are elements in *my* theory, as applicable to developing countries, which can be related to List. The Germany of List's time was, of course, a developing country, or group of countries. There is, however, hardly any continuity from List to the present day, simply because the neo-classical theory became completely dominant.

material resources by investing in new types of equipment. Therefore we assume that future products cost less than present products.

Quasi-rent is the return to capital which arises when production is measured at constant prices, even if the price structure in each single time period is proportional to the one which equalizes the prices of all product streams in all time periods to their costs. The zero-profit condition, measured at constant prices can be restored by calculating interest as a cost factor.

Society must not only find out which productive activities are efficient from a technical point of view and which are inefficient and hence unprofitable. It is necessary also to choose how and when to use the available resources, which types of products to produce, and when they are to be available.

The building of a certain type of factory may be technically efficient, and there may be a 'perfectly competitive' price structure which allows a firm to build it and recover its costs. Yet the construction of this factory at this particular time may be uneconomical, because its construction competes with the construction of houses and other claims on present production capacity.

The 'perfect-competition' solution to this problem would be to raise the rate of interest and the construction of the factory would become unprofitable. On the other hand, the factory might be undesirable because its operation would deplete valuable natural resources at the cost of later generations.

Again, an adjustment in the price system can make the investment unprofitable, this time by calculating a higher cost for the natural resources, thereby bringing the return on the investment down to a figure below the calculated rate of interest. One cannot well see how one can have a complete theory of value and income distribution without at the same time considering economic growth.

It is true that, among the authors of the period in which the neo-classical theory was dominant and in a more or less complete form, only Schumpeter [42] placed a considerable emphasis on innovation as a cause of growth, as well as on the income effects of innovation.

Provided one accepts the (classical) proposition that a stationary technology results in a stationary economy the imputation of interest on the lines of section 1.12 above is a direct application of the neo-classical approach to valuation, economic growth, and technical change.

What cannot be denied is that *Keynesian* economists, including

Keynes himself, were so preoccupied with the traumatic experience of the Great Depression that they came to identify production with employment. Keynes writes in his *General Theory* (Chapter 20): 'The *employment function* only differs from the aggregate supply function in that it is, in fact, its inverse function and is defined in terms of the wage-unit . . .' True, the last words *are* a qualification since any change in productivity would be reflected in the wage-unit.

It is legitimate, I suggest, to assume that any apparently correct features of earlier theories which are not explicitly denied by later writers are included in their own theories, otherwise we would never be able to relate a consistent and correct theory to a previously existing one, without explicitly stating a fairly large number of established propositions.

The neo-classical theory to be stated below is held to be an approximation of the real world even by its protagonists. No one has ever seriously suggested that its restrictive assumptions are *strictly* true. What matters is whether the theory gives an approximately true picture of reality. The neo-classical theory rests on the following assumptions concerning the world around us, and the reactions of people.

Firstly, one assumes that there is at any point in time a given, limited availability of physical means of production, human labour, land, etc., which enables the economy to produce certain products, but only to a limited amount, by means of a limited collection of known technical processes.

The amounts of the various production factors and the methods which are available to process them into products are most relevant for the state of the economy, but they are assumed to be *exogenous*, that is, not themselves the result of economic events.

This may seem a rather self-evident assumption, but it is not so self-evident as one might think. For example, Ricardo made the contrary assumption concerning human labour. People are 'produced', like cattle, by feeding them. The cost of a labourer is the food, clothing, etc., needed for him to stay alive and fit and able to support a family of sufficient size to ensure continuation of the labouring class.

If the demand for labour increases, the price will rise, and as a result the supply will increase as well, because more labourers can support larger families. That, however, is not part of the later neo-classical model although there are reminiscences of it in the writings of neo-classical authors.

The second neo-classical assumption is the postulate of divisibility (*see also* section 1.7). Any activity which can be pursued at all, can be pursued at any desired scale. If we can build a factory of a certain specification, we can also build a thousand similar factories, provided the inputs are available. Conversely, if we want less of a certain product, we assume that we can reduce the cost of production, the cost of procuring the various production factors and semi-finished products, by the same factor as the output.

One knows that there are indivisibilities. One cannot obtain half the output from one-half of a factory, but one assumes that the size of production units is relatively small and that therefore such indivisibilities as there are do not have important economic consequences.

Thirdly, one postulates the existence of a 'utility' or personal welfare function for every single individual. One assumes that people obtain the maximum 'utility' from the income which they have available by always buying a given product at the lowest price for which they can obtain it, and that they always buy the combination of products which they find most satisfying.

Fourthly, one assumes that firms always maximize the profit which they can obtain from the amounts of production factors which are at their disposal. Furthermore, they will hire or buy more production factors—or alternatively resell or cease hiring production factors which they already employ—if such a disposition is more lucrative than their present use of these factors.

This is related to a fifth assumption, that of a perfect market for production factors. Each owner of a production factor, or of a certain amount of some factor, is assumed to sell or let the service of this factor at the maximum price he can obtain for it. Conversely there is always a firm which, at a slight price concession, could do with an additional unit of any production factor. Therefore the alternative value of the production factors used by any firm is essentially the same as their external price in case of new acquisition. The combination of these assumptions leads to the requirements of *perfect competition*, *zero profit*, and *equilibrium between supply and demand.*

If no restrictions on 'free' competition (like tariffs or special entry requirements for new firms wishing to enter certain sectors of the economy) exist, each firm can produce each product by the most efficient method and at the lowest possible cost. Hence a firm can only expect to sell it at precisely that lowest possible cost and no more.

The product will not be made at less than the lowest possible cost and cannot be sold at more because other firms will offer it at the lowest possible cost.

It is stated here without proof that a set of incomes and prices (including prices of production factors) which allows market equilibrium under perfect competition does exist, given suitable assumptions about the production functions and utility function. As indicated already in this book, increasing returns to scale is the one major and realistic case where these assumptions about the specification of production functions are at odds with reality.

If we wish to apply the zero-profit requirement in a realistic context, that is, if we want to calculate the costs of various products, we face the complication that both production and consumption take place in time. There are two major cases where present production decisions influence the availability of consumer goods and other products for later generations. They are investment (production of capital equipment, machines, buildings, roads, pipelines, etc., now for productive use later) and the use of exhaustible resources.

In the first case, present production and revenue accruing to present production factors can be used either directly for consumption by producing and purchasing consumer goods, or the production factors can be used to produce capital goods and the income to finance the investment needed to produce consumer goods later on. In the second case the production factors themselves are not attributable to any particular time period.

In both cases, the present generation must make up its mind about its priorities between its own present consumption, its own consumption in later years, and the consumption of later generations. Most people would prefer immediate consumption over future consumption, if the amounts were equal.

There is, however, no strict requirement here. Indeed, Keynes, in his *General Theory* ([21], p. 214), made the following, very neo-classical remark that '. . . if the desire to postpone consumption were enough . . . would a process become advantageous, merely because it was lengthy . . . '

Under conditions of economic growth, there is an additional reason for preferring present consumption to future consumption. The utility of yet more consumer goods drops with their number.

Suppose that, by not buying a second suit now, one can enable one's children to buy two extra suits. If those extra suits are going to be a fourth and a fifth one, one might still prefer one extra (second) suit now relative to saving the money and enabling one's son to buy two suits, a fourth and a fifth, from the savings plus interest, quite apart from any preference for one's own immediate consumption. The corresponding interest charge, calculated as cost of production, will make a machine unprofitable, if it does not create more future productive value (i.e. two suits) than just the cost of its initial investment. As we saw in section 1.12, the rate of interest as a cost factor also serves to maintain orderly market conditions when production methods of different degree of mechanization are temporarily serving side by side.

During most of the nineteenth and twentieth centuries the literature (*see* [27]) has paid much attention to capital and investment, but not all that much to the other intertemporal allocation problem, the use of exhaustible raw materials. Yet the two are obviously related. Should, for example, the rate of interest in real terms, after subtracting that part of the nominal rate which is merely compensation for the loss in value of the capital by inflation, be 10 per cent, it would imply we hardly cared what happens in 50 years' time. One unit of value set out at 10 per cent compound interest for 50 years would yield a value after 50 years equal to just over 30 times the initial sum.

Therefore, if we are not prepared to save now in order to finance capital equipment at a real return of less than 11 per cent, and refuse an investment opportunity yielding 10 per cent, we sacrifice 30 units of our grandchildren's consumption in favour of one unit of our own. However, if the real rate of interest is only 1 per cent, the corresponding figure is 1·65 times the initial saving.

Hence, being prepared to invest money in machines and other capital equipment, despite a return of only 1 per cent per annum, reveals an apparent concern about the welfare of our children and grandchildren. Investment at a low rate of interest is rational behaviour, only if we are also prepared to restrict our present consumption of exhaustible natural resources to ensure their availability to our grandchildren.

The penalization of production methods which do not respect such a priority by the price mechanism is a direct generalization of the principle of perfect competition. The conclusion, that a concern for the living conditions, environment, and mineral supplies of our grandchildren and great-grandchildren implies a relatively low rate of return to capital, seems inescapable.

Such a reduction in the return to capital would come about because of the increased costs of raw materials, because of mineral-deposit rents, and possibly because of the higher costs of 'clean' environment-sparing methods of production.

If current prices of raw materials do not reflect the possibility that mineral resources may run out in the future, then there is profit in the speculative acquisition of mineral concessions; this will drive up their price for present exploitation. (*See also* section 8.5.)

The reason that relatively little attention has been paid to the intertemporal allocation of natural resources by neo-classical economics is, no doubt, the fact that the neo-classical authors envisaged that at the relatively low labour productivity of their time, exhausting of natural resources was likely to be a remote problem, far in the future. This is no longer so.

The conclusion that, if we face a threat of pollution and of running out of mineral supplies, the price system ought to make environment-sparing production methods profitable* and material-wasting production methods unprofitable, is a direct generalization of the neo-classical model. The model, however, assumes that the price mechanism will automatically reflect the community's preferences.

I have submitted the contrary proposition that it may be necessary for the state to intervene and enforce, by decree, a price which should 'in theory' have been the result of perfect competition.

The neo-classical conclusion, that price adjustment always equalizes the demand and the supply, is not upheld by me, at least not as a factual conclusion but only as a desideratum. It is desirable to regulate the economy in such a way that demand equals supply, but disequilibrium does unfortunately occur. One particular disequilibrium, unemployment of labour, has, of course, been observed as a fact. It is often resolved in a somewhat tautological way. One postulates a 'labour supply function'. This supply function is assumed to have the 'normal' positive slope, i.e. if people are seen to be not working, they

* The bankruptcy of Rolls-Royce, on the development of a *quiet* engine, is a public scandal. Airports should charge landing rights, not only according to the size of an aircraft, but also according to its noise rating, and pay indemnities to householders for noise nuisance. That would make the development of quieter aircraft profitable!

are assumed to be *unwilling* to work at the prevailing wage rate, preferring free time instead.

9.2 MONETARY VERSUS FISCAL KEYNESIANISM

The essential policy conclusion which Keynes has recommended to his fellow-economists and which has greatly influenced economic thinking since his time is the necessity for the government to regulate the level of economic activity. This regulation was to be effected by means of suitable financial devices.

There are two schools of thought which share this common ground—'the principle of effective demand'—but they have different opinions about the most suitable means to the agreed end.

I shall call these schools 'monetary Keynesianism' and 'fiscal Keynesianism' according to their preferences for the fiscal instrument (the public budget) or the monetary instrument (the manipulation of the capital market by the central bank and by means of the government's own lending policy).

If fiscal regulation is used, spendable income is influenced directly, and people will spend more (or less) according to their changed after-tax income. Monetary policy on the other hand affects in first instance only expenditure by stimulating (or discouraging) the use of credit facilities.

The legitimacy of fiscal Keynesianism's parentage to Keynes is open to questioning, but two circumstances make it impractical to classify it as anything else than Keynesian. There is a large element of common ground with monetary Keynesianism and, secondly, post-Keynesian adherents of the neo-classical system, such as Friedman ([10], section 5), have attacked the theory which was the more radical departure from their own views, *and have presented this as an attack on Keynes's theory.*

In other words, fiscal Keynesianism, although containing more deviations from the neo-classical model than can be found with Keynes, at least in his major work, *General Theory* [21], has been legitimated as Keynesian by the opponents of Keynesianism.

9.3 MONETARY KEYNESIANISM AND THE DEMAND FOR NEW INVESTMENT

There are two ways in which a limited stock of money, and the financial situation in general, influence the real physical part of the economy. The Radcliffe Report [8] distinguishes these two effects as the 'interest incentive effect' and the 'general liquidity effect'.

The interest incentive effect arises because, one assumes, a low interest rate as cost factor influences the decision to invest, favouring financing with borrowed money or even persuading a firm to invest its own money in capital goods, machines, buildings, etc., instead of in interest-bearing titles. The same would presumably apply to durable consumer goods. The general liquidity effect on the other hand means that decisions to purchase goods and services are influenced primarily by the simple availability of money.

As the reader will have noted, I have argued in this book that the influence of money, as far as there is any, is largely direct, through the availability of money as such—the general liquidity effect. Furthermore, I hold that money regulates the nominal income which circulates in the real economy, and that the real physical volume of the level of economic activity is therefore dependent on price and income controls as well. There is so far no agreed opinion among economists about the impact of money or the rate of interest on the real sphere of the economy. Not only is there disagreement about which of the two monetary effects is the more important, but even the relevance of money as such is an object of controversy.

For example, Walters ([50], p. 16), arguing that money *does* matter, 'accuses' Keynes's 'disciples' of suggesting that money has little effect on the level of income. I will, in this and in the next two sections, indicate the logical premises on which a particular view about this problem can be based.

According to the classical (neo-classical) model the price of labour, like the price of any production factor or semi-finished product, is equalized by competition to its marginal productivity, i.e. the excess of the price of any product which could be produced additionally if an additional unit of labour was employed, over the other costs associated with such possible additional production. This is the zero profit condition applied to any activity which would imply increased employment of labour.

If there is unemployment this is 'voluntary'. If unemployed labourers desire to be employed, they should be prepared to work for less than the prevailing, apparently too high, wage rate. This argument has an element of persuasiveness. In an open economy, with a considerable part of the domestic production being sold for export to other countries, it may even be substantially correct. There, excessive wage demands by organized labour may cause unemployment.

In a closed economy without foreign trade (or a nearly closed economy with only little foreign trade), the problem is more complicated. The wage rate is not only a cost factor but also an income determinant. Hence, unless prices drop in proportion to wages, any drop in wages means a drop in consumption of those who must live from the reduced wages. Profits accrue to a large extent either to impersonal institutions, which will retain a large portion of them for some time, or to wealthy people who do not have so much need for an immediate increase in their consumption. Therefore, any reduction in consumption by the labouring class is incompletely compensated by consumption out of profit, if consumption out of profit rises at all, and the money demand for consumer goods drops with wages.

In an open, export-orientated economy such a fall in the demand for consumer goods would be compensated by a rise in exports, but this would not be the case in a closed economy. In a closed economy the long-term effect of a change in wages on *consumption* would be neutral, once the prices had adjusted themselves and assuming no change in investment. This means that one *cannot change* the real level of wages.

Which of the neo-classical assumptions are correct and should be upheld, and which are not and should be rejected? It is quite clear that the actual behaviour of labourers and organized labour has not confirmed the neo-classical model. The price of labour does *not* automatically adjust itself to the requirement that the demand for labour equals its supply. It could be argued that if organized labour is not prepared, for whatever reason, to accept the price which would equalize the supply and demand for labour, then the state should step in with administrative powers and regulation and prescribe certain rates of pay. I have, in the preceding chapters, argued the desirability of such intervention by the state. It is, however, important to distinguish the two arguments for such a policy.

In an *open* industrially developed economy with foreign trade, and a requirement to maintain an external balance of payments (and that, if at all possible, at the prevailing exchange rate, without resort to import controls, duties, and the like), the original neo-classical argument is valid. In an open economy the link between domestic consumption, as a destination of products to be sold, and domestic production is loosened. The concept of a circular flow, where labour income is both cost and income, is the core of Keynes's argument against lower wages as a cure for unemployment of labour. This argument is valid only in a closed economy with little or no foreign trade.

The original neo-classical argument concerning the supply-and-demand equilibrium in the labour market is more valid in an open economy, the more so the greater the dependence of that economy on international trade. The point is explicitly mentioned by Keynes. His *General Theory*, Chapter 19, section ii (2) reads: 'If we are dealing with an unclosed system, and the reduction in money-wages is a reduction relative to money-wages abroad when both are reduced to a common unit, it is evident that the change will be favourable to investment.' Since the Great Depression and especially after World War II, international trade has increased much faster than production, because more efficient and relatively cheaper methods of transport are available. Therefore the neo-classical proposition is now relatively more valid than it was in Keynes's time.

The other quite separate argument concerns the desirability of maintaining *price stability* in the interest of rational calculation* and protecting people with fixed incomes. If prices are already rising, while there is simultaneously unemployment, fiscal and monetary policies alone cannot cure both evils at the same time. They can only redress the one by making the other worse.

One can restore full employment by an expansionist fiscal and monetary policy—increase public expenditure, reduce taxation, reduce the official lending rate, etc.—although this may, and probably will, imply devaluation of the national currency. However, the result of restored full employment and rising prices will probably be a new rise in money wages, resulting in a further rise in prices and also quite possibly unemployment of labour again. Once there is inflation, there is no rational criterion about an appropriate increase in incomes if

* This point is also mentioned by Hansen, following Lerner. *See* A. H. Hansen ([14], end of Chapter 8) and A. P. Lerner [25].

there is no possibility of increasing production. Control over incomes is necessary in order to maintain full employment *and* stable prices.

This argument went the opposite way in the 1930s, since prices were already falling. Since various prices (rents, long-term contracts, etc.) were already fixed, both rational calculation and social cohesion called for stabilization, i.e. the prevention of any further fall in the general price level.

In any case it is one of the assumptions of Keynes and Keynesian economic theory that the price of labour does not automatically equate its supply and demand. One can assume either that the price of labour is 'change resisting', largely fixed by tradition and long-term contracts (clearly Keynes's own assumption), or that it is controlled by incomes policy. The neo-classical assumption that the price equalizes the supply of and the demand for *products* is, so far, upheld.

The supply of total production, if it is not the actually realized output is, to my mind, the production capacity in a technical sense, that is, the output which can be produced with the help of the employed labour and the installed capacity.

The implication is that there is no such thing as underemployed capital equipment. I find this assumption hard to swallow and I have some doubts if Keynes, as a politically engaged citizen, genuinely believed the policy conclusions which are the logical outcome of the assumptions of monetary Keynesianism. There are, however, some good reasons for assuming that it is the correct interpretation of Keynes's economic theory. Even if—as I am inclined to believe—Keynes and many of his followers had not seriously thought about this particular problem, we later users of economic theories require a logically consistent version, irrespective of the actual opinions of its author. The economic theory, to which I have attached the name 'monetary Keynesianism', is such a theory.

We must also consider the tradition and Keynes's place in the transmission of ideas from earlier writers to a later generation. His *General Theory* opened, in its very first chapter, with a frontal attack on the tautological argument of unemployment being voluntary, because actual employment is the equilibrium between supply and demand at the prevailing price. No similar attack is made against the same proposition with respect to other production factors and produced capital equipment. Should we not, from his silence on this point, infer that Keynes accepted the neo-classical conclusion that the price equalizes the supply and the demand in each product market?

The assumptions of perfect competition certainly imply just that. In a perfectly competitive market an individual firm serving only a tiny fraction of the total market can, and will, ensure full-capacity operation of its equipment by underbidding its rivals by a tiny margin and thereby increasing its sales at their cost.

The theory which arises if one assumes perfect price-adjustment in all markets except one, the labour market, is perfectly consistent from a logical point of view. Its conclusions depend to a certain extent on whether or not one admits substitution between capital and labour. If it is possible to increase labour productivity merely by adding machines, then the productivity of employed labour will increase during a depression or recession. Some firms will go into liquidation and their surviving competitors will buy their equipment for use by their own labour force. Alternatively, one can assume complementarity, at least for existing machines. Existing machines can only be worked at a specific labour productivity. In that case the assumption of perfect competition leads to the conclusion that even if demand in money terms drops, and the realized rate of return on capital drops with it, this does not correspond to a reduction in physical production, except with respect to those productive activities where the return to capital drops below zero. Then production is stopped and the equipment is scrapped. Bankruptcy may have occurred long before that but, in a perfectly competitive economy, it would have been worthwhile for the holders of the various bonds, bank loans etc., to take over the ownership of a firm's assets and to run it at a return below their legal right to interest, rather than receiving nothing.

The consequence of full-capacity utilization of all equipment which is in productive use at all is that a reduction in the rate of interest would always make new investment profitable, although at a lower return to capital. As long as there is any return to real capital, any positive difference between proceeds from sales and current operating costs—and this positive difference is expected to remain positive in the future—it pays to invest. The return to capital may be small, but as long as it is there at all* one can find a low enough rate of interest at which it is profitable to invest.

* There is a theoretical possibility that a machine would earn itself a return insufficient to repay the initial investment. However, the case *against* the regulation

In this respect the eleventh chapter of the *General Theory* ('The marginal efficiency of capital') is still the original source text from which later economists have developed the investment evaluation technique known as *discounted cash flow.*

Suppose an investment ('an asset', to use Keynes's terminology) is expected to produce a yield—a surplus of the proceeds of the sales of its products over its operating cost—of £10 million in each of ten successive future years. Then, at a rate of interest of 5 per cent a year, the present value of the prospective yield of this investment is:

$$10\left(\frac{1}{1{\cdot}05}+\frac{1}{1{\cdot}05^2}+\frac{1}{1{\cdot}05^3}+\ldots\frac{1}{1{\cdot}05^{10}}\right)=80$$

If the cost of purchasing or producing the asset (e.g. building a factory, ordering a machine, etc.) is also 80, this investment will be profitable for a rate of interest of less than 5 per cent per annum and unprofitable if the rate of interest is in excess of 5 per cent.

Potential investment projects vary and the rate of interest at which they are just profitable is different from project to project. The list of investment opportunities will then give rise to a demand schedule for finance capital, just like an ordinary price. If the rate of interest drops, projects are added to the list of profitable projects, and if the rate of interest rises some projects become unprofitable because of the high cost of financing them.

The idea of a finance-capital demand function and a corresponding supply function, with the rate of interest as a price which equalizes the demand for finance capital by industry and its supply by capitalists and investors, is not a fundamentally new innovation by Keynes. He 'only' spelled out in detail the implications of the neo-classical model for capital theory. If Keynes's theory on money and interest, to be discussed in the next section, and his investment theory, as discussed in this section, are combined with the classical assumption that the price equates the supply and the demand in each (sub)market, the classical policy conclusion of non-intervention stands. Any consistent monetary policy, including the metallistic system, generates the same price structure (according to the classical model). Even the real rates

---

of the level of investment by means of the rate of interest, assumes, just as monetary Keynesianism, that there is a return to capital. The real limit on investment is given by the sales prospect of the end-product.

of interest would be the same, once the price systems were brought on a common footing by introducing appropriate deflators. The mechanism by which this equilibrium establishes itself had not been fully spelled out by the (neo)-classics. Keynes's theory completes the classical system on this point. (*See also* R. L. Crouch [9], Chapter 7.) The only actual deviation from the neo-classical model which we have met until now is the relaxing of the perfect-competition assumption concerning the price of labour.

9.4 THE KEYNESIAN THEORY OF MONEY AND INTEREST*

Let us recall section 1.14 and the quantity of money theory (in connection with international liquidity) in section 8.2. The quantity of money theory assumes that the amount of money needed to circulate a given total income is a fixed fraction of that income. In section 1.14 we discussed the simple example of monthly payment.

The ratio between the money needed for circulation, and the income to be circulated, is assumed to be given by the institutions and customs of a society, namely, the percentages of workers paid per week, per month, per year, the structure of the trade channels, etc.

Traders require cash holdings just as much as private persons. Hence, if it is customary for factories to sell directly to shops, less money is needed for circulation than if there are intermediate wholesale traders, who also require cash balances. 'Circulation requirement' is, however, not the only reason for holding money.

People, and firms, keep some cash available because they *may* want to spend it at some time. How much they will deem to be a prudent reserve depends also on the return they are likely to make by investing the money, putting it in an interest-yielding deposit account, buying a bond, etc.

A family may normally spend £100 each month. Then £100 is the necessary cash reserve. At a fairly low rate of interest they may, however, find it desirable to keep about £300 ready in cash or in a current-account bank balance. At a much higher rate of interest they would want to invest a part of the £200 'extra cash' in some interest-bearing title. This 'liquidity-preference' effect will give rise to a demand function for holdings of extra cash. The lower the rate of interest, the

* *See also* Chapter XIV of G. Ackley [1].

more money people, and firms, will want to hold as extra cash. Conversely, the higher the rate of interest, the less extra cash is kept, and more money is invested in interest-bearing titles. The demand function for liquid reserves *is therefore at the same time the supply function for finance capital.* At any given level of income and a given stock of money, the amount of money people are willing to invest in interest-bearing titles is a function of the rate of interest.

A noticeable (but not a logically necessary) feature of the Keynesian theory of money and interest is the assumed absence of an interest-response of consumers' intertemporal distribution of expenditure. According to the neo-classical theory (and any theory which postulates rational welfare-maximizing behaviour of consumers), people will put money in a deposit account on interest, or buy themselves an interest-bearing bond or certificate, so as to spend the initially saved money and the interest with it at some later stage. The fact that interest is paid is one of the things which persuade people to save for later consumption, instead of spending their money now. Keynes flatly denies this.

I quote: 'An act of individual saving means—so to speak—a decision not to have dinner today. But it does *not* necessitate a decision to have dinner or to buy a pair of boots a week hence or a year hence or to consume any specified thing at any specified date.' (*General Theory*, the first two sentences of Chapter 16.)

Instead, there is the concept of the 'propensity to consume'. This means people will spend a certain percentage of their income and save the rest, quite independent of the yield on any investment which they may obtain from their savings.

There may be an element of reality in this contention, in particular if a large part of private saving is more or less involuntary, like repaying a mortgage on one's house or paying pension premiums; but it is a departure from the neo-classical model, which is the more noticeable in *monetary* Keynesianism because some other, certainly not more realistic, elements of the neo-classical model are upheld.

The particular combination of assumptions we have described—a fixed (exogenous) price of labour, perfectly competitive price adjustment in product markets, and zero interest-elasticity of the demand for consumer goods—leads to the conclusion that the rate of interest is *the* most suitable instrument to control the level of investment and economic activity in general.

A reduction in the rate of interest, to be brought about by increase in bank credit to the business sector or by the purchase of its own bonds by the Treasury, is associated with an increase in the amount of money in circulation. That increase in the money supply should *not*, according to the 'monetary' school, be brought about via the public budget, which ought to balance. Other instruments that could be used to stimulate consumption, such as a deficit on the public budget, created by paying old-age pensions and unemployment benefit, or a direct increase in public expenditure on roads, public buildings, etc., or a cut in taxation, are deemed by monetary Keynesianism to be inflationary. For they affect in the first instance only consumption, and they stimulate investment (according to this particular theory) only after prices have risen, making investment profitable. If Keynes's special assumption of zero interest-response of consumption is dropped, the rest of the theory of monetary Keynesianism still stands. The effectiveness of monetary policy as an instrument of economic regulation is even enhanced, now affecting investment *and* consumption. The special claim of 'sound' finance is, however, lost. Stimulation of consumption by means of easy hire-purchase cannot be called a particularly 'sound' financial policy.

9.5 FISCAL KEYNESIANISM

There are some concessions to the policy recommendations of fiscal Keynesianism which can be obtained from the theory which underlies monetary Keynesianism.

Keynes had placed a considerable emphasis on *expectation* as a criterion for investors' current decisions: *see*, for example, *General Theory*, Chapter 13, section ii. Now one result of an (attempted) reduction in the rate of interest by deliberate policy might be uncertainty about future rates and, in particular, speculative anticipation of a recovery to the former higher level. In that situation it is simply impossible to reduce the effective rate of interest once it is considered to be already below normal. The business community would prefer to hold cash rather than interest-bearing titles. The monetary authorities would buy bonds, thereby bringing cash into the economy, but the prices of bonds would not rise.

There can be no question of a 'general liquidity effect' of the increased stock of money under those circumstances. The money is held for speculative purposes, whereas a general liquidity effect assumes that the money is used for transactions and is spent. In other words, the stock of money increases, but nothing else happens. This effect is known as the *liquidity trap*.

The actual deviation from Keynes's original theory comes with the assertion that the rate of interest itself is not all that important. For example, in his book *The Keynesian Revolution* ([22], p. 117) L. R. Klein writes: 'Economists are . . . coming to the conclusion that the rate of interest is not a very important variable in the modern world, but that theories of the rate of interest are in a most unsatisfactory state.' They are indeed, if one drops the notion of market equilibrium by the price without offering a logically consistent alternative.

It is quite possible to drop Keynes's (i.e. the neo-classical) theory for the determination of the level of real investment and at the same time maintain Keynes's theory of money and interest. But *one needs another alternative theory which explains the level of real investment.* Klein does not offer us much indication of one, at least not in the publication cited.

It is, however, clear from other publications that Klein's opinion in this respect originates from his econometric work. The Klein-Goldberger model ([23]; *see also* Goldberger [11]) contains an investment-demand function, which relates the demand for new investment to the previous period's income from sources other than employment (profits, rents, etc.) and to business liquidity. This may or may not be adequate as a means to *forecast* the level of investment at a particular time. It cannot be the full explanation. We must assume firms invest not only because they have money available, but because they want the capital goods for their future contribution to production. The timing of the actual execution of investment programmes can, of course, be determined by the availability of funds.

Klein does not stand alone in this respect. If all was well, econometrics would be the quantitative expression of the economics appearing in the textbooks. In fact, econometricians have rarely been able to obtain statistical estimates of economic theory in the form in which it figures in the general economics textbooks.

One assumes that Klein and Goldberger have investigated the impact of the rate of interest on investment but have been unable to find any.

Back in the 1930s a group of Oxford economists investigated the impact of the rate of interest on businessmen's investment decisions by means of a survey [31]. They reported that the majority of businessmen did not consider the rate of interest an important factor in their investment decisions.

In 1959 the official *Radcliffe Report* [8] commented at p. 131 about the interest incentive effect: 'We have sought, without much success, for convincing evidence of its presence in recent years.' But more recently Evans [9*a*], pp. 133–42, conducted a survey of econometric work. Evans, and following him Glahe [10*a*], p. 102, claim that this survey shows that the rate of interest *does* influence firms' investment. It does not prove this to me. Rates of interest are high when money is scarce and the figures do not show whether investment drops because credit is dear, or because it is not available. Moreover, if the rate of interest is raised, by deliberate act of policy, the government is clearly of the opinion that investment ought to be curtailed. Firms might well take notice, before the government resorts to the use of the fiscal instrument as well. It does not prove that the monetary theory is intrinsically true.

There is no clearly distinguishable authoritative theory associated with fiscal Keynesianism, but only a measure of common ground on certain issues of economic regulation.

It may be summarized by the following points:

(i) The rate of interest as such does not significantly influence the level of investment, except possibly investment in certain specially low-yielding assets.

(ii) The stock of money does not under normal conditions have a significant influence on economic conditions, and the abnormal conditions of liquidity crisis should preferably be avoided.

(iii) The main instrument of economic regulation, given a certain income- and price-structure, is the public budget, in order to ensure that the total demand for products is approximately equal to the cost of full-employment production.

9.6 PRICE INFLEXIBILITY AND UNCERTAINTY

Under this heading we discuss a theory which R. L. Crouch, in the final, sixteenth chapter of his *Macroeconomics* [9], calls the Clower–Leijonhufvud reinterpretation of Keynes. This theory ascribes the failure of a real economy to function in the manner of the (neo)-classic 'perfect competition' model to the fact that price adjustments require time. In this connection Clower [7] and Leijonhufvud [24] refer to Hicks, who in the tenth chapter of his *Value and Capital* [18] had introduced the term 'false prices'.

Hicks and Clower–Leijonhufvud assume that the price maintains some sort of long-run equilibrium between supply and demand. This is related to Walras's [49] concept of 'tâtonnement', i.e. blind search for equilibrium.

A price which is the continuation of a previous period's price will not, however, equate the demand and the supply in a particular market in a particular time period. Here Leijonhufvud introduces the term 'false trading'. He goes one step farther than Hicks, in that he analyses the impact of transactions at non-equilibrium prices on incomes and on the supplies and demands for separate products. Here the Keynesian multiplier mechanism, for example, comes into place.

The position of the accelerator mechanism needs some further discussion. I have defended the accelerator principle by assuming a systematic discrepancy between the market rate of interest and the higher return to fully-employed real capital. This is a more radical departure from the neo-classical model than Clower and Leijonhufvud are prepared to make.

One can defend the accelerator with arguments much nearer to both Keynes and the neo-classical school. Indeed, one chapter of the *General Theory* (22, 'Notes on the trade cycle') seems to indicate that Keynes's own theory was as follows.

Recall the position of monetary Keynesianism, which holds that a change in the current demand for goods and services causes price adjustment, and that this price adjustment in its turn causes a change in the profitability of new investment. Now if, for whatever reason, the assumed price response does not actually materialize, the *expectation* of a future price change is as good as the actual change itself.

Expectations are not necessarily consistent and the expectation of higher prices of product *X* would lead to orders for new investment by firms in industry *X* but not in other industries which supply semi-finished inputs to industry *X*. Clearly there is ample room for 'false trading' caused by business cycles generated by the accelerator.

Actually, Clower and Leijonhufvud did not pay much attention to this problem, even though Keynes himself placed some emphasis on expectations. Yet the accelerator argument would greatly strengthen the case for the next step in the Leijonhufvud interpretation of Keynesianism. *Because* 'false trading' occurs, a temporary discrepancy between supply and demand is not a reliable guide to the true equilibrium price. Therefore firms will postpone price adjustment until it becomes evident that a discrepancy between supply and demand is more than just an occasional fluctuation, easily bridgeable by a temporary variation in stocks. This uncertainty about future market conditions is assumed to prompt firms to adopt a 'wait and see' attitude in their pricing policies. Under such conditions the prevailing prices have a tendency towards self-perpetuation, except in the presence of a persistent discrepancy between supply and demand. The result is a theory which admits that there is temporary, short-term disequilibrium, and that this short-term disequilibrium has its own momentum, while at the same time maintaining the classical model as a condition for long-term equilibrium.

I suppose many adherents of fiscal Keynesianism would gladly adhere to this theoretical framework. The words 'false prices' and 'false trading' have, however, normative overtones to which one might wish to take exception. These terms assume that complete equilibrium between supply and demand is the normal case, the temporary disequilibrium the exception.

The central notion of fiscal Keynesianism is, however, that one cannot expect the price system to fulfil its market-clearing function precisely in any separate time period. Therefore, 'temporary' disequilibrium is the normal situation and it is the job of the regulating government to keep such discrepancies within a reasonable order of magnitude by means of appropriate manipulations of aggregate demand.

9.7 FISCAL KEYNESIANISM AND OLIGOPOLY

In this section I give my own theory on the demand for investment, as it arises from the theory of the oligopolistic market equilibrium. The policy inferences, as far as they refer to the capitalistic free-enterprise economy, are broadly similar to those I listed in section 9.5 as fiscal Keynesianism. This is not to say that it is *the* theory of fiscal Keynesianism since there will be adherents of the policy recommendations who do not share my view on the economic theory. Also, an economic theory with greater similarity to the neo-classical model would conclude that a moderate degree of regulation restores the supposed results of the neo-classical theory: full-capacity utilization of both labour and capital.

I find that such a modest amount of regulation (*see* section 6.3) restores full employment in the social sense, while leaving a systematic under-utilization of capital, even where we may be prepared to accept such under-utilization.

There is also one noticeable difference in the theory itself, at least with one version of fiscal Keynesianism. Most adherents of fiscal Keynesianism, following the *General Theory*, relate investment to the level of income (or to profits). If this is meant to be an expenditure multiplier, I beg to differ. The availability of funds cannot be the full explanation of why firms invest. We must distinguish between investment programmes and the level of investment at a particular time. Investment programmes are affected by the prospects of profitable use of new equipment, while the pace of implementing existing programmes is influenced by firms' ability to finance an investment budget in a particular time period. This means that expenditure multipliers can serve reasonably well for *forecasting* the immediate future, without giving a complete explanation.

I now proceed to describe my own theory. I submit, first of all, that there is no automatic price adjustment in each product market and that a discrepancy between supply and demand is normal. Potential supply, industry's capacity to produce, is normally greater than the demand which is realized at the prevailing price. One can, if so desired, 'translate' this situation in the terms of monetary Keynesianism. The prospective return on any investment project consists of two components. One is the estimated benefits from the technically possible full-capacity production; the other is the expected degree of utilization of that production capacity.

A contraction in the demand for the end-product will, of course, reduce the expected yield on new investment.

If one assumes that product prices equate supply and demand, a contraction of demand in money terms will push prices downwards and the financial return of full-capacity production drops. This is the theory of monetary Keynesianism. The contention of (my version of) fiscal Keynesianism is, however, that the calculated return on planned investment drops in case of a stagnating market, because firms cannot expect to operate additional capacity to its technical limit. There may, and probably will be, some price adjustment in response to a disequilibrium between production capacity and demand for the product, but the main result of variations in demand is likely to be variation in the level of plant utilization, not price adjustment.

Surplus capacity is more or less unavoidable in an oligopolistic market and can be classified under three headings: random, systematic, and recessionary. Random surplus capacity is the result of 'false trading' as discussed in the previous section. If that were the full story, one might conclude that full-capacity utilization would be attained, at least in some important sectors of the economy, at some time during the top of each phase of the business cycle.

I submit, however, that this is not generally true. Unless the government maintains a fairly comprehensive system of planning, backed up by controls like price regulation and capital rationing, surplus capacity is the rule and temporary attainment of physical full-capacity production the exception.

The systematic component arises because, for reasons which I explained in some detail earlier in this book, the return to fully-employed real capital of the most modern type is well above the cost of financing new investment. It therefore pays to build a new factory, even if its degree of utilization is likely to be well below full-capacity production. Firms considering new investment will therefore add new facilities to their production capacity, until it has increased to well beyond the point where the actual production of the industry would be limited by demand factors rather than by the (increased) supply capacity. In a partially regulated oligopolistic market there is an apparent asymmetry between full employment of labour in the social sense and surplus production capacity inside the average oligopolistic firm. This asymmetry is enhanced because full employment of labour in the social sense is a major yardstick of effective economic regulation and because a maximum price for labour (an incomes policy) is one of the major instruments of economic regulation.

The random and the systematic surplus capacity together constitute the normal surplus capacity, as distinct from recessionary surplus capacity. It will not always be possible to distinguish clearly between the two components of normal surplus capacity, the random and the systematic. The normal level of surplus capacity is determined by two, often interlocking, factors: general uncertainty about future market conditions and the relation between price and marginal cost. The ratio between the price of the product and the marginal full-production cost is determined, via the oligopolistic market equilibrium, by the technology of the industry. If there are substantial indivisibilities and if the 'know-how' of the industry is complicated, there are only a relatively low number of firms; in a strongly concentrated oligopolistic market it does not pay to compete. With a high degree of concentration the marginal cost, even the marginal full-production cost of newly created production capacity of the most efficient type, is well below the price of the product.

Therefore, if future market conditions are uncertain, it pays to invest in new production capacity in a strongly concentrated market even if the likely outcome is that the new production capacity will not be operated to the full for some time. One can afford to risk investing without much return, because if perchance the market is better than expected, there is good profit.

The recessionary surplus capacity is associated with downward price rigidity, i.e. the oligopolistic market is incapable of adjusting supply capacity by means of price reduction (recall section 1.9).

The profit of a separate firm is maximal if the additional revenue to be obtained from increasing the planned full-capacity production, less the price concession needed to obtain the increased market share required to sell it, is equal to the marginal full-production cost. This marginal full-production cost includes the cost of new investment and research but not the overheads of the firm's central administration and research establishment. At the same time the number of firms in the market is stable if the sales price just covers the total cost per unit for the least efficient firm in the industry. However, if there is a substantial surplus capacity, the number of firms in the industry is not in stable equilibrium.

Most firms will find it desirable to have some surplus capacity, better indicated as 'normal standby capacity', even at a moment when demand is relatively high. If, due to recessionary tendencies in the economy, demand drops to well below production capacity, the 'abnormally high' part of this surplus capacity is the recessionary surplus capacity.

The established firms in an oligopolistic market can react to such a situation of disequilibrium in two different ways. If they continue to behave competitively in the limited oligopolistic sense, there is a certain price adjustment which may not be sufficient to restore the equilibrium between production capacity and the demand for the product. With surplus capacity, the profit of a firm which continues to compete is maximal if the price, less the average price concession needed to sell an additional unit of product, is equal to marginal operating cost. There will in that case be a partial adjustment, a reduction of the industry's production capacity, since some firms will be unable to finance interest charges on external finance capital, and they will be driven out of business. If the remaining firms continue to behave competitively, the reduction in the number of firms in the market will continue, until one of the two following limits is reached first. Either the surplus capacity is eliminated, or a new temporary oligopolistic equilibrium is reached with persisting surplus capacity and a lower number of firms in the market. A reduction in the number of firms makes the price elasticity of the demand for the output of each individual firm again consistent with the ratio between average and marginal cost, which is now marginal operating cost. In section 1.9, we found that the profit of an individual firm is maximal if the price elasticity of the demand for its product equals the reciprocal of the ratio between its fixed costs and its total costs.

When the firm is operating well below full capacity, the capital charge on its technical installations becomes part of its fixed cost, since expansion is not considered and no additional investment costs are associated with an increase in output.

For example, if marginal full production cost is 90 per cent of average cost, and marginal operating cost is 80 per cent of average cost, the equilibrium number of firms at full-capacity production corresponds to a price elasticity for the demand for the product of a single firm of $1:(1-0{\cdot}9) = 10$. With surplus capacity this figure drops to $1:(1-0{\cdot}8) = 5$. We should, however, remember that one of the conditions which determines the oligopolistic market equilibrium is the potential threat of outside competition.

The price at which it would pay an outsider to enter the market is inversely related to the degree of capacity-utilization in an industry. If there is surplus capacity, it will pay an outsider to enter the market only if the price is well above the cost per unit of full-capacity production. This means that surplus capacity limits competition to the competition between the established firms in an industry.

Under conditions of surplus capacity the established firms can therefore try to come to agreement with each other and form a *cartel*, and prevent the full market-adjustment to happen. Firms can undertake not to sell below an agreed minimum price, or not to sell more than an agreed quotum, or to limit their operations to certain submarkets, leaving the rest of the market reserved for other members of the cartel.

The possibility of cartel formation limits competition under surplus capacity even more than the presence of oligopoly does.

If there were a clear-cut distinction between the conditions of normal capacity-utilization and recessionary under-utilization, there would probably be two models of price determination, each valid under its own specific conditions.

At normal capacity production the price equates the supply capacity to demand plus a normal standby capacity, and firms behave competitively in the limited oligopolistic sense. Under conditions of substantial (i.e. recessionary) surplus capacity, the market condition is less competitive and price adjustment in a downward direction is blocked by cartel formation, informal understanding, and price leadership. As long as the condition of recessionary surplus capacity prevails, the price is a function of costs, the cost per unit of the least efficient firms being the lower limit.

In the extreme, this can even imply a negative price elasticity of supply, because a cartelized market reacts to a contraction of demand by increasing the price per unit, in order to recover costs from a lower turnover. Price-regulating cartel behaviour of this type is, however, a disequilibrium symptom associated with a temporary recession in demand.

Should a given percentage of surplus capacity persist for a longer period of time, the cartel will, as long as it lasts, keep all its members in business. The stronger and more progressive firms will, however, be in a position to increase their efficiency in the course of time and eventually the cartel will break down because the stronger firm can afford to outbid the weaker and keep a normal return for itself, even at the lower price needed to outbid a weaker rival. If this happens, it means that a new oligopolistic equilibrium has established itself with, in a smaller market, a lower number of firms.

I argued earlier in the book that the accelerator mechanism (*see* section 6.4) presupposes the presence of surplus capacity as a normal condition. I have now given the theoretical argument why this is so.

The adaptation of firms' production capacity to the expected demand for the end-product by means of the flexible accelerator mechanism *can*, I submit, be used as the sole method of regulating the total demand for investment in an oligopolistic economy. The percentage of an investment programme implemented in a particular time period would in that case depend on technical factors. These could be delivery times, gestation lags, administrative delays in implementing individual investment projects, and so on. General caution could also operate with firms adapting their production capacity only gradually to the expected demand for the end-product.

This would presuppose regulation of total demand in the first instance by primary demand, i.e. consumption and public expenditure only. Loan capital would always be available to a creditworthy borrower at the going rate of interest.

In reality the limited availability of funds restricts investment to a certain extent.

We cannot, however, assume that the availability of funds is the *main* determinant of the level of investment. If a restrictive monetary policy kept investment substantially below its technical demand for a somewhat longer period of time, while the demand for the end-product continued to increase, the systematic surplus capacity would disappear.

Full-capacity utilization, if attainable at all, is a stable situation only in a system of comprehensive planning with strict rationing of capital and not in a free-enterprise capitalist economy.

If full-capacity utilization existed under conditions of free-enterprise oligopoly, it would pay firms to bid for loan capital, thereby driving up the rate of interest, the return on fully employed capital of the most modern type being higher than the rate of interest. The result of both the full-capacity utilization itself and of the rising cost of interest would be a general upward pressure on prices. Then, if costs were controlled (and the demand for the end-product continued to expand), the non-labour share in the national income would increase to such an extent that increased savings would permit a higher level of investment. The restrictive monetary policy, if combined with an expansive fiscal policy, would not bite. The higher level of investment would then once more permit the creation of a systematic surplus capacity, as is normal under conditions of oligopoly.

If costs were not kept in check, the same result would arise from a stagnating volume of demand, for the reasons discussed in section 3.2.

Conceivably, periods of purely fiscal regulation and monetary 'stop' could alternate.

During the periods of fiscal regulation total demand would be regulated only by incomes control and fiscal policy, and during shorter periods of squeeze, investment would be less than its technical demand because of the limited availability of funds.

Such a 'go-stop'* policy is obviously undesirable. The realistic case for an effective contribution of monetary policy to the control of total demand is its use as an auxiliary to the fiscal instrument, while the more active use of a restrictive monetary policy is held in reserve. This would be achieved by combining a mildly restrictive monetary policy with regular expansion of primary demand.

Budget restrictions would limit the investment of some firms but not of all, and total investment would be marginally less than if the same technical demand for investment was combined with a completely elastic supply of loan capital. Eventually an equilibrium would establish itself, the same level of realized investment being the result of a somewhat stronger technical demand for investment than would have arisen without monetary restrictions.

A mildly restrictive monetary policy would also ensure that no large sums of excess liquidity were available in the economy. Should therefore the government decide to resort to a temporary squeeze of credit or some other more strongly restrictive monetary policy, investment would indeed be curtailed.

Positive stimulation of total demand on the other hand would have to rely primarily on fiscal regulation.

9.8 THE THEORY OF OLIGOPOLY

This section is concerned with the theory of oligopoly itself. It deals with the systematic reasons for the existence of oligopolistic market structures, rather than with macro-economic implications. Oligopolistic market structures are caused by two groups of phenomena: by technical obstacles to new firms entering the market, and by factors which limit the competition between firms already in it. The technical aspect is discussed first.

Suppose there are at least two firms in a perfect market for a product

* This term is used by me, rather than the more common 'stop-go', to emphasize the element of imbalance in the 'go' phase.

of uniform quality and that buyers buy always from the cheapest suppliers, thereby compelling all firms to sell at the same price. Oligopoly is then explained by the fact that the most efficient methods of production require a certain size of plant and that this most efficient size corresponds to a sizeable share of the market for the product.

An entrepreneur, who considers whether to enter the market for a certain product and to build a factory for its production, has to consider the impact of his own entry on the price of the product.

For example, if the lowest cost per unit of product is obtained at a scale of operations determining a supply of 10 per cent of the market, a plant of the corresponding size will not be built unless there is a prospect of profit even *after* the price has adjusted itself to a 10 per cent increase in the supply. If the price elasticity of the demand for the product is 0·5, then a 10 per cent increase in the demand can be obtained only by a 20 per cent reduction in the price. This puts the 'maximum oligopoly rent' at 20 per cent, i.e. existing operators of plants of the most economical size can enjoy a surplus profit of up to 20 per cent before this will attract investment in a new plant of a similar scale.

The oligopoly rent may be reduced to a more modest figure when an outsider enters at a smaller scale with higher cost per unit than the technically possible minimum.

Suppose an outsider enters the market with a factory producing a 5 per cent addition to the supply, at a cost per unit 5 per cent above the lowest possible cost that can only be realized when operating on a larger scale. This will reduce the price of the product by 10 per cent, leaving the larger and most efficient producers a residual oligopoly rent of 10 per cent and the newcomer 5 per cent. Assuming that the newcomer chose the plant size most profitable under the prevailing conditions, the resulting moderation of the oligopoly rent will prevent further new entries, until the rising demand for the product has again increased that rent.

The theory of oligopoly, as described above, is due to Bain [3*b*] and can also be found, condensed in a much shorter paper, in Modigliani [32*a*] who wrote a review article summarizing both Bain and the Italian original of Sylos-Labini [44].

Chamberlin [5], [6], who created the very notion of oligopoly, is not so easy to place, because there are elements of several alternative theories in his work. There is a central notion in Chamberlin's work which is also a logically necessary element of Bain's theory and I shall, therefore, speak of the Chamberlin–Bain theory. This is the notion of the U-shaped cost curve.

Up to a certain 'optimal' scale, costs per unit of product are a decreasing function of the scale of operations, i.e. the output-return per unit of input is an increasing function of the scale. When the scale of operations is increased beyond this 'optimal point', the opposite tendency of decreasing returns to scale prevails.

I quote (Chamberlin [5], p. 21):

> 'The cost curve of an individual producer must always have these general characteristics, no matter what the commodity (or the service), since there must always be a scale of production which is more efficient than any other, and on either side of which costs will be higher.'

In fact, the relevant distinction is whether this most efficient scale results in production which is a minuscule fraction of the total demand in the market, a sizeable part of the total demand, or more than the whole market can absorb.

If the production of the optimum-size plant is a minuscule fraction of the market, the result is perfect competition. If the market share of the optimum-scale plant is sizeable, we have a Chamberlin–Bain type oligopoly. If in a continuous range of technically possible scales the lowest possible cost per unit of product requires a scale in excess of the capacity of the market to absorb, the result is monopoly.

A logical corollary of the Chamberlin-Bain oligopoly theory is the *merger theorem*, which does not appear to be well developed in existing literature on the subject.

If one assumes rational behaviour—profit maximization—it follows that a firm which is too small to attain the most efficient scale will solicit merger with another firm, whenever the market structure makes its own displacement by a larger firm possible. This phenomenon does not arise under perfect competition. In an atomistic market, new firms using the most efficient methods of production enter the market all the time, and a plant of sub-optimal size can only be operated at a loss. In an oligopolistic market the presence of the oligopoly rent makes it possible for a firm of sub-optimal size to continue operating if it so chooses. In any case the purchase of a firm of sub-optimal size by a larger firm gives the new combination the same possibilities as the where $\rho_{LM} = \rho[\mathbf{L},\mathbf{M}] = \{\mathbf{a}_L{}^T\mathbf{a}_i\}$, $\mathbf{a}_L$ is the design unit gradient vector of the limit state function of target safety, $\mathbf{a}_i$ is the design unit gradient vector of limit state of the ith inspection event, β_L is the reliability index of the limit state of interest, and β_M is the reliability index corresponding to the limit state function of the crack measurement.

Summary

The updated reliability indexes for the three inspection events are now available. The information can be used to develop the maintenance strategy.

Updating Inspection Interval

Suppose that based on the inspection outcome, doing nothing is not a viable option and some other strategy must be developed. Updating the inspection interval could be one such option.

Selection of the inspection interval depends not only on the underlying reliability but also on economic constraints. Mandatory periodic NDIs with a constant interval are easy and simple, but may not always be an ideal choice, since the chance of crack non-detection is very high in the early stage of fatigue life. Theoretically, the optimal inspection plan should be based on safety and economy; however, its usage is very limited due to the complexity of the fatigue failure analysis and the optimization procedures.

In the permissible maintainability approach discussed earlier, the inspection interval can be determined by the permissible maintainability level. Considering the severity of fatigue failure, its prevention can be considered as the optimal solution for structural maintenance purposes. The principle of the permissible maintainability approach can be expressed as:

$$P\left[\alpha\left(N_i + \Delta N_{up}\right) \leq \alpha_c \middle| H\left(N_i\right)\right] \leq \Phi\left(-\beta_c\right) \tag{23}$$

where α_c is the critical crack size to define the fatigue failure, $H(N_i)$ is the inspection event at the N_i^{th} stress cycles, ΔN_{up} is the updated inspection interval between i^{th} inspection and next inspection, and β_c is the permissible maintainability index.

Once the permissible maintainability index is determined and the appropriate inspection schedule is established, the updated inspection interval can be estimated using reliability updating techniques and inverse reliability analysis. However, this is expected to be complicated. To overcome the shortcomings of the permissible maintainability approach, an approximate approach is proposed next.

As stated earlier, the limit state of interest, statistical characteristics for each of the basic random variables, and the reliability index can be updated after an inspection. The predicted reliability index at the next scheduled inspection can also be evaluated. Once a permissible maintainability index is selected, the time when the reliability index approaches β_c can be determined. Theoretically, the structure should be inspected at this time.

Due to numerical difficulty, an exact solution for this inverse reliability analysis is impractical. As an alternative, the following equation is proposed to update the next inspection interval based on the updated reliability index, i.e.,

$$\Delta T_{inp,up} = Min\left[\frac{\beta_{up}-\beta_c}{\beta_i-\beta_c}\Delta T_{inp}, \Delta T_{inp}\right] \quad (24)$$

where ΔT_{inp} is the constant inspection interval, $\Delta T_{inp,up}$ is the updated inspection interval, β_c is the permissible maintainability index, β_i is the initial designed reliability index, β_t is the target reliability index, and β_{up} is the updated reliability index.

If the updated reliability index is very small compared with either the initial or the target reliability index, the repair or replacement option needs to be considered. In some cases, it is not easy to repair a damaged structural element due to accessibility problem or because the repair process may cause additional damage. In other cases, the intended function of a structure may not recover entirely after the repair. Considering the high cost of repairs and other associated risks, complete replacement may be warranted in some cases.

Example

To elaborate the proposed procedure, a plate girder with a welded cover-plate is considered. According to the AASHTO Fatigue Design Specifications (1989), the welded connection between the cover-plate and the flange can be classified as either Category E or E'. These are the most critical structural details under fatigue loading. The thickness of the cover-plate will indicate whether the detail belongs to Category E or E'. If the thickness of the cover-plate is greater than 0.8 inch (2.03 cm), the detail is considered to belong to Category E'. It is the most critical fatigue detail in highway bridges according to the current AASHTO Guide.

Considering a fatigue truck and the cross sectional properties of the plate girder, the mean stress range of 13.80 Mpa (2.0 ksi) is assumed to be produced at welds between the cover-plate and the flange. Typically, the fatigue load produced by a truck is a narrow band Gaussian process. Therefore, the stress range in this fatigue analysis will follow the Rayleigh distribution. The distribution parameter, S_0 of the Rayleigh distribution required to define the stress range parameter is assumed to be lognormally distributed with a mean of 10.96 MPa (1.59 ksi) and a COV of 0.1. Although the magnitude of the mean stress range is small, it is still significant for the problem under consideration (AASHTO Category E and E') subjected to a long spectrum of variable-amplitude stress range. The total number of stress cycles for the detail considered can be estimated as

$$N = T \times 365 \times ADTT \times P \quad (25)$$

where T is the design life in years, ADTT is the average daily truck traffic volume, and P is the number of stress cycles per truck passage. According to the current AASHTO guidelines (1990), ADTT varies with location and time. In this study, ADTT is considered to follow a lognormal distribution with a mean of 2500 and a COV of 0.10. The number of cycles per truck passage P is assumed to be one in accordance with the suggestions made in the Guides for a simple span girder of 40 ft or more. Zhao and Haldar (1996) discussed the geometry functions necessary to represent the AASHTO E and E' details. The information on deterministic and random parameters required to evaluate the fatigue reliability is summarized in Tables 1 and 2, respectively.

Reliability Analysis and Updating of Cover-plate Detail

Considering the cover plate with thickness 2.54 cm (1 inch) making it a category E' detail, the reliability index is evaluated using the LEFM-based method proposed by the authors. It is found to be 3.338. The target reliability index is considered to be 3.0. Thus, the initial reliability index is greater than the target reliability index, and the detail is acceptable. It is assumed that the detail will be inspected once every two years using ultrasonic equipment, i.e., T = 2, 4, ... , 50 years. It is further assumed the detectability of the ultrasonic equipment is modeled by a lognormal distribution with a mean of 0.254 cm (0.1 inch) and a COV of 0.50.

In the following discussions, two crack detection cases are considered to demonstrate how the information from imperfect NDIs can be incorporated in developing the maintenance strategy.

First, it is assumed that no crack is detected during all the inspections. The reliability index is updated after each inspection, and the updated reliability indexes are plotted in Figure 1. As expected, the non-detection of cracks during the periodic inspections increases the reliability index, indicating the benefit of inspections. Each inspection costs some money; but it also increases the reliability of the bridge if no crack is detected. It may not be that simple if cracks are detected during some of the inspections.

The benefit of inspections can also be evaluated by considering single and multi-inspection plans. The single inspection plan indicates that the structure is inspected for the first time without conducting previous required inspections, and the multi-inspection plan indicates that all the previous and present inspections were conducted on a regular basis. Figure 2 shows the difference in the updated reliability indexes for the event of crack non-detection between the single inspection event and the multi-inspection events. The figure indicates that the fatigue reliability will be higher for the multi-inspection plan than for the single inspection plan. As more inspections are conducted, more information about the structural integrity is obtained, and for the case of crack non-detection, the fatigue reliability is expected to be much higher, particularly as it approaches the design life. Although inspections cost money, they provide valuable information.

In the second case, suppose a crack is detected during an inspection. The problem is much more complicated if cracks are detected during some of the inspections. It is not possible to discuss all possible cases of detection and non-detection of cracks during sequential inspections. For the sake of discussion, one possible scenario is considered here. Assume that the weld in the 2.54 cm (1 inch) thick cover plate will be inspected every two years. The design life of the bridge is 50 years. No crack was detected in the first seven inspections. During the eighth inspection, i.e., after 16 years of service life, a crack of size A was measured. The proposed method can update the reliability of the connection for different crack sizes. When the detail was initially built, the reliability index was 3.338. As shown in Figure 3, if no crack were detected during the 16 years of service life, the reliability index would increase to about 3.685. If a crack size of 0.305 cm (0.12 inch) is measured, the updated reliability index will drop to 2.615, which is far below either the initial reliability index (3.338) or the target reliability index (3.0). If a crack size of 0.19 cm (0.075 inch) is measured during the eighth inspection, the updated reliability index is estimated to be 3.092 which is larger than the target reliability index and smaller than the initial reliability index. Although a certain level of fatigue damage has occurred to the structural detail under consideration, the structural safety is not compromised. Repair is not needed immediately but a further close watch is recommended.

Updating of Inspection Interval

This is the case of updating the inspection interval. Using Eq. 21, the new inspection interval for the next inspection can be estimated to be 7 months, as shown conceptually in Figure 4. However, if a crack size of 0.06 inch (0.1524 cm) is measured during the eighth inspection, the updated reliability index is found to be 3.344. This is almost the same as the initial reliability index. It indicates that a certain amount of cracking or damage can be tolerated in the proposed fatigue evaluation procedure. Thus, the event of crack size measurement does not always indicate that structural safety has been compromised, although the existence of a fatigue crack would have a negative effect on the structural integrity. This example clearly indicates that the information on crack size alone without considering the time of detection is inadequate for the complicated fatigue maintenance problem.

Concluding Remarks

A fatigue reliability updating method incorporating information from nondestructive inspections is presented. Using a linear elastic fracture mechanics approach and the first-order reliability method, the reliability index is first evaluated for fatigue damage. The reliability index is then updated using the information from the nondestructive inspections using the Bayesian approach. The method is capable of considering all major sources of uncertainties in the fatigue damage evaluation model as well as in the nondestructive inspections. The updated reliability index is then used to make maintenance decisions to mitigate fatigue damage. Information on the initial reliability index, target reliability index and permissible maintainability index is used to implement this risk-based concept. The method addresses the overall problem of risk evaluation, maintenance, and rehabilitation of fatigue sensitive structures by combining old owners, i.e. continued operation of the small high-cost plant. The greater financial strength of the larger firm also gives rise to the additional option of replacing the small plant at a suitable moment by a bigger plant with lower costs per unit of product. Not only do both parties together never lose anything by merging, they also gain in security against outside competition.

Suppose a firm *X* operates a single plant with a production capacity of 2 and a cost price of 0·9 per unit of product; suppose the prevailing price is 0·95, including an element of oligopoly rent. Another firm, say *Z*, considers entering the market with a cost price of 0·8 per unit of product and a production capacity of 5. This is an attractive prospect for *Z*, particularly if the likelihood is that its own (*Z*'s) entry will depress the price to something between *Z*'s own cost price of 0·8 and *X*'s cost price of 0·9. It will mean that *Z*'s venture is immediately viable, but *X* is driven into bankruptcy. After the elimination of *X*, the oligopoly rent will be partially restored, but the price will not re-attain its previous level of 0·95 since *Z*'s supply is 5 and *X*'s was only 2.

In an oligopolistic market the possibility of such market entry by an outsider is probabilistic rather than certain, but it is a risk whenever it is at all possible. *X* would be well advised to pre-empt it by merger with another established firm. The larger established firms would also find it to their advantage to buy *X* for the same reason.

After the merger the enlarged concern may well frighten off would-be entrants, simply by announcing plans to replace the old factory *X* by a newer and bigger plant. The actual building of a larger factory would probably be postponed until the oligopoly rent was quite near its maximum value and the new plant would be built on a correspondingly larger scale, demand for the product having risen in the meantime.

The upshot of this is that the Chamberlin–Bain assumptions lead us to expect only a very moderate degree of variation in plant size. In other words, competition and profit maximization in a Chamberlin–Bain type of oligopolistic market work much the same as perfect competition. The one major difference is that an industry as a whole enjoys a specially high return on its investments, and elimination of less than fully efficient production units is by take-over rather than by bankruptcy.

This is, I submit, a flaw in the Chamberlin–Bain theory since, in fact, plant sizes within industries show quite a noticeable range of variation, as documented by Bain himself [3*a*].

A group of alternative theories of oligopoly arises if one drops the assumption of a 'perfect market'.

The product of one firm is a relatively close substitute for a similar product of another firm in the same industry, although not a perfect substitute.

The product of one firm must obviously be a substitute more close to the product of another firm in the same industry, than to anything produced by another industry. (Otherwise the concept of an industry loses its significance.) Likewise, it is approximately correct to speak of 'the' price of an industry despite the fact that there are minor differences between the prices charged by different firms in the industry.

One consequence of assuming imperfect competition is the following. The fact that one firm is able to produce at a lower cost per unit of product than another no longer implies that the more efficient firm will be in a position to drive the less efficient one out of the market; nor does it follow that the more efficient firm has an incentive to do so, even if it were possible.

Hence it is quite possible for a monopolistic market form to be efficient from a purely technical point of view, because increasing returns to scale prevail for all possible sizes of firm and an oligopolistic market structure prevails nevertheless.

The point does not seem to be discussed in any detail in the literature. As a result it is not altogether clear whether, for example, Sylos-Labini [44] shares Chamberlin's assumption of the U-shaped cost curve, or my assumption of increasing returns to scale applying to all possible sizes of firm. The reader will have noticed that this assumption of increasing returns to scale at all possible sizes of firm is essential for my conclusion that the return to fully employed real capital is greater than the cost of financing new investment.

There are different causes of imperfect competition, usually assumed to operate in combination with economies of scale, and giving rise to different theories of oligopoly. We may, for example, assume that the product of one firm is an imperfect substitute for the similar product of another firm, because of minor differences in the product itself. Different models and styles of motor cars and different flavours of cigars are examples of this type of intrinsic product differentiation.

The resulting theory is, from a strictly formal point of view, a theory of monopoly: only Vauxhall makes Vauxhall motor cars. We speak of competition between different manufacturers, nevertheless, because Ford motor cars are a closer substitute to Vauxhall motor cars than to any other type of product. This theory of oligopoly, based on product differentiation, is developed by Hilhorst in his published thesis [19*a*]. Since, again, most of the underlying ideas can be found in the earlier work of Chamberlin, I propose to call the theory the Chamberlin–Hilhorst theory of oligopoly. An important special case of this theory arises if one considers transport costs rather than differences in the product itself as the product-differentiating factor.

To have a ship repaired by Harland & Wolff, Belfast, is a different service from having the same repair done by a Japanese firm, because it is impractical to have the repair done in Japan if the ship is used on the North Atlantic shipping route. This is the theory of oligopoly developed by Hilhorst in his published lecture notes [19] as a by-product of his theory of location and regional concentration. The two main oligopoly-supporting factors together determine the oligopolistic market equilibrium, and the following points may now be added to our earlier analysis of this equilibrium. In section 4.6 we discussed the existence of *two* rates of profit, an upper limit demanded by profit-maximizing finance capital and a lower limit. It seems valid to associate the surplus element in the higher rate with the Bain oligopoly rent, and the operation of the lower limit with the merger theorem.

Next, let us consider the role of brand-names and advertising on behalf of a specific brand made by only one manufacturer.

Advertising fulfils two roles, It supplies information, so that the buyer or potential buyer is informed of specific properties of the product offered for sale, where he can buy it, and what price will be charged for it. This 'rational' kind of advertising constitutes a cost of production and is not relevantly different from, for example, the heating and lighting of a factory or the cost of transporting the product. It gives rise to an oligopolistic market structure only because the cost of informing the public does not increase proportionally with the amount sold. In other words, costs of rational information are a cause of increasing returns to scale and come under that heading within the framework of the Chamberlin–Bain theory of oligopoly.

Now consider the case of 'persuasive advertising'. In that case one assumes that a particular seller can differentiate his own product from similar products made by other firms, despite the fact that the only difference consists in a box with a particular brand-name printed on it, the content being physically indistinguishable.

The distinction between persuasive advertising and rational information of the public may be clear in theory; but in practice it is often difficult to establish where information about genuine differences between the product of one firm and similar ones made by competitors ends and where persuasive advertising begins. In both cases a firm can sell its own product, despite the fact that a close substitute produced by another firm is offered for sale at a slightly lower price.

There is one remaining major work on the theory of oligopoly, that of Sylos-Labini [44]. His conclusions clearly imply limited competition, i.e. Chamberlin–Hilhorst, and there is a case for indicating the theory as Chamberlin–Sylos-Labini rather than Chamberlin–Hilhorst, since Sylos-Labini is the older author even where Hilhorst does not refer to him. Sylos-Labini does not, however, clearly state that he assumes imperfect competition, placing most of the emphasis on technical factors instead.

A common element between both my theory of oligopoly and the older work of Sylos-Labini, not found with either Chamberlin, Bain or Hilhorst, is the emphasis on technical change, that is, innovation as an oligopoly-creating factor. Only a few firms employ the newest and most efficient methods of production.

9.9 A MODEL OF MACRO-ECONOMIC EQUILIBRIUM

We discuss first a formal presentation of a more or less neo-classical theory of economic equilibrium, and the amendments necessary to convert this system into one representing monetary Keynesianism, Leijonhufvud's version of fiscal Keynesianism, and the oligopolistic version of fiscal Keynesianism.

The 'central' version of the neo-classical model which I give is not quite 'the' neo-classical model. It contains some amendments which accommodate objections I would otherwise make against a model based on textbook *communis opinio*. These objections do not, however, strike at the basic proposition that the price mechanism equates the demand and the supply in each market.

Accordingly I have made some 'concessions' on behalf of the neo-classical school in order to highlight the points where non-classical assumptions give rise to model-features which cannot be reconciled with the neo-classical assumptions.

The model is presented in fifteen equations, with fifteen jointly dependent variables and five exogenous variables, the values of which are determined outside the equilibrium model. Of these exogenous variables, four (the quantity of public expenditure, the taxes on the two major income categories, and the amounts of new loans issued) are, or are assumed to be, instruments of public policy. One variable, the (demographic) supply of labour, is assumed not to be the result of economic factors at all; it is simply a given amount.

The model is presented in Figure 3. Since the names of the equations and the variables are given at the margins of the tableau, it is not necessary to repeat them here.

The model contains a fair share of the usual simplifying assumptions.

There is only one homogeneous type of product, which can be used as consumption, as investment, or by the government as public expenditure.

There is no foreign sector, but there is a public sector.

There are two prices: one for labour, the wage rate, and one for products. The products price is applicable to all types of expenditure.

There are only two types of taxes: on wages and on profits. There are no indirect taxes like purchase tax or turnover tax.

Despite these simplifications, an attempt has been made to account properly for the various channels by which policy instruments operate, and for the fact that nominal values are not identical to quantities, as the price can change. This attempt at realistic accounting is responsible for nine out of the fifteen relations (1–8 and 14). Even so, the monetary sector of the model is incomplete. There is at least one possible way for the capital market to malfunction, which cannot be adequately discussed without distinguishing between bonds and shares. Stock exchange speculation considerably aggravated the depression of the 1930s, especially in the United States.

The model lumps together as 'bonds': (i) public loan certificates and (ii) banks' titles to the repayment of overdrafts by clients. It does not recognize private industrial bonds at all. There is some justification for this, because no feedback from the stock of bonds to the rest of the economy is assumed.

The amalgamation of banks' titles to repayment of overdrafts with government bonds means that the model assumes public control over the private capital market; otherwise the exogenous nature of the variable *BI* (= bonds new issue) must be questioned. It is clear that the government has at its disposal one more financial instrument besides the public budget.

This is seen if we rearrange the variables, making the rate of interest exogenous and the creation of new money (*BI*) endogenous. The algebra is the same as in the main version presented in the tableau, but the institutional assumption now is that the government commits itself to buy and sell its own bonds at a specific published rate of interest, i.e. at parity value irrespective of the amount of money created or absorbed by such transactions. This makes the published rate of interest effective irrespective of the amount of money created by the banking system on behalf of the private sector. The amount of money created or absorbed by these open-market operations is thus whatever is needed to make the total stock of money consistent with the money demand equation (13). This is the 'compensation effect' discussed in section 3.4.

Among the economic reaction functions the consumption demand function (9) and the money demand function (13) are not particularly controversial. Relation (9) says that workers spend a fraction α_1 of their disposable income and the capitalist class a fraction α_2, and that the timing of consumption is affected by the rate of interest, hence the term $-\alpha_3 ri$. Relation (13) is Keynes's demand for money function, as discussed in section 9.4. This relation is accepted by a wide range of authors—adherents of monetary Keynesianism, the neo-classical school after its absorption of Keynes's theory on this point, and also by myself.

Now consider the three remaining economic relations. Equation (11), the labour demand function, differs from what some other authors give as the neo-classical model by mentioning output directly as an argument in the labour demand function.

For example Aschheim and Ching Yao Hsieh [3], p. 54, have a labour-demand as well as a labour-supply function, both of which list wages and prices as the only arguments. Crouch [9], p. 142, has the same for labour supply, and lists wages and prices and the capital stock as the arguments of the labour demand function. Crouch's version of the labour demand function could perhaps be interpreted

Names of equations \ Names of variables	Jointly dependent variables 1 Id Labour demand	2 L Wage bill	3 pq Produced quantity	4 pr Price	5 PV Production value	6 c Consumed quantity	7 C Consumption value	8 i Investment quantity	9 I Investment value	10 k Capital stock	11 DL Disposable labour income	12 DP Disposable profit	13 M Money stock	14 ri Rate of interest	15 wr Wage rate	Exogenous variables 1 qpe Quantity of public expend.	2 TP Taxes on profit	3 TL Taxes on labour income	4 BI Bonds issue	5 ls Labour supply
1 Definition of wage bill	ld =	L	•	•	•	•	•	•	•	•	•	•	•	•	÷ wr	•	•	•	•	•
2 Definition of produced quantity	•	•	pq =	•	•	c	•	+ i	•	•	•	•	•	•	•	+ qpe	•	•	•	•
3 Definition of production value	•	•	pq ×	pr =	PV	•	•	•	•	•	•	•	•	•	•	•	•	•	•	•
4 Definition of consumption	•	•	•	pr	• ×	c =	C	•	•	•	•	•	•	•	•	•	•	•	•	•
5 Definition of investment value	•	•	•	pr	•	•	• ×	i =	I	•	•	•	•	•	•	•	•	•	•	•
6 Definition of capital stock	•	•	•	•	•	•	•	i	=	Δk	•	•	•	•	•	•	•	•	•	•
7 Definition of disposable labour income	•	L =	•	•	•	•	•	•	•	•	DL	•	•	•	•	•	•	+ TL	•	•
8 Definition of disposable profit	•	−L	•	•	+ PV	•	•	•	•	•	•	= DP	•	•	•	•	+ TP	•	•	•
9 Consumption demand function	•	•	•	•	•	•	C =	•	•	•	α_1 DL +	α_2 DP	•	$-\alpha_3$ ri	•	•	•	•	•	•
10 Investment demand function	•	•	•	•	•	•	•	•	I =	•	•	β_1 DP	•	$-\beta_2$ ri	•	•	•	•	•	•
11 Labour demand function	ld =	•	γ_1 pq +	γ_2 pr	•	•	•	•	•	•	•	•	•	$+\gamma_3$ ri −	γ_1 wr	•	•	•	•	•
12 Production supply function	$-\delta_1$ ld	•	+ pq =	•	•	•	•	•	•	δ_2 k	•	•	•	•	•	•	•	•	•	•
13 Money demand function	•	•	•	•	ϵ_1 PV	•	•	•	•	•	•	•	M	$-\epsilon_2$ ri	•	•	•	•	•	•
14 Definition of money supply	•	•	•	see qpe	•	•	•	•	•	•	•	•	ΔM =	•	•	qpe × pr −	TP −	TL +	BI	•
15 Labour market equilibrium cond.	ld =	•	•	•	•	•	•	•	•	•	•	•	•	•	•	•	•	•	•	ls

Note: The definition of the wage bill is presented as ld = L ÷ wr, this is equivalent to L = ld × wr, similar to the other value-flows PV, C, and I

FIGURE 3 Economic equilibrium in fifteen equations

as having more or less the same significance as mine. One would assume that as long as a particular price structure prevails, the demand for both labour and capital equipment varies in proportion to the quantity of product to be produced.

No similar reconciliation with my specification is possible in the case of Aschheim and Ching Yao Hsieh. Their specification implies that an autonomous increase in demand from, say, export or public expenditure would not influence the demand for labour in any way until adjustments in the price structure and income distribution took place.

That goes a bit far. One can disagree with this version of neo-classical theory, while accepting the main proposition that competitive behaviour leads to adjustments in the income and price structure, as a result of which the demand is equal to the supply in each market at the prevailing price.

The assumption I made when I wrote equation (11) is that a given quantity of product is produced at the lowest possible real cost, and that accordingly there is a substitution effect between capital and labour. The same coefficient γ_2 occurs for both the wage rate and the price of production, with opposite signs, because the net effect of the two, the real wage rate, is meant. Of the two other coefficients, γ_2 represents the technical fact that more output requires more capital and more labour, and γ_3 the other leg of the substitution effect, the cost of capital. The combination of the labour demand function (11) with the production function (12) means that the production function is at the same time an implied investment demand function.

In the neo-classical model, the operation of the production function as an implied investment demand function is restricted by the presence of an explicit investment demand function. This explicit investment demand function then works as a condition of equilibrium to be satisfied by its arguments. We know how much investment is required to sustain the equilibrium level of production, therefore the market factors which actually determine the amount of investment must be adjusted accordingly.

The specification of the investment demand function which I have listed as equation (10) is not quite neo-classical. I would have been nearer the neo-classical tradition if I had listed production value rather than disposable profit as the main argument in addition to the rate of interest.

It is, I believe, more or less agreed among present-day adherents of the neo-classical theory that an increase in national income causes a corresponding shift in the investment demand function. The specified function (10) is, however, a mixture of supply and demand factors. The term $\beta_1 DP$ presents the supply of investable funds. A more truly neo-classical investment demand function would be specified as:

$$i = \beta_1 pq - \beta_2 ri/pr$$

instead of

$$I = \beta_1 DP - \beta_2 ri$$

as shown in (10).

However, if one neglects the problem of the adjustment between capital stock and investment flow, the production function can be written as

$$pq = \delta_1 ld + \delta_2 i$$

or presented as implied investment demand function:

$$i = 1/\delta_2 pq - \delta_1/\delta_2 ld$$

The combination of the implicit investment demand function with the explicit investment demand function allows us to eliminate investment itself, to obtain:

$$(\beta_1 - 1/\delta_2)pq = -\delta_1/\delta_2 ld - \beta_2 ri/pr$$

The significance of this result depends to a certain extent on our interpretation of the coefficient β_1. If it is assumed that an increase in production shifts the investment demand function, because increased production requires more capital equipment, the coefficient β_1 is in substance the same as the reciprocal of δ_2, the ratio between production and its capital requirement. Even if no such assumption is made, one can imagine quite reasonable parameter values which will make β_1 nevertheless approximately equal to $1/\delta_2$.

The model then says that the demand for labour depends *only* on the deflated cost of interest, i.e. the cost of financing new investment. This statement should be qualified because δ_2 does not refer directly to the investment flow, but to the capital stock and there may be short-term variations due to adjustment discrepancies between the capital stock and its operative use in production. This qualification uses, however, an argument which is not admissible in the neo-classical system, since it assumes temporary non-equilibrium.

The result

$$ld = -\frac{\delta_1}{\delta_2} \times \beta_2 \frac{ri}{pr}$$

is nevertheless unrealistic.

We ought to take into account the possibility that public interference in the secondary income distribution—by means of its fiscal policy (the use of the variables *TL* and *TP*) or in the capital market (via *BI*)—shifts the level of employment corresponding to a particular price structure.

We cannot, however, assume that the investment demand function simply transmits the available savings of the private sector to productive investment. That assumption would lead to the specification

$$I = (1-\alpha_1)DL + (1-\alpha_2)DP + \alpha_3 ri$$

i.e. the complement of the consumption function (9). Together the two functions require:

$$C + I = DL + DP$$

Despite its apparent reasonableness, this specification leads to an unreasonable result:

Replace *DL* by its equivalent from (7), $L - TL$, and *DP* by its equivalent from (8), $PV - L - TP$, and the result is

$$C + I = PV - TL - TP$$

Replace *C*, *I*, and *PV* by their definitions in terms of quantity and price given in (3), (4), and (5), to obtain

$$c \times pr + i \times pr = pq \times pr - TL - TP$$

Replace the production quantity *pq* by $c + i + qpe$, from (2), and obtain, after cancellation of $c \times pr$ and $i \times pr$ on both sides:

$$qpe \times pr - TL - TP = 0$$

In other words, the assumption that the private sector exactly matches its expenditure to its disposable income implies an automatically balanced budget. Hence, if the government increased the variable *qpe*, the quantity of public expenditure, without changing taxes, the supposed perfect market would oblige the government with a fall in the price level, allowing the government to obtain an increasing quantity of public expenditure for a non-increasing sum of money.

The specified investment function

$$I = \beta_1 DP - \beta_2 ri$$

has a much more reasonable result in this respect, namely

$$qpe \times pr - TL - TP = (1-\alpha_1)DL + (1-\alpha_2-\beta_1)DP + (\alpha_3+\beta_2)ri$$

From this relation a deficit on the public budget would almost certainly imply that investment, and to a lesser extent consumption, would be discouraged by a rising rate of interest.

According to this basically neo-classical model, there is full employment of labour, no matter what the government does. The spontaneous adjustment of the price structure, and if necessary the income distribution, takes care of that. The government can in that case use its instrument-variables to further other desirable goals, such as stable prices, economic growth, or an equitable income distribution.

Now consider the non-classical proposition that the price structure does not always adjust itself to the requirement of economic equilibrium.

This leads to alterations in the model. Firstly, the wage rate becomes an exogenous variable, instead of being automatically at the level which equates the demand for labour to the available supply. Against this, the equilibrium condition of the labour market has to be dropped, except in the case where regulation ensures that the effective demand in value equals the cost of full-employment production. This is, in fact, the theory which we have described as monetary Keynesianism.

At this point it is necessary to say something about the assumed numerical values of the coefficients in the economic relations. There is a version of fiscal Keynesianism which maintains that, given certain unfavourable conditions, full-employment income results in a level of private savings well in excess of any reasonable level of investment, even at a zero or near-zero rate of interest. Among modern authors Lindauer [25*a*] is the one who comes nearest to being a representative of this school. It is, to my knowledge, the only version of fiscal Keynesianism which can claim a legitimate parentage from Keynes's *General Theory* without adding non-classical assumptions.

One takes, first of all, Keynes's concept of the marginal propensity to consume, i.e. $\alpha_3 = 0$. Secondly, one assumes that the magnitude of the propensity to consume is so low that savings out of full-employment income exceed the level of investment even at a near-zero rate of interest, irrespective of the precise specification of the investment function.

The result is that, even while the formal structure of monetary Keynesianism is largely accepted, a solution to the model which combines full employment with a balanced budget can only be obtained by assuming unrealistic and politically impractical values for the wage rate and the rate of interest. People just save too much.

Thus, if the state does not spend the difference between private savings and a reasonable level of private investment, the only solution is to allow production and income to drop to a level where an impoverished people will save less.

One may ask what *is* a reasonable level of investment? Keynes (*General Theory*, Chapter 16) argued the case of this version of fiscal Keynesianism against the background of the particular historic circumstances of Great Britain and the United States in the 1930s. In particular he assumed that the preceding boom of the 1920s had largely exhausted the available economically viable investment opportunities. This is a valid argument only if one assumes a basically static or at best slowly changing technology. It is just not true in a time of rapidly changing technology, which opens up new opportunities for investment all the time.

The next inroad into classical assumptions comes with the assertion that *prices* do not necessarily respond to supply and demand for products, but rather are directly related to the cost of production.

For example Sirkin [42*a*], p. 171, quoting source evidence by Blair [3*c*], argues that prices are often 'administered', i.e. calculated and charged to the customer on the basis of a predetermined rate of return to the firm's investment. Blair, an official of the U.S. (Senate?) Committee on the Judiciary, Subcommittee on Antitrust and Monopoly, bases his explanation of the factual situation which he reports squarely on the presence of oligopoly.

The assertion that prices are a direct function of costs rather than the result of a market equilibrium means that we should add a *price equation* to our model. The introduction of an additional equation means that we must drop one of the existing equations.

Consider first the labour demand function. Keynes, in his *General*

Theory [21], p. 280, assumes that the labour demand function is the implicit form of the production function. This would mean that, in our model, (12) is written as $pq = \delta_1 ld$ and that the explicit labour-demand function (11) is dropped.

The implication is that substitution between capital and labour, which was the reason for the presence of the coefficients for price variables in (11), is denied.

Unfortunately, this theory of employment is inconsistent with the theory of capital explained in the sixteenth chapter of the same book. Here Keynes follows the (neo)-classical theory and assumes that the relative prices of capital and labour influence the choice between the direct use of labour in labour-intensive methods of production and its indirect, but more efficient, use in 'roundabout' (capital-intensive) production methods.

One can resolve this contradiction, once it is recognized, by assuming that the conditions for economic equilibrium depend on the lapse of time.

In the *short* run one assumes complementarity between capital and labour, and rigid prices which are purely a function of costs, irrespective of equilibrium or disequilibrium between supply and demand.

The assumption of short-run rigidity can exist side by side with an assumption of substitutability, given sufficient lapse of time. The most logical explanation for such a time-lag is a technological one, that substitution is possible only after new types of machines have been designed.

Hence the Clower–Leijonhufvud reinterpretation of Keynes is upheld as a theory for short-run equilibrium, and monetary Keynesianism as the correct theory of long-term equilibrium. This is a logically correct combination of theories, but it is not the theory defended in this book.

The theory which has been defended here maintains that both the labour demand function and the production supply function are valid and separate from each other as long-term equilibrium conditions.

Under normal financial conditions, the redundant equation is the explicit investment demand function (10), and the rate of interest has no significant short-term effect. The long-term effects of the rate of interest come under two headings, the impact on the capital-labour ratio, as expressed by the price-terms in the labour-demand function (11), and presumably a certain impact on the market structure. One has to assume that a policy of low or high rates of interest, if followed for a long period, will mitigate or enhance the impact of increasing returns to the scale of capital investment on the degree of concentration.

A change in the degree of concentration does not by itself influence the total amount of investment. The long-term investment demand function is the implied investment demand function given by the production function. The short-term equivalent is the flexible-accelerator adjustment mechanism.

If, during a financial crisis, this relation is temporarily replaced by a restriction on the supply of investable funds, the implication is that production is determined by the demand side only. As long as this situation lasts, the redundant relation is the production function (12) and realized production is less than the figure indicated by equation (12).

References

1 ACKLEY, G. *Macro-Economic Theory*. New York: Macmillan, 1961.

2 ARROW, K. J. 'The Economic Implications of Learning by Doing' *in:* J. E. Stiglitz and J. Uzawa (eds.) *Readings in the Modern Theory of Economic Growth*. Cambridge, Mass., and London: M.I.T. Press, 1969.

3 ASCHHEIM, Joseph, and CHING YAO HSIEH. *Macro-economics, Income and Monetary Theory*. Columbus, Ohio: Merrill, 1969.

3*a* BAIN, Joe S. *International Differences in Industrial Structure*. New Haven and London: Yale University Press, 1966.

3*b* BAIN, Joe S. *Barriers to New Competition, their Character and Consequences in Manufacturing Industries*. Cambridge, Mass.: Harvard University Press, 1956.

3*c* BLAIR, J. M. 'Administered Prices: A Phenomenon in search of a Theory'. *American Economic Review*, Conference-supplement to Vol. 49, supplement No. 71, pp. 431–50. (A.E.A. conference, 1958.)

4 CENTRAAL PLAN BUREAU (Netherlands Ministry of Economic Affairs). *Centraal Economisch Plan 1955*. The Hague, March 1955.

5 CHAMBERLIN, E. H. *The Theory of Monopolistic Competition*. Cambridge, Mass.: Harvard University Press, 1933.

6 CHAMBERLIN, E. H. *Towards a more General Theory of Value*. New York: Oxford University Press, 1957.

7 CLOWER, R. W. 'The Keynesian Counter-Revolution: A Theoretical Appraisal' *in:* F. H. Hahn and F. P. R. Brechtling (eds.). *The Theory of Interest Rates*. London: Institute of Economic Affairs, 1965.

8 COMMITTEE ON THE WORKING OF THE MONETARY SYSTEM 'REPORT' (also known as RADCLIFFE REPORT, after its Chairman). London: HMSO, 1959. Cmnd. 827.

9 CROUCH, Robert L. *Macroeconomics*. New York: Harcourt Brace Jovanovich Inc., 1971.

9*a* EVANS, Michael K. *Macroeconomic Activity, Theory, Forecasting and Control*. New York: Harper and Row, 1969.

10 FRIEDMAN, Milton. *A Theoretical Framework for Monetary Analysis*. National Bureau of Economic Research (U.S.A.) Occasional Paper 112. New York: Columbia University Press, 1971.

10*a* GLAHE, Fred R. *Macroeconomic Theory and Policy*. New York: Harcourt Brace Jovanovich, 1973.

11 GOLDBERGER, A. S. *Impact Multipliers and Dynamic Properties of the Klein-Goldberger Model*. Amsterdam: North Holland Publishing Co., 1959.

12 GREENHUT, M. L. 'A Theory of the Firm in Economic Space'. New York: Appleton-Century-Crofts, Meredith Corporation, 1970.

13 GOODWIN, R. M. 'The Non-linear Accelerator and the Presence of Business Cycles'. *Econometrica*, Vol. 19 (1951), pp. 1–17.

14 HANSEN, Alvin H. *A Guide to Keynes*. New York: McGraw-Hill, 1953.

15 HARVEY, J. and JOHNSON, M. *Introduction to Macroeconomics*. London: Macmillan, 1970.

16 HEESTERMAN, A. R. G. *Forecasting Models for National Economic Planning*. Dordrecht, Holland: D. Reidel, 1972.

17 HEESTERMAN, A. R. G. *Allocation Models and their use in Economic Planning*. Dordrecht, Holland: D. Reidel, 1971.

18 HICKS, J. R. *Value and Capital*. Oxford: Clarendon Press, 1939; 2nd edn., 1948.

19 HILHORST, Jos. G. M. *Regional Planning*. Rotterdam: Rotterdam University Press, 1971.

19*a* HILHORST, Jos. G. M. *Monopolistic Competition, Technical Progress and Income Distribution*. Rotterdam: Rotterdam University Press, 1965.

20 INTERNATIONAL MONETARY FUND. *Summary Proceedings Annual Meeting, 1969*. Washington, 1969.

21 KEYNES, J. M. *The General Theory of Employment, Interest and Money*. London: Macmillan, 1936.

22 KLEIN, L. R. *The Keynesian Revolution*. London: Macmillan, 1952; 2nd edn., 1962.

23 KLEIN, L. R. and GOLDBERGER, A. S. *An Econometric Model of the United States 1929–1952*. Amsterdam: North Holland Publishing Co., 1955.

24 LEIJONHUFVUD, Axel. *On Keynesian Economics and the Economics of Keynes*. London: Oxford University Press, 1968.

25 LERNER, A. P. 'The Essential Properties of Interest and Money'. *Quarterly Journal of Economics*, May 1952.

25*a* LINDAUER, J. *Macroeconomics*. New York: Wiley, 1968.

26 LIST, Friedrich. *The National System of Political Economy*. Translated by S. S. Lloyd (London: Longmans Green, 1885). German original: *Das National System der Politischen Ökonomie*. Stuttgart-Tübingen: J. G. Gotta'scher Verlag, 1842. Posthumous edition in List's collected works, Vol. 6 (Berlin: Reimar Hobbin, 1930).

27 LUTZ, Friedrich A. *The Theory of Interest*. Dordrecht, Holland: D. Reidel, 1967. Translation from the German original *Zinstheorie*, 2nd edn. (Zürich: Polygrafischer Verlag and Tübingen: J. C. Mohr, 1967).

27*a* MAHDAVI, H. 'The Patterns and Problems of Economic Development in Rentier States: The Case of Iran' *in*: M. A. Cook (ed.). *Studies in the Economic History of the Middle East*. London: Oxford University Press, 1970.

28 MARSHALL, A. *Principles of Economics*. London: Macmillan, 1895.

29 MEADOWS, Dennis L. *The Limits to Growth, A Report on the Club of Rome Project on the Predicament of Mankind*. New York: Universe Press, 1972.

30 MEADE, E. M. *The Growing Economy*. London: Allen and Unwin, 1968.

31 MEADE, J. S. and ANDREWS, P. W. S. *Summary of Replies to Questions on Effects of Interest Rates*. Oxford Economic Papers, Vol. 1, 1938, pp. 14–31.

32 MERHAV, M. *Technological Dependence, Monopoly and Growth*. Oxford: Pergamon Press, 1969.

32*a* MODIGLIANI, F. 'New Developments on the Oligopoly Front'. *The Journal of Political Economy*, Vol. LXVI, June 1958.

33 MUSGRAVE, R. A. 'Principles of Budget Determination' *in:* J. Scherer and J. A. Papke (eds.). *Public Finance and Economic Policy*. New York: Houghton Mifflin, 1966.

34 NATIONAL BOARD FOR PRICES AND INCOMES, Report 150. *Pay and other Terms and Conditions and the Prices charged by the London Brick Company*. London: HMSO, July 1970. Cmnd. 4422.

35 NATIONAL PLAN, THE. London: HMSO, 1965.

36 NOURSE, H. O. *Regional Economics*. New York: McGraw-Hill, 1968.

RADCLIFFE REPORT. *See*: Committee on the Working of the Monetary System.

37 REYNOLDS, L. G. *The Three Worlds of Economics*. New Haven and London: Yale University Press, 1971.

38 RICARDO, David. *The Principles of Political Economy and Taxation*. London: John Murray, 1819. Reprinted in Everyman's Library, No. 590. London: J. M. Dent and New York: E. P. Dutton, 1957.

39 SAMUELSON, P. A. *Economics, An Introductory Analysis*. New York: McGraw-Hill.

40 SANDEE, J. 'Possible Economic Growth in the Netherlands' *in*: R. C. Geary (ed.). *Europe's Future in Figures*. Amsterdam: North Holland Publishing Co., 1962.

41 SANDSTRÖM, G. E. *Man the Builder*. New York: McGraw-Hill, 1970.

42 SCHUMPETER, Joseph. *The Theory of Economic Development*. Cambridge, Mass.: Harvard University Press, 1934. Translated by R. Opie from the German original *Theorie der wirtschaftlichen Entwicklung* (Munich: Duncker und Humbolt, 1911; 2nd edn., 1926).

42*a* SIRKIN, G. *Introduction to Macroeconomic Theory*. Homewood, Illinois: Richard D. Irwin Inc., 1961.

43 SOLOW, R. *Growth Theory, an Exposition*. Radcliffe Lectures, University of Warwick, 1969. Oxford: Clarendon Press, 1970.

43*a* STAMP, E. 'The End of Cheap Food'. *New Internationalist*, April 1973, p. 6.

44 SYLOS-LABINI, Paolo. *Oligopoly and Technical Progress* (translated from the Italian original). Cambridge, Mass.: Harvard University Press, 1962.

45 UNITED NATIONS FOOD AND AGRICULTURAL ORGANIZATION. *World Outlook and State of Food and Agriculture, 1950*. Washington, D.C., October 1950.

46 UNITED NATIONS STATISTICAL OFFICE. *A System of National Accounts and Supporting Tables*. 59 XVII.II.

47 UNITED NATIONS STATISTICAL OFFICE. *Statistical Yearbook of the United Nations*.

48 UNITED NATIONS STATISTICAL OFFICE. *Yearbook of International Trade Statistics*.

VAN DER WERF, D. *See*: WERF, D. van der.

48*a* VICKREY, William S. *Metastatics and Macroeconomics.* New York: Harcourt, Brace and World Inc., 1964.

49 WALRAS, Leon. *Elements of Pure Economics.* London: Allen and Unwin, 1954. Translated from the French original *Elements d'Economie Politique Pure* (1926 edn.).

50 WALTERS, A. A. *Money in Boom and Slump.* London: Institute of Economic Affairs, 1970 (Hobart Paper 44, 2nd edn.).

51 WERF, D. van der. 'The Economy of the Federal Republic of Germany in Fifteen Equations'. *The German Economic Review* Vol. 10, 1972, pp. 216–32.

52 WILES, P. J. D. *Communist International Economics.* Oxford: Blackwell, 1968.

Index